# CYBER SECURITY EDUCATION

This book investigates the goals and policy aspects of cyber security education in the light of escalating technical, social and geopolitical challenges.

The past ten years have seen a tectonic shift in the significance of cyber security education. Once the preserve of small groups of dedicated educators and industry professionals, the subject is now on the frontlines of geopolitical confrontation and business strategy. Global shortages of talent have created pressures on corporate and national policy for workforce development. *Cyber Security Education* offers an updated approach to the subject as we enter the next decade of technological disruption and political threats. The contributors include scholars and education practitioners from leading research and education centres in Europe, North America and Australia. This book provides essential reference points for education policy on the new social terrain of security in cyberspace and aims to reposition global debates on what education for security in cyberspace can and should mean.

This book will be of interest to students of cyber security, cyber education, international security and public policy generally, as well as practitioners and policy-makers.

**Greg Austin** is a Senior Fellow and leader of the Cyber, Space and Future Conflict Programme for the International Institute for Strategic Studies, while maintaining a professorial appointment at the University of New South Wales Canberra, Australia.

T0384740

# ROUTLEDGE STUDIES IN CONFLICT, SECURITY AND TECHNOLOGY

Series Editors: Mark Lacy, *Lancaster University*, Dan Prince, *Lancaster University*, and Sean Lawson, *University of Utah*

The *Routledge Studies in Conflict, Security and Technology* series aims to publish challenging studies that map the terrain of technology and security from a range of disciplinary perspectives, offering critical perspectives on the issues that concern publics, business and policymakers in a time of rapid and disruptive technological change.

**Cybersecurity Discourse in the United States**
Cyber-Doom Rhetoric and Beyond
*Sean T. Lawson*

**National Cyber Emergencies**
The Return to Civil Defence
*Edited by Greg Austin*

**Information Warfare in the Age of Cyber Conflict**
*Edited by Christopher Whyte, A. Trevor Thrall, and Brian M. Mazanec*

**Emerging Security Technologies and EU Governance**
Actors, Practices and Processes
*Edited by Antonio Calcara, Raluca Csernatoni and Chantal Lavallée*

**Cyber Security Education**
Principles and Policies
*Edited by Greg Austin*

For more information about this series, please visit: https://www.routledge.com/Routledge-Studies-in-Conflict-Security-and-Technology/book-series/CST

# CYBER SECURITY EDUCATION

## Principles and Policies

*Edited by Greg Austin*

Routledge
Taylor & Francis Group

LONDON AND NEW YORK

First published 2021
by Routledge
2 Park Square, Milton Park, Abingdon, Oxon OX14 4RN

and by Routledge
52 Vanderbilt Avenue, New York, NY 10017

*Routledge is an imprint of the Taylor & Francis Group, an informa business*

*British Library Cataloguing-in-Publication Data*
A catalogue record for this book is available from the British Library

*Library of Congress Cataloging-in-Publication Data*
Names: Austin, Greg, 1951- editor.
Title: Cyber-security education : principles and policies / edited by Greg Austin.
Description: London ; New York : Routledge/Taylor & Francis Group, 2021. |
Series: Routledge studies in conflict, security and technology |
Includes bibliographical references and index.
Identifiers: LCCN 2020013078 (print) | LCCN 2020013079 (ebook) |
ISBN 9780367421922 (hardback) | ISBN 9780367421915 (paperback) |
ISBN 9780367822576 (ebook)
Subjects: LCSH: Computer security--Study and teaching. |
Computer networks--Security measures--Study and teaching.
Classification: LCC QA76.9.A25 C91813 2021 (print) |
LCC QA76.9.A25 (ebook) | DDC 005.8071--dc23
LC record available at https://lccn.loc.gov/2020013078
LC ebook record available at https://lccn.loc.gov/2020013079

ISBN: 978-0-367-42192-2 (hbk)
ISBN: 978-0-367-42191-5 (pbk)
ISBN: 978-0-367-82257-6 (ebk)

Typeset in Bembo
by Taylor & Francis Books

# CONTENTS

# ILLUSTRATIONS

## Figures

## Tables

## Boxes

# CONTRIBUTORS

**Greg Austin** is Senior Fellow for Cyber, Space and Future Conflict at the International Institute for Strategic Studies. He concurrently holds a professorial post with the University of New South Wales. Greg is a member of the Advisory Board for the Global Foundation for Cyber Studies and Research, registered in the United States. He has authored books on *Cyber Policy in China* (2014) and *Cybersecurity in China* (2018) and has edited a volume on *National Cyber Emergencies* (2020). His other publications include five books on Asian security affairs (four are on China), each with a strong interdisciplinary focus, and one additional edited volume on energy security. He has held appointments at the War Studies Department at King's College London (Senior Visiting Fellow), Peace Studies at Bradford (Principal Research Fellow), and International Relations at ANU in Australia (Fellow). He has served in Australian security policy as a Ministerial adviser, parliamentary committee secretary, international intelligence liaison officer and intelligence analyst. He has worked as a consultant on projects for the Australian and British governments.

**Jean R.S. Blair** is Professor of Computer Science at the U.S. Military Academy, West Point, and is currently the Distinguished Professor for Innovation in the Department of Electrical Engineering and Computer Science. Her research interests include computing and cyber security education, the design and analysis of algorithms for combinatorial problems, graph algorithms, and parallel computing. Blair received a Ph.D. in computer science from the University of Pittsburgh.

**William J. Caelli** is Emeritus Professor at the Queensland University of Technology and an Adjunct Professor at Griffith University, Australia. He has over 50 years' experience in industry, research and education, in information and data network technologies, more than 43 years of which have been in cyber security in Australia and overseas. His interests lie in the areas of cryptology and its application, trusted systems and networks and management/policy/legal aspects of information security. He has published extensively in the area and has been a consultant nationally and internationally, including participating in Rand Corporation activities in the USA. He received his PhD in 1972 in Nuclear Physics from the Australian National University and was made an Officer in the Order of Australia in 2003. His latest book (edited with L. J. Janczewski) was *Cyber Conflict and Small States* (Routledge, 2016).

**Jamie Collier** is a Research Affiliate at the Centre for Technology and Global Affairs, the University of Oxford, Oxford, UK, where he is also a cyber security DPhil Candidate. His research focuses on the role of private actors in cyber security. In 2017, Jamie was based at the MIT as a Cyber Security Fulbright Scholar. He is a strategic intelligence analyst with Digital Shadows, and has work experience with the NATO Cooperative Cyber Defence Centre of Excellence and PwC India.

**Daria Daniels Skodnik** currently serves as an Advisory Board Member, for Defence and Security Policy, at the World Research Centre, a group holding company comprised of research centres registered in Canada, the United States, France, Japan, and India. From 2013 to 2016, she was Deputy Commandant and Dean of the North Atlantic Treaty Organization (NATO) Defense College. Dr Daniels Skodnik is the first woman to have been elected by the NATO Military Committee to a senior leadership role at the NATO Defense College. As Dean, she was the functional head of all academic matters and was responsible for Professional Military Education (PME) and through research and outreach for the advancement of NATO policies. As Deputy Commandant, she advised on political, diplomatic, and complex security issues in support of NATO's strategic priorities and challenges to the security of the Alliance. She has held many leadership and management roles in the defence and military sectors dealing with international security, and more recently, with PME as well as NATO policy. She continues to teach, mentor, and advise in the fields of international security, NATO policy, and the European Union's Common Security and Defence Policy. She holds a PhD in Political Science (Political Theory) from LUISS Guido Carli University, Rome (2012), an MA in International Law from the University of Maribor (2006), and a BA in Political Science (International Relations) from the University of Ljubljana (2002). Her teaching focuses on geopolitics, the impact of the Fourth Industrial Revolution on international security policy and defence, the future of war, and senior professional military education. Her current research emphasis is on executive coaching.

**Tommaso De Zan** is a Research Affiliate at the Centre for Technology and Global Affairs and a PhD Researcher at the Centre for Doctoral Training in Cyber Security at the University of Oxford, Oxford, UK. His dissertation analyses the effectiveness of public policy interventions aimed at tackling the cyber security skills shortage. He has worked for the European Union Network and Information Security Agency, the European Union Institute for Security Studies and the

International Affairs Institute in Rome. He is a member of the Working Group on Cyber Security Culture and Skills of the Global Forum on Cyber Expertise. He holds a Master's degree in International Relations and a Bachelor's degree in Political Science and International Relations from the University of Bologna, and he was an exchange student at the Hertie School of Governance, the Josef Korbel School of International Studies and Université catholique de Louvain.

**Andrew O. Hall** was commissioned in 1991 in the U.S. Military Academy as an Infantry Officer. He has a BS in Computer Science, an MS in Applied Mathematics, and a PhD in Management Science. After command, Andy was selected to study at the Naval Postgraduate School and teach at the U.S. Military Academy at West Point. He taught in the Department of Mathematical Sciences at West Point where he was Career Field Designated as an Operations Research/Systems Analyst (ORSA). He has since served as a Manpower Analyst in the Strength Forecasting Division of the Army G-1 (Personnel), and as an Assessment and Effects analyst for the XVIIIth Airborne Corps/Multi National Corps-Iraq, and as a global force management analyst in the Joint Operations Division on the Joint Staff. He last served as the Chief of the Military Personnel Structure and Plans Division in the Army G-1 where he was instrumental in the establishment of the Cyber Branch and Cyber Scholars program. He is currently assigned as the Director of the Army Cyber Institute at West Point, USA.

**Adam P. Henry** is Director of Education and Research Programs at Fifth Domain, focusing on partnerships with education institutions and industry. He is an Adjunct Lecturer at the UNSW Canberra Cyber, and participates in other key projects and programs. He is a cyber security education, skills and workforce development expert and researcher. He has presented widely at major conferences in Australia and abroad. He has extensive experience in digital and cyber leadership, including transformation, developing, leading and executing technology business solutions and strategies. He is a new thought leader in this field, pushing the boundaries with his research while implementing practical solutions to this global issue.

**Monica Kaminska** is a DPhil Candidate in Cyber Security at the Centre for Doctoral Training in Cyber Security, the University of Oxford, Oxford, UK. Her doctoral research focuses on the attribution of cyber operations. Monica has previously investigated election interference through social media and the presence of misinformation and automated activity on technology platforms. Within the Centre for Technology and Global Affairs, Monica contributes to the work of the Cyber Studies Programme. Monica previously has worked in the professional services sector in London and also has experience with the UK Foreign and Commonwealth Office. She currently co-organises interdisciplinary cyber crisis simulation exercises for UK universities and private sector organisations and collaborates with Oxford Analytica as an expert contributor. Monica holds an MPhil in Geographical Research from the University of Cambridge and a BSc in International Relations from the London School of Economics.

**Anne Kohnke** is Associate Professor of Cybersecurity in the Department of Cybersecurity and Information Systems at the University of Detroit Mercy, USA, and teaches courses in both the information technology and organisation development/change management disciplines at the bachelor through doctorate levels. Anne's research focus is in the areas of cyber security, risk management, threat modelling, and IT governance. After a 25-year career in IT, Anne transitioned from a Vice President of IT and Chief Information Security Officer (CISO) position into full-time academia in 2011. She holds a PhD from Benedictine University.

**Wenze Lu** recently completed his PhD in the School of Humanities and Social Sciences at UNSW Canberra at the Australian Defence Force Academy. He received his Bachelor's and Master's degrees from Northeastern University (NEU) in China and the Australian National University (ANU). He has a Bachelor's degree in Automation, and he has Master's degrees in Financial Management, in Business, and in Control Theory and Control Engineering (by research). He has held posts in China's Ministry of Industry and Information Technology (MIIT) and its Academy of Telecommunications Research. His primary research interests are in the areas of internet political participation and cyber policies. In the area of internet political participation, he focuses on China's online political protests, including grassroots anti-corruption protests, online environmental movements, and online protests against police brutality. He also conducts research related to China's cyber policies. This research has focused on China's cyber security strategies, internet censorship regime, and the cultivation of Chinese cyber security talents.

**Andrew Martin** is Professor of Systems Security in the Department of Computer Science at the University of Oxford, Oxford, UK. He has set up and run several initiatives on cyber security within the university, including an MSc in Systems Security, and his current venture, the Centre for Doctoral Training in Cyber Security. His core research area is in co-designing hardware and software to build complex distributed systems which exhibit the property of being "secure by design", with applications such as trusted cloud computing and secure Internet-of-Things. Though pursuing cross-disciplinary cyber security, he now explores research in many broader areas.

**Dan Shoemaker** is Principal Investigator and Senior Research Scientist at the Center for Cyber Security and Intelligence Studies, at the University of Detroit Mercy, USA. Dan has served 30 years as a professor at UDM, with 25 of those years as department chair. He served as a co-chair for both the Workforce Training and Education and the Software and Supply Chain Assurance Initiatives for the Department of Homeland Security, and was a subject matter expert for the NICE Workforce Framework 2.0. Dan has co-authored six books in the field of cyber security and has authored over one hundred journal publications. Dan holds a PhD from the University of Michigan.

**Ken Sigler** is a faculty member of the Computer Information Systems (CIS) program at the Auburn Hills campus of Oakland Community College in Michigan, USA. His primary research is in the areas of software management, software assurance, and cloud computing. He developed the college's CIS program option entitled "Information Technologies for Homeland Security." Until 2007, Ken served as the liaison for the college with the International Cybersecurity Education Coalition (ICSEC), of which he is one of three founding members. Ken is a member of IEEE, the Distributed Management Task Force (DMTF), and the Association for Information Systems (AIS).

**Jantje Silomon** is a researcher at the Institute for Peace Research and Security Policy in Hamburg (IFSH), Germany, having joined as part of the Arms Control and Emerging Technologies Research Project in April 2019. Previously, Jantje was based at the University of Oxford, conducting her doctoral research on the topic of software as a weapon. She completed her BSc in Computer Science, before spending some time in South-East Asia. Upon returning to the UK, she worked in academia and industry, while also gaining an MRes in International Security and Global Governance.

**Edward Sobiesk** is the Senior Civilian Faculty Member in the Army Cyber Institute, West Point, USA, and is Professor of Computer and Cyber Science in the Department of Electrical Engineering and Computer Science. Dr Sobiesk spent 28 years in the U.S. Army, retiring as a colonel. He has over two decades of experience as an educator, leader, and practitioner within the Cyber Domain. Dr Sobiesk has directed three different computing programs at West Point; has run a 200-person computer support directorate; and has over 30 invited or refereed academic publications. His research interests include online privacy and usable security, computing and cyber security education, artificial intelligence and machine learning, and complex interdependency.

**Glenn Withers** is a Distinguished Honorary Professor at the Australian National University and Visiting Professor at the University of New South Wales Canberra. His PhD from Harvard University was on the topic of human resources for defence. He has held appointments at Harvard University and Cambridge University, and has consulted widely for governments and companies from the OECD and the North-West Shelf Consortium to the U.S. Defense Department and the Prime Minister of Malaysia. In Australia, he has been Chair of the National Population Council and the Commissioner of the Economic Planning Advisory Commission and helped to establish the Bureau of Labour Market Research, the Bureau of Immigration Research, the Productivity Commission, the Crawford School of Government, and Universities Australia. He was awarded honours by the Australian government for developing the Australian Immigration Points System. He is immediate past President of the Academy of the Social Sciences in Australia and the Australian Council of Learned Academies.

Currently, he is Chair of the Global Board of the Global Development Learning Network, a World Bank affiliate that operates in 60 countries. He has a wide range of publications in books, academic journals, government reports and consultancy reports, particularly focusing on education, skills, workforce, and population issues.

# ACKNOWLEDGEMENTS

The editor would like to acknowledge: the University of New South Wales Canberra, who first published Chapter 2, "Mastering the cyber security skills crisis" as a Working Paper under a digital commons framework; the U.S. Military Academy as the publisher in 2019 of the initial version of Chapter 4, "Educating future multidisciplinary cyber security teams" under a digital commons framework; Taylor and Francis Group for permission to republish the initial version of Chapter 5, "What the profession of cyber security needs to know and do", first published in *EDP Audit, Control, and Security Newsletter* (59) 2 (2019); the Social Cyber Institute, who first published Chapter 6, "Creating social cyber value as the broader goal" under a digital commons framework and a different title; and the Global Cyber Security Centre in Rome who first published "Mind the Gap: The Cyber Security Skills Shortage and Public Policy Interventions" from which Chapter 12, "Future research on the cyber security skills shortage", draws some material.

# ABBREVIATIONS

| | |
|---|---|
| ABET | Accreditation Board for Engineering and Technology |
| ACCS | Australian Centre for Cyber Security |
| ACCSE | Academic Centres of Cyber Security Excellence |
| ACE | Academic Centres of Excellence |
| ACE-CSR | Academic Centres of Excellence in Cyber Security Research |
| ACI | Army Cyber Institute |
| ACM | Association of Computing Machinery |
| ACOLA | Australian Council of Learned Academies |
| ACS | Australian Computer Society |
| AFR | Australian Financial Review |
| AI | Artificial Intelligence |
| AIS | Association for Information Systems |
| AISA | Australian Information Security Association |
| AIS SIGSEC | Association for Information Systems Special Interest Group on Security |
| APT | advanced persistent threat |
| ASD | Australian Signals Directorate |
| AUSTRAC | Australian Transaction Reports and Analysis Centre |
| BCS | British Computer Society |
| BYOD | bring your own device |
| C3T | Cadet Competitive Cyber Team |
| CAC | Cyberspace Administration of China |
| CAE | Centers of Academic Excellence |
| CAE-2Y | Centers of Academic Excellence in Cyber Defense Two-Year Education |
| CAE-CD | Centers of Academic Excellence in Cyber Defense |
| CAE-CDE | Centers of Academic Excellence in Cyber Defense Education |

| | |
|---|---|
| CAE-CO | Centers of Academic Excellence in Cyber Operations |
| CAE-IAE | Centers of Academic Excellence-Information Assurance Education |
| CAE-R | Centers of Academic Excellence in Cyber Defense Research |
| CAICT | China Academy of Information and Communications Technology |
| CCA | Centre for Cyber Assessment |
| CCP | Chinese Communist Party |
| CCS | competitive computer security |
| CDT | Certified Degree Providers and Centres for Doctoral Training in Cyber Security |
| CE | computer engineering |
| CEO | Chief Executive Officer |
| CERDEC | Communications-Electronics Research, Development and Engineering Center |
| CERIAS | Center for Education and Research in Information Assurance and Security |
| CERT | Computer Emergency Response Team |
| CESG | Communications-Electronics Security Group |
| CIC | China Investment Corporation |
| CIO | Chief Information Officer |
| CIMA | Cyber Incident Management Arrangements |
| CISM | Certified Information Security Manager |
| CISO | Chief Information Security Officer |
| CISSE | Colloquium for Information Systems Security Education |
| CISSP | Certified Information Systems Security Professional |
| CITSEC | China Information Technology Security Evaluation Centre |
| CLDP | Cyber Leader Development Program |
| CNI | critical national infrastructure |
| CNKI | China Knowledge Resource Integrated Database |
| CNSS | Committee on National Security Systems |
| CNSSI | Committee on National Security Systems Instructions |
| COAG | Council of Australian Governments |
| COAST | computer operations, audit and security technologies |
| COBR | Cyber Crisis Response Committee |
| CPNI | Centre for the Protection of National Infrastructure |
| CS | Computer Science |
| CSC | Capability Systems Centre |
| CSEC | cyber security education curriculum |
| CSEC-JTF | Cyber Security Education Curriculum-Joint Task Force |
| CSPRI | Cyber Security and Privacy Research Institute |
| CSSS | cyber security skills shortage |
| CSX | cyber security expert |
| CTF | capture the flag |
| CTO | Chief Technology Officer |
| CTT | cyber table top |

| | |
|---|---|
| CUAA | Chinese Universities Alumni Association |
| CyBOK | Cyber Security Body of Knowledge |
| DCAT | defence cyber aptitude test |
| DCMS | Digital, Culture, Media and Sport |
| DHS | Department of Homeland Security |
| DFAT | Department of Foreign Affairs and Trade |
| DNC | Democratic National Committee |
| DoD | Department of Defense |
| DPMC | Department of the Prime Minister and Cabinet |
| ECQs | executive core qualifications |
| ECU | Edith Cowan University |
| EE | electrical engineering |
| ENISA | European Network and Information Security Agency |
| EO | Executive Order |
| EPSRC | Engineering and Physical Sciences Research Council |
| EU | European Union |
| FAANG | Facebook, Amazon, Apple, Netflix, Google |
| FBI | Federal Bureau of Investigation |
| FEMA | Federal Emergency Management Agency |
| FIT | Faculty of Information Technology |
| GCHQ | Government Communications Headquarters |
| GCSCC | Global Cyber Security Capacity Centre |
| GGE | Group of Governmental Experts |
| GIAC | Global Information Assurance Certification |
| GSP | government-wide security profession |
| GWU | George Washington University |
| HASS | Humanities, Arts, and Social Science |
| HCI | human-computer interaction |
| HEO | High Executive Officer |
| HMG | Her Majesty's Government |
| HR | Human Resources |
| IA | information assurance |
| ICAO | International Civil Aviation Organisation |
| ICITST | International Conference for Internet Technology and Secured Transactions |
| ICT | Information and Communications Technology |
| IEC | Israel Electric Corporation |
| IEEE | Institute of Electrical and Electronics Engineers |
| IEEE-CS | Institute of Electrical and Electronics Engineers Computer Society |
| IFE | Institute for Future Environments |
| IFIP | International Federation for Information Processing |
| IFIP WG | International Federation for Information Processing Working Group |
| IISP | Institute of Information Security Professionals |

| | |
|---|---|
| IISS | International Institute of Strategic Studies |
| IJCWT | International Journal of Cyber Warfare and Terrorism |
| INFOSEC | information systems security |
| ISACA | Information Systems Audit and Control Association |
| $(ISC)^2$ | International Information System Security Certification Consortium |
| ISG | Information Security Group |
| ISI | Information Security Institute |
| ISRC | Information Security Research Centre |
| IT | Information Technology |
| ITiCSE | Innovation and Technology in Computer Science Education |
| ITMO | Information Technologies, Mechanics and Optics |
| ITPA | Information Technology Professionals Association |
| JTF | Joint Task Force |
| KSA | knowledge, skills, abilities |
| MBA | Master in Business Administration |
| MIIT | Ministry of Industry and Information Technology |
| MLPS | Multi-Level Protection Scheme |
| MOD | Ministry of Defence |
| MoE | Ministry of Education |
| MOOC | Massive-Open-Online-Course |
| NATO | North Atlantic Treaty Organisation |
| NCISSE | National Colloquium for Information Systems Security Education |
| NCSC | National Cyber Security Centre |
| NCTIB | National Cybersecurity Talent and Innovation Base |
| NHS | National Health Service |
| NIAC | National Infrastructure Advisory Council |
| NICCS | National Initiative for Cyber Security Careers and Studies |
| NICE | National Initiative for Cyber Security Education |
| NISA | National Information Security Authority |
| NIST | National Institute of Standards and Technology |
| NSA | National Security Agency |
| NSF | National Science Foundation |
| NSTISSC | National Security Telecommunications and Information Systems Security Committee |
| NSTISSI | National Security Telecommunications and Information Systems Security Instruction |
| NSW | New South Wales |
| NUST | National University of Sciences and Technology |
| OECD | Organisation for Economic Cooperation and Development |
| OMB | Office of Management and Budget |
| OPM | Office of Personnel Management |
| OS | operating system |
| OSI | open systems interconnection |

| | |
|---|---|
| OST | out-of-school time |
| PCCIP | President's Commission on Critical Infrastructure Protection |
| PGP | pretty good privacy |
| PLA | People's Liberation Army |
| PME | Professional Military Education |
| PNNL | Pacific National Northwest Laboratories |
| PRC | Privacy Rights Clearinghouse |
| QIT | Queensland Institute of Technology |
| QUT | Queensland University of Technology |
| RACF | Resource Access Control Facility |
| RCT | randomised control trial |
| RHC | Royal Holloway College |
| ROTC | Reserve Officers' Training Corps |
| RUSI | Royal United Services Institute |
| S&P | Standard and Poor's |
| SAGE-AU | System Administrators Guild of Australia |
| SANS | SysAdmin, Audit, Network and Security Institute |
| SAST | Static Application Security Testing |
| SCI | Social Cyber Institute |
| SCP | Sector Competitiveness Plan |
| SE | South-east |
| SEF | Science and Engineering Faculty |
| SEO | Senior Executive Office |
| SFS | Scholarship for Service |
| SIGCAS | Special Interest Group on Computers and Society |
| SIGSAC | Special Interest Group for Security, Audit and Control |
| SME | small and medium-sized enterprises |
| SQA | Software Quality Assurance |
| SSRN | Social Science Research Network |
| STEM | Science, Technology, Engineering and Mathematics |
| SWEBOK | Software Engineering Body of Knowledge |
| TAFE | Technical and Further Education |
| TGSP | Transforming Government Security Programme |
| UCD | University College Dublin |
| UK | United Kingdom |
| UN | United Nations |
| UNGGE | United Nations Group of Governmental Experts |
| UNSW | University of New South Wales |
| USA | United States of America |
| USAA | United Services Automobile Association |
| USMA | United States Military Academy |
| VALUE | valid assessment of learning in undergraduate education |
| VET | vocational education and training |
| VP | Vice President |

# INTRODUCTION

*Greg Austin*

This book aims to help reposition global research and debates on cyber security workforces of the future. The book is to help leaders in business, government, the armed forces, and civil society to respond to the global shortage of cyber guardians. In China's case alone, by 2020, this shortage has been estimated to reach 1.4 million cyber security posts for which no suitably trained applicants are available. Both structured research and personal reflections of leading researchers in the field and several early career researchers are presented. It exposes the breadth of the field of capital formation for security in cyberspace: from basic philosophy to education policy and corporate choices for a variety of settings, as diverse as big business and military force structure. In doing so, the essential interdisciplinarity of cyber security education is revealed. The material presented here cannot presume to be comprehensive across all relevant aspects of the subject, but rather aspires to reorient thinking about human capital accumulation for security in cyberspace.

The problem set has been transformed in the last decade since the Stuxnet attack on Iran was revealed in 2010. Edward Snowden's leaks in 2013 from the National Security Agency (NSA) redefined the political and policy challenges of cyber security around the world. In 2015 and then again in 2016, weeks before he left office, former US President, Barack Obama declared a national emergency in cyberspace. The second Obama cyber emergency was in large part the result of the Russian cyber-based influence campaign in the presidential election the previous year. In 2017, one randomised attack by a single piece of malware cost a single firm as much as US$300 million, with known total costs for the same attack reaching well in excess of US$10 billion. Even the wealthiest corporations find themselves continually upgrading and expanding not only their workforce but also their stable of external service providers, just to keep up with known threats. There is no better example of this than the diverse problems besetting Facebook through 2018, which saw its share value drop as it struggled to meet reshaped global expectations for privacy and security.

In 2018, the White House and the Pentagon issued companion strategy documents for cyberspace which put human capital development at the forefront of international security competition on all fronts. The White House Strategy, issued in September, observed that the country's "peer competitors are implementing workforce development programs that have the potential to harm long-term United States cybersecurity competitiveness" (White House 2018: 17). The Pentagon document (in fact, a seven-page summary) declared the country's intention to remain dominant in cyberspace and build a military and civilian force that could "defend forward, shape the day-to-day competition, and prepare for war" in cyberspace (DoD 2018: 7). One-tenth of the summary document was devoted to specific workforce development measures, in a section that was the equal longest in the short document. Through these measures, the Trump administration in effect declared a cyber workforce "arms race". In 2019, President Trump declared another national emergency in cyberspace, and then extended it in March 2020.

Future disruptions to current security practices, which are mostly designed to respond to known threats, are inevitable. These disruptions can come from technology shifts, new sources of attack, and from the complexity of systems we now rely on. Earlier preferences globally for a cyber security workforce model and education system premised largely on technology skills have swiftly been overtaken by the equally important need to consider non-technical aspects, especially privacy and ethics, but also management, psychology, and marketing. No country has been able to develop the human capital to match the scope of this challenge, though Israel may have delivered a focus and capability not seen elsewhere, benefiting from both a small well-educated population and unique security challenges.

The book provides an essential grounding (an introduction) for leaders in cyber security education and human capital formation in the face of rapid change and a global shortage of formally educated talent. It provides guideposts in education policy to the technical aspects of cyber security, as classically understood. At the same time, it opens up social and ethical aspects of the field that have emerged with great force in the past decade. Human capital formation for cyber security in the broad scope (ethics, economic, and business models, and radical social uses of information technology) all demand a redesign of education. Interdisciplinarity has become the catchphrase in universities, while in government and corporations, change management has taken on a new sharp edge of defending against state-sponsored cyber attacks. This is one of the first books to offer an updated approach, both reflective and collective, to the problem set as we enter the next decade of technological disruption and escalating threats in cyberspace, from criminal attack, threats to privacy, and state-based information warfare. Its well-referenced chapters by leading scholars and practitioners will help key stakeholders shape human capital for a more secure future in cyberspace.

The book has had an extended provenance, with first steps taken early in 2017 by the Australian Department of the Prime Minister and Cabinet and the University of New South Wales Canberra to convene international specialists in November of that year to look at "realigning cyber security education" in connection with the country's follow-up on its national cyber security strategy. Over the following six months, as we reflected on our combined effort, UNSW Canberra decided to add another stream of research and analysis to address the problem set. This was the aspect of education for national cyber emergencies and cyber disaster response. To that end, we convened a second international research conference in February 2019 under the rubric of "Preparing for the Cyber Storm", and this included a stream of papers on education issues, a stream on simulation, and a stream on a broad set of policy issues around disaster preparedness and national resilience. We have prepared two edited volumes from the papers at the two conferences. The first was published in February 2020: *National Cyber Emergencies: The Return to Civil Defence* (Routledge). This book is the second of the two volumes.

## The structure of the book

This book includes contributions from the 2017 conference, two of which have not been updated. Chapter 1, "History and Philosophy of Cyber Security Education", offers a set of reflections from Professor Bill Caelli, who started his career in nuclear physics as a graduate student in 1967, and who in 1984 published his first paper on cyber security. Bill is one of the pioneers of the subject. This chapter has an enduring value despite the passage of two and a half years between its presentation and the submission of this manuscript. The chapter as presented offered some reflections on the Australian case. Remarkably, or perhaps not, little has changed in Australian policy settings or formal education offerings between November 2017 and the time this manuscript was completed. The few changes had occurred prior to that date. In 2016, the Australian federal government allocated an incredibly modest $1.4 million over four years for a programme around "centre of excellence" branding in several universities. One of the important insights in this chapter is the concept of nano-credentialisation, the idea that industry and business were more interested in credentials offered outside traditional channels of education.

In Chapter 2, Adam Henry offers a framework for analysing cyber security education that also has an enduring value, regardless of its provenance in 2017. It introduces a multi-level approach to education in this sector through consideration of five discrete categories of analysis: (1) level of education (e.g. primary through tertiary and continuing education); (2) expertise (basic through expert and super expert); (3) field of study (such as technology, law, business, management); (4) purpose (national security, commercial, law enforcement, among others); and (5) application (as team leader, team member, senior executive in business, or executive official in government, or the armed forces). The chapter's analysis is supported by one of the few scholarly surveys of graduate students in the field. In this case, the survey population were Master's degree students at UNSW Canberra, one of the leading centres in the world for its diversity of Master's degrees in cyber security. For example, in 2015, UNSW Canberra approved a new Master's degree in Cyber Security, Strategy and Diplomacy ("cyber war and peace"), a university-based degree with few if any peers in the world. All UNSW Canberra undergraduates (officer cadets at the Australian Defence Force Academy) need to take a semester unit in Cyber Security, regardless of the discipline of the degree. Diversity is not everything, however, and Henry usefully compares the value of this range of offerings with a more specialist offering by University College Dublin in cyber crime, an offering that has received global recognition unlike that of any other Master's degree in the field. The contrast is between breadth at UNSW Canberra and depth at UC Dublin.

Innovation in doctoral studies in cyber security is the subject of Chapter 3 by Oxford-based scholars, Andrew Martin and Jamie Collier. They address the challenge of finding the suitable middle ground between the view that cyber security is the preserve of technically educated professionals and the view that everyone must understand cyber security. From the perspective of education in one of the world's leading universities, they discuss the best educational response to types of expertise in professional settings and the scholarly challenge of the emerging inter-disciplinarity in a field that is barely two to three decades old. The chapter reflects on the Cyber Studies Programme set up in the Department of Politics and International Relations at the University of Oxford. It also references the experience of the establishment of the Centre for Doctoral Training in Cyber Security at the University of Oxford, which was based on a pre-existing model within the university for such centres in other disciplines. Of some note, the Centre was set up in the Oxford Martin School, a new institution endowed by IT pioneer author James Martin for just the sort of challenge presented by cyber security education and research – a subject that did not and still does not, in its interdisciplinary manifestations, sit comfortably in most universities. The authors of this chapter argue for deep changes in thought and practice.

Addressing the demand side of the educational need, in Chapter 4, three educators from the U.S. Military Academy at West Point look at the challenge of constructing multidisciplinary teams. Jean Blair, Andrew Hall, and Ed Sobiesk provide a useful review template for evaluating cyber security education programmes from this perspective. The authors present a first-principles approach which is sorely lacking both at the practitioner level and in the education sector. Their purview includes such things as graduate attributes and programme characteristics.

With the role of practitioners and professionals so firmly established in the earlier chapters, the analysis by Dan Shoemaker, Anne Kohnke, and Ken Sigler in Chapter 5 on that question is a particularly valuable contribution. These scholars have a notable history of contributing to policy development in the field. They make a case for "adoption of a complete, correct, and highly effective set of well-defined and commonly accepted controls". This proposition about the mentality of the practice of cyber security is essential and one that is not as dominant in educational programmes as it probably needs to be. They argue for the "amalgamation of all of the essential concepts of cyber defense into a single unifying practice model, one that has real-world currency". They see professional societies both as developers of fundamental ideas in the field but also as "final sanction" for those ideas.

Building on the case being made in earlier chapters for multidisciplinary approaches and the involvement of industry practitioners, in Chapter 6, Greg Austin and Glenn Withers make the case for an approach that more explicitly integrates the social and technical dimensions of the cyber security challenge. They argue that few scholars have been prepared to recognise the full social science implications of the well-worn idea that cyber security is a socio-technical phenomenon. They want to see their novel concept of "social cyber value" placed at the core of all education and practice in the field. There is little direct reference to educational practice in the chapter, rather a plea for a more wide-eyed recognition of the non-security dimensions of cyberspace that are impacting security. These include digital transformation and legacy systems. The authors argue for study not just of cyber competence, but also of cyber incompetence, especially those elements of social organisation and human behaviour that can distort more technically oriented systems for managing security and bring about ever more costly cyber failures.

In addition to planning for cyber security education broadly defined, comprehensive and multidisciplinary, there are some niche mission sets that deserve attention. In Chapter 7, Adam Henry addresses the requirement for education that might equip graduates and practitioners for cyber disaster scenarios. The need goes further than organisations looking after their own networks or government legislation that covers critical infrastructure. This chapter calls for a focus not just on specific cyber education practices, but on using current disaster recovery methods and case studies to inform responses in situations of cyber crisis. Henry highlights the disconnect between national cyber emergencies as a policy priority, especially since 2016, and the lack of engagement by university educators with the issue at the level of intensity and urgency suggested by the shift in policy needs. The author canvasses elements of a new approach in this area of education for cyberspace security.

The next chapter introduces the escalating sense of international security crisis around cyberspace. It raises the question of the type of leadership skills and abilities, not to mention knowledge, needed for those in government and the armed forces to deal with the inter-state cyberspace confrontations that are now occurring on a daily basis. Based in part on her experience as Deputy Commandant of the NATO Defense College in Italy, Daria Daniels Skodnik looks, in Chapter 8, at the role of professional military education (PME) in preparing high-level decision-makers in national security policy for the geopolitical face-offs now occurring in the cyber domain. The author challenges educators in the armed forces to understand the leadership demands of cyber conflict. The chapter offers a view on the attributes of leaders, both military and civilian, working in national security. She sets a very high bar for new approaches, based on recent research, that can feed into novel education approaches in national and multilateral war colleges. Part of the answer, the author asserts, is first working out what sort of society we want to become as we continually equip ourselves with such transformative technology.

Governments have been rushing to develop new strategies to expand their cyber workforces with talent needed to safeguard digital infrastructures and cyber-physical systems. Chapter 9 surveys such initiatives taken in the UK, focusing particularly on university programmes, government strategies, and national and regional competitions. The authors, Monica Kaminska of Oxford University and Jantje Silomon, now of the Institute for Peace Research and Security Policy in Hamburg (IFSH), conclude that while the UK has significantly expanded its repertoire of cyber training initiatives in the last six years, there is still a significant skills gap in the public sector. New initiatives should pay attention to skills provision for national-scale cyber emergencies.

In Chapter 10, Blair, Hall, and Sobiesk offer an additional chapter with a radical proposal to integrate cyber knowledge into all levels of education, both through in-class and extra-curricular activities. They present a multi-level, multidisciplinary approach for holistically integrating cyber into a student's academic experience. Their approach suggests formally integrating cyber studies throughout an institution's curriculum, including within the required general education programme, in electives from a variety of disciplines, as multi-course threads, as minors, and in numerous cyber-related majors. Their holistic approach complements in-class curricula with both a pervasive cyber-aware environment and experiential, outside-the-classroom activities that apply concepts and skills in real-world settings. The aim of their approach is to provide all educated individuals with a level of cyber education appropriate for their role in society. Throughout the description of their approach, they include examples of its implementation at the U.S. Military Academy.

China's ambition to become a cyber power, declared in 2014, has led to reforms in its cyber security education policy. In Chapter 11, Greg Austin and Wenze Lu outline some of the more prominent measures, but assess that the country will need more time for them to have much effect. The challenges for the country are magnified by its massive population scale and its level of development relative to advanced economies, especially the United States. The chapter reviews the reform measures, particularly in universities since the Chinese government regards this education sector as the foundation both of knowledge development and for delivering the well-qualified educators in the numbers needed. They note two trends: more attention to artificial intelligence as an important area of education policy for information security; and some embryonic recognition that recourse to foreign talent may have to be a larger part of China's policy mix than has been acknowledged to date. The country's education policies in this field recognise some of the issues raised by other chapters in this volume, such as the need for multidisciplinary approaches and more attention to social science approaches, including management and psychology. Yet such influences have not penetrated deeply into China's education system for cyber security.

In Chapter 12, Tommaso de Zan reflects upon future directions that research on the cyber security skills shortage might take and argues that it should primarily concentrate on two aspects: the incidence of the shortage and the effectiveness of policy interventions. He also discusses the need to anchor analysis on the cyber security skills shortage in more established research traditions in the social sciences, such as labour economics, skills policy, and impact evaluation. A "dream team of experts" composed by specialists in relevant disciplines should be gathered to blend their expertise to have a common and solid conceptualisation of the cyber security skills shortage.

In an epilogue to the volume as whole, in Chapter 13, Greg Austin offers some reflection on the contents of the book. He presents 12 dilemmas of reform for cyber security education. These start with philosophical questions, such as what sort of cyberspace do we want, through to the balance between formal and informal training. The final dilemma he mentions is how we incorporate personal resilience into education for cyberspace security. Austin asserts that while few of these dilemmas are ever made explicit when discussing cyber security education, they play an invisible role in shaping the debate and the outcomes.

This is one of the first books to reflect on cyber security education since the United States, Russia and China mutually elevated this field of endeavour into a new and vital element of the geopolitical competition between them.

## References

DoD. 2018. Summary: Department of Defense Cyber Strategy, 2018. Available at: http s://media.defense.gov/2018/Sep/18/2002041658/-1/-1/1/CYBER_STRATEGY_ SUMMARY_FINAL.PDF.

White House. 2018. National Cyber Strategy of the United States of America. Available at: www.whitehouse.gov/wp-content/uploads/2018/09/National-Cyber-Strategy.pdf.

# 1

# HISTORY AND PHILOSOPHY OF CYBER SECURITY EDUCATION

*William J. Caelli*

More than 50 years ago, in October 1967, the US Defense Science Board set up a Task Force to examine and recommend appropriate computer security safeguards that would protect classified information in multi-access, resource-sharing computer systems. The study, led by Dr Willis Ware, was published initially as a government document in a classified version in 1970 (DSB 1970) and then declassified several years later.[1] This ground-breaking report, still amazingly relevant, heralded the start of study into what we now call cyber security. Moreover, it ushered in a recognition of the overall need for training, education and further research and development activities in the area, including research into cyber security education practice. The 1960s and 1970s, however, should be regarded as the two decades when cyber security education was largely confined to "in-house" resources in both the private and governmental sectors, especially in the latter for defence and intelligence entities.

However, ICT vendors to military/intelligence entities, government, and business did play a major role in the internal provision of education and training in the area, such as IBM's courses on the RACF access control system for its OS/360 mainframe system and defence-related courses in cryptology. The question internationally was a simple one of whether or not open universities had the human/academic and laboratory/technical resources and the will to provide that education, even as the ICT industry became commoditised. By the 1980s, traditional tertiary education had at last entered the arena. This included universities in Europe, the United States and Australia. Change was rapid and various associations/groups dedicated to cyber security education also formed globally, such as Working Group 11.8 of IFIP, the International Federation for Information Processing.

This chapter provides some personal reflections based on decades of engagement as an academic researcher and educator in this field. The sweep of change has been broad: from the formation of the US National Colloquium for Information

Systems Security Education (NCISSE); the involvement of commercial bodies, ICT suppliers, and not-for-profit enterprises with partial to full dedication to cyber security education, such as $(ISC)^2$, ISACA, SANS Institute, the US Cybercorps/ Scholarship for Service (SFS) and the programme for Centers of Academic Excellence (CAE) in cyber security.

The main philosophical questions to be considered include:

- just how "industry certification", both supplier and broad arena providers, is considered and accepted against formal academic/university/tertiary qualifications
- the role of government in fostering and supporting cyber security education and training at all levels, including scholarship programmes
- acquiring and retaining teachers and researchers in the area by public universities
- to what extent open universities can or should participate in classified cyber security education programmes, including cyber operations, cyber warfare/ terrorism studies
- the role that open and free, or low cost, on-line courses play and their acceptance as sufficient qualification for professional practice in cyber security
- what lessons can we learn from at least the past 30 years or more of accelerated cyber security education efforts?
- how does cyber security education relate to today's IT environment of outsourcing, open, local and hybrid "cloud" computing and the global influence of the largest corporations: FAANG (Facebook, Amazon, Apple, Netflix, Google), or the "Frightful Five" (Amazon, Apple, Facebook, Microsoft and Alphabet-Google) (Manjoo 2017).

## Departure points in three countries

In the United States, the first known course in computer security at an open and public university appears to be that created and delivered by Professor Lance Hoffman in 1970. He went on later to establish a computer security education programme at George Washington University (GWU) in Washington, DC, in 1977 (Hoffman 2017). The Cyber Security and Privacy Research Institute (CSPRI) was later formed at GWU in 1993, with Professor Hoffman as its founding director. Interestingly, CSPRI appears to have had a varied history resulting in its "relaunch" in 2016 (CSPRI 2017).

COAST (Computer Operations, Audit and Security Technologies) was officially commenced in 1991 (CERIAS 2017a), formed out of a small research group in the Computer Sciences Department at Purdue University, West Lafayette, Indiana. It appears to have rapidly grown over the next six years, to become what it says was in 1997 the "largest research group in computing security in the country, reaching a peak research budget of over one million dollars per year". COAST was absorbed into the Center for Education and Research in Information Assurance and Security (CERIAS) in 1999. CERIAS has claimed a premium position in education and research in cyber security: "one of the world's leading centers for research and education in areas of information security" through its multidisciplinary approach "ranging from purely technical issues (e.g., intrusion detection, network security, etc.) to ethical, legal, educational, communicational, linguistic, and economic issues, and the subtle interactions and dependencies among them". As of 2017, the research conducted through CERIAS includes faculty from six different colleges and 20+ departments across campus (CERIAS 2017b).

In Australia, in July 1998, the Faculty of Information Technology at the Queensland Institute of Technology (QIT)[2] established the Information Security Research Centre (ISRC) to provide a consultancy, training, research and development service to industry, government and commerce in the areas of data and computer security, in addition to more traditional tertiary level education and training services (FIT 1989). The ISRC was formed as a joint venture between industry and FIT. The ISRC developed its educational role by offering research Master's and PhD programmes as well as by teaching specialist subjects for post-graduate course work and some undergraduate students (QUT 1991). It was merged into the Information Security Institute (ISI) in the mid-2000s but the ISI was later disbanded. The main problems appeared to be lack of financial support from entities external to the university itself as well as the availability of appropriate academic staff. By 2017, cyber security was no longer mentioned as a "research strength" by QUT's Science and Engineering Faculty (QUT 2017a) or its Institute for Future Environments (IFE) (QUT 2017b).

In the United Kingdom, the Information Security Group (ISG) was founded at Royal Holloway University in 1990, to "pioneer cyber security education, research and industry engagement" (RH 2017). It created the world's first Master's programme in information security (Martin 2013). In 2017, ISG claimed to have "hundreds of post-graduate students, undergraduate teaching and world class academic staff" and to maintain a "Systems Security Lab" which "uses multi-disciplinary techniques to perform industry-relevant research on systems and software security". This is still one of the oldest continuing cyber security education and research centres in the world and is today acknowledged as a leader in the field.

## US cyber security education: workforce or profession?

From 13–18 November 2017, the US National Institute of Standards and Technology (NIST) of the US Department of Commerce designated a special week of activity related to careers in cyber security, described as follows: "The National Cyber Security Career Awareness Week is a celebration to focus local, regional, and national interest to inspire, educate and engage children through adults to pursue careers in cyber security" (NIST 2017a). This week of activities aimed to show the broad range of careers possible in the now critical cyber security realm, a discipline perceived as vital to the security of individuals, enterprises, both public and private, and the nation as a whole. The diversity is captured in Figure 1.1, from the documents of the US National Initiative for Cyber Security Education

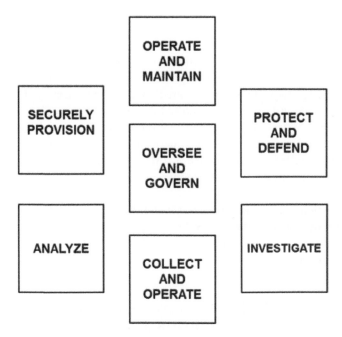

**FIGURE 1.1** NIST/NICE Cybersecurity Workforce Framework, 2017

(NICE), itself under NIST. It immediately indicates a broad base for education and training, ranging from legal and investigatory matters to computer science and engineering to data and telecommunications systems to mathematics. This follows the 12 July 2016 publication by the US Office of Management and Budget (OMB) and Office of Personnel Management (OPM) of the first ever US "Federal Cyber Security Workforce Strategy" (Donovan et al. 2016).

However, in education and training terms:

> For any discipline to be regarded as a professional undertaking by which its members may be treated as true 'professionals' in a specific area, practitioners must clearly understand that discipline's history as well as the place and significance of that history in current practice as well as its relevance to available technologies and artifacts at the time.
>
> *(Caelli et al. 2013)*

Such respect for and understanding of the history and broad philosophy of any discipline are obvious in many other fields from medicine to physics and more. In the United States, prior to the formation of NICE, the National Security Telecommunications and Information Systems Security Committee (NSTISSC) was established under National Security Directive 42, "National Policy for the Security of National Security Telecommunications and Information Systems", dated 5 July 1990. On 16 October 2001, President George W. Bush signed Executive Order

13231, Critical Infrastructure Protection in the Information Age, redesignating the National Security Telecommunications and Information Systems Security Committee (NSTISSC) as the Committee on National Security Systems (CNSS). This entity, still operating, sets out a series of standards related to cyber security for the US Government, including several related to required education and training. For example, document CNSSI-4014, entitled "National Information Assurance Training Standard for Information Systems Security Officers" was issued in 2004 and claims to describe "the process used to aid in the systematic development of training to serve as the first line of defense in Information Assurance (IA)." This document lays out a series of essential curricula for cyber security education as follows:

- Information Systems Security (INFOSEC) Professionals NSTISSI 4011
- Senior Systems Managers CNSS 4012
- Senior Systems Administrators CNSS 4013A
- System Certifiers NSTISSI 4015
- Risk Analyst CNSS 4016A.

A diagram from the Defense Science Board report of 1970 mentioned above, reproduced as Figure 1.2, illustrates the areas of interest in relation to cyber security which has remarkable relevance even today. It gives an indication of the type and depth of topics to be included in any cyber security education process and thus the levels of expertise needed by any teacher.

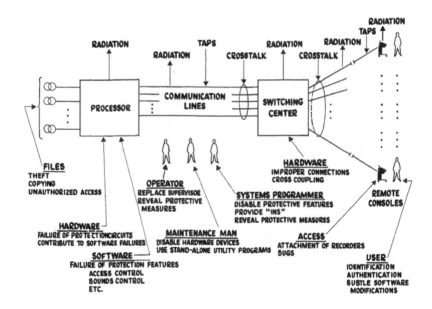

FIGURE 1.2 Security controls for computer systems: 1970 view

As prescient as it was, the 1970 graphic does not capture the added complexity that has emerged in the field of cyber security in the last 25 years following the advent and development of both the Internet and the "World Wide Web", as well as mobile devices and other radical technologies. These changes have added new burdens for all countries in framing cyber security education and training, particularly for their defence and public sectors. The United States has been in the lead on many of the technologies and has also therefore been forced into a leading position on security education. The field of cyber security has massively changed over this period as the usually isolated computer systems of both enterprises and individuals alike became connected to a global "information super-highway", the Internet, and the "personal computer" and then "smart phone" revolutions rapidly emerged.

In summary, cyber security education and training have had a mixed history over the past 50 years with the majority of entities involved being related to defence/intelligence/government support or to specific product demands in the ICT private sector. A broad education philosophy has only recently arisen whereby publicly funded tertiary institutions appear to "go it alone" in financially supporting cyber security education and research even if not supported by the number of various private sector and government/defence programmes. This contrasts with the situation for more classical disciplines, e.g. medicine, law, science, etc. where financial resources external to a university may be vital for research but basic undergraduate and postgraduate education programmes are funded through university resources, often involving student fees. There is recent evidence demonstrating that "market demand" for cyber security education may have had an influence on universities, particularly in Australia, to separately support such activity on the basis of current and projected student numbers, particularly over the next 5–10 years.

Terminology for the field of cyber security has changed over time but the term "information assurance" has probably proved the most durable. It is a softer sounding and more marketable term, being most prominent until the second decade of the twenty-first century. This also resonates with such terms as "cyber/information resilience" and others all apparently aimed at that more marketable and acceptable approach to the problem for commerce and industry and, indeed, all outside the strict defence/intelligence/government areas.

Identification of the need for a clear definition of cyber security and for education and training in that area was emphasised in 1997 in the report of the US President's Commission on Critical Infrastructure Protection (PCCIP), as follows:

> NIST, NSA, and the U.S. Department of Education work in collaboration with the private sector to develop programs for education and training of information assurance specialists and for the continuing education as technologies change. This effort should also support "training the trainers" to provide an adequate cadre of qualified instructors to teach technicians.
>
> *(PCCIP 1997)*

Meanwhile, the terminology used still largely reflected the classifications and areas of interest derived from the original Ware report from the Rand Corporation as published in 1975. Interestingly the same broad areas of concern largely survived in the security architecture of the Open Systems Interconnection (OSI) model via the IS 7498–2 standard. That standard has now been abandoned for the most part in favour of the ARPANET/DARPANET/"Internet" structures standards.

In traditional terms, cyber security education has been largely oriented towards, and thus provided by, science, technology, engineering and mathematics (STEM) disciplines at the university level. However, by the 1990s, this had changed somewhat and matters of cyber security in relation to business, management, society, policy, politics, international relations and law had all arisen and some academic programmes had been developed and offered (CSPRI 2017). This is now acknowledged internationally, as demonstrated, for example, in the case of the Australian Computer Society (ACS), which has two separate professional certification processes, one in the technology area and the other in the management/policy area.

This separation is again exemplified by a course offered by the Harvard Kennedy School in 2018 on cyber security: "The Intersection of Policy and Technology" (Harvard Kennedy School, 2017). It was billed as the "first program of its kind to focus on the intersection of policy and technology and how, together, they can address the critical threats of a cyber world". The objective would be to "bring together technologists and policymakers and provide them with a conceptual framework for the design of both cyber security policy and technology". The claim of "first" is, however, arguable, given the earlier such multidisciplinary activity work in the United States at George Washington University (GWU), for example. The full-time, intensive nature of the Harvard Kennedy School course demonstrates a difference in style compared to traditional university/tertiary semester-long programmes. Interestingly, the Harvard Kennedy School six-day intensive residential course, priced at US$8,500, illustrates quite different approaches to the discipline. It offers "Executive Core Qualifications (ECQs)", which are described as

> [Meeting] the professional training needs of U.S. federal managers and their military, corporate and international counterparts. The curricula for many of these programs incorporate the Office of Personnel Management (OPM) Executive Core Qualifications (ECQs) and their associated core competencies. These five ECQs (Leading Change, Leading People, Results Driven, Business Acumen and Building Coalitions) are the fundamental prerequisites for selection to, assessment of and continued assignment within the Senior Executive Service.
> *(ibid.)*

One example of professionalisation can be found in the Australian experience. The Australian Information Security Association (AISA), formed in 1999, declares cyber security activity as a profession and provides the usual professional "code of ethics" which governs its members (AISA 2016). It clearly states its aims as follows: it "champions the development of a robust information security sector by building the capacity of professionals in Australia and advancing the cyber security and safety of the Australian public as well as businesses and governments in Australia". It "was created to provide leadership for the development, promotion, and improvement" of the new profession, including through further work "in the areas of advocacy, diversity, education, and organisational excellence".

## Demand-driven pathways: nano-certification

NIST/NICE sees pathways to a cyber security career as being linked to processes for "obtaining cyber security work experience" (NICE 2017). These processes that need to exist for the student include "Internships, Cooperative Education, and Apprenticeships", according to NICE. This observation reflects the apparent Australian market-demand for professionals in cyber security where, as already mentioned, specific product/system skills are requested along with associated experience. However, the educational needs of a person entering the profession are answered in some ways by a highly variable set of options. These include:

- self-study, using Internet-based facilities such as YouTube, etc.
- enrolment in a Massive-Open-Online-Courses (MOOC), offered by traditional tertiary institutions, commercial enterprises or others for varying fees and with or without a form of certification, such as a "nano-degree", e.g. UDACITY, Coursera, edX, Udemy, etc.
- enrolment in a course offered by a not-for-profit enterprise or by an IT systems or services vendor, e.g. CompTIA, the SANS Institute, Microsoft, RedHat, CISCO, etc.
- enrolment in the same courses as above but offered by or through the assistance of a traditional tertiary education enterprise and with the potential for certification under traditional terms, e.g. a certificate/diploma/Master's degree
- traditional university/tertiary institutions in either in-house or online form or a combination of both.

For example, edX (www.edx.org) appears to be offering 13 full cyber security courses in early 2018. At another point in the education spectrum, the University of Washington, via edX, offered a series of four four-week courses, 2–5 hours per week of involvement, entitled "Essentials of Cyber Security", "Cyber Security: The CISO's View", "Building a Cyber Security Toolkit" and "Finding Your Cyber Security Career Path" for US$284.40 in total (University of Washington 2017). This is claimed to be a Professional Certificate Program: "Created by leading companies and top universities, Professional Certificate programs are a series of in-demand courses designed to develop the critical skills needed for today's top jobs." This exemplifies an educational move to "nano-degrees": small intense courses aimed at specific topics such as cyber security. However, the acceptance, value and recognition of such educational experiments and their associated certificates are still not certain despite their use of the words "professional" and "certificate". Indeed, the discipline of cyber security is showing one of the largest ranges of education/training offerings in any discipline for a potential student and wildly varying costs to the student with extreme variations in recognition and certification.

Over the past 10 years or more there has been the rapid development of not only cyber security programmes from the usual not-for-profit and vendor organisations but a newer phenomenon of education entities who offer courses that profess to make students ready for the examinations required by the main not-for-profit entities in this area, such as $ISC^2$, ISACA, etc. For example, the USCyber Security Academy makes the bold claim that "when you train with us, we not only guarantee that you will pass the related certification exam, we also guarantee that you will learn some pretty cool stuff" (CSA 2017).

In 2017, Cyber Security Ventures of California offered a listing[3] of those enterprises offering cyber security education/training in the United States and elsewhere. It included some 29 such entities, with enterprises such as $ISC^2$, the SANS Institute, Global Information Assurance Certification (GIAC), EC-Council, and others. Much will depend upon acceptance of these cyber security education schemes not only by employers but also by relevant associations in the profession (such as IEEE and ACM). As of 2017, this acceptance appears solid and, in many cases, industry-level certification may be seen as being superior to traditional university/academic awards. Some universities claim that their courses prepare the student for industry certification examinations.

## Multidisciplinary curriculum development

The concept of an internationally agreed curriculum for the now acknowledged profession of cyber/information security had gained momentum by 2015. A number of high profile professional associations[4] with international memberships set up the Joint Task Force on Cyber Security Education (JTF).[5] It was launched in September 2015 with the purpose of developing comprehensive curricular guidance in cyber security education that would support future programme development and associated educational efforts. "The JTF is a collaboration between major international computing societies" (JTF 2017). The important point to note here is that this activity involves a group of ICT professionals from a diverse set of nation states, often with varying political and policy settings in relation to national information infrastructure. The JTF goes further by offering a definition of cyber security which clearly sets out a multidisciplinary concept, as follows:

> a computing-based discipline involving technology, people, information, and processes to enable assured operations. It involves the creation, operation, analysis, and testing of secure computer systems. It is an interdisciplinary course of study, including aspects of law, policy, human factors, ethics, and risk management in the context of adversaries.
>
> *(ACM 2017: 17)*

Interestingly three of the acknowledged four aspects of science, technology, engineering and mathematics (STEM) education are not mentioned, viz. science, engineering and mathematics. Of note also is that this activity is sponsored by the US National Science Foundation (NSF) as well as the international professional societies of the Association for Computing Machinery (ACM), the IEEE Computer Society (IEEE CS), the Association for Information Systems Special Interest Group on Security (AIS SIGSEC), and the International Federation for Information Processing Technical Committee on Information Security Education (IFIP WG 11.8) and the US Intel Corporation.

An important consideration is the one of placement of cyber security learning in any academic curriculum and programme. It could be argued, using an analogy, that cyber security for the IT professional is rather like the required ability of a qualified civil engineer to confidently build a bridge that is safe to use and is constructed following a recognised set of appropriate standards as against an amateur who may feel competent to do the same. In this sense, cyber security studies must form an integral part of any undergraduate/certificate/diploma studies in IT at any tertiary institution. Specialised cyber security curricula may obviously exist for specific dedicated roles with a far more extensive mandate in assessing the management and security of an information system.

## Collective organisation of education: the US case

For two decades, cyber security researchers and educators at the tertiary level worked largely as individual academics. One can identify the pioneers who have worked over the last 40 years, for example, Professor Matt Bishop of the University of California Davis whose publications in the area date back to 1979 (Bishop and Snyder 1979). However, it was not until more recently that fully designated cyber security research and education centres were created and financially supported, for example, under the US Centers of Academic Excellence (CAE) programme, as described below.

The National Colloquium for Information Systems Security Education (NCISSE) was created in 1996 to provide a forum for dialogue between leading figures in government, industry and academia. In June 2002, NCISSE expanded its mission to include greater international participation. To reflect this, the organisation formally changed its name to The Colloquium for Information Systems Security Education or simply "The Colloquium". This organisation states as its goal "to work together to define current and emerging requirements for information assurance education and to influence and encourage the development and expansion of information assurance curricula, especially at the graduate and undergraduate levels" (CISSE 2017). It brings together those interested in overall cyber security education at annual conferences and offers associated activities with a potential for academic job opportunities to be made known and advertised.

### National Centers of Academic Excellence

In 1999, the US National Security Agency (NSA) established its programme for Centres of Excellence in Information Assurance Education (CAE-IAE) and in 2004 it was joined in the effort by the US Department of Homeland Security (DHS). By 2017, the programme had the following streams:

- Cyber Defense (CAE-CD)
- Cyber Defense Education (CAE-CDE)
- Cyber Defense Two-Year Education (CAE-2Y)
- Cyber Defense Research (CAE-R)
- Cyber Operations (CAE-CO)

The programme's goal was to "reduce vulnerability in our national information infrastructure by promoting higher education and research in cyber defense and producing professionals with cyber defense expertise for the Nation" (CAE Community 2017).

As of November 2017, there appear to be over 200 institutions designated as CAE-CD entities in some 44 States of the United States. Most recently the concept of "designated CAE-Cyber Defense (CAE-CD) Resource Centers" has emerged and 14 such centres have been announced. These centres are a network of participating CAE-CD institutions that will provide resources and guidance to applicant institutions. Three categories of resource centres are positioned to assist at a regional and national level: Hub, Consultation and National.

A separate "cyber operations" activity is also supported as follows: "CAE-Cyber Operations program focuses on technologies and techniques related to specialized cyber operations (e.g., collection, exploitation, and response)." This activity accentuates educational requirements in "computer science (CS), computer engineering (CE), and/or electrical engineering (EE) disciplines" (NSA0217B) with an emphasis on laboratory-led learning activity (NSA2017B).

### CyberCorps: Scholarship for Service Program.

Closely related to the CAE programme in the United States is the CyberCorps: Scholarship for Service (SFS) scheme (OPM 2017a). This programme is described as

> a unique program designed to increase and strengthen the cadre of federal information assurance professionals that protect the government's critical information infrastructure. This program provides scholarships that may fully fund the typical costs incurred by full-time students while attending a participating institution, including tuition and education and related fees.

Funding is provided through the US National Science Foundation (NSF) and varies between undergraduate and postgraduate programmes from around US

$22,000–34,000 per annum. Much discussion occurred at the time of formation of this scheme as to the nature of any obligation to be placed on the recipient of such a scholarship. This was essentially resolved as per OPM statements as follows:

> In return for their scholarships, recipients must agree to work after graduation for a Government agency or, subject to approval of the NSF program office, for a State, Local, Tribal, or Territorial Government; or a Federally Funded Research and Development Center, in a position related to cyber security for a period equal to the length of the scholarship. An academic year (the fall and spring semesters) is equivalent to a calendar year of employment.
>
> *(OPM 2017b)*

## The Australian case

A 2017 press report indicated a massive growth in jobs in IT security in Australia over the previous five years or so, as follows: "Census data showed that ICT security specialist roles were up 50 percent from 2011, while ICT manager roles were up 89 percent from 2011" (Arboleda 2017a). This same report went on to quote Robert Hudson, President of the Information Technology Professionals Association (ITPA 2017), an organisation formed in 2016 from the original System Administrators Guild of Australia (SAGE-AU), established in 1993, referring to a government survey that indicated that "Australia would need another 11,000 cyber security specialists in the next ten years." In addition, in a radio broadcast of 11 June 2017, the following summary was given of Australia's cyber security situation in relation to trained, educated and experienced cyber security professionals: "Australian governments and businesses have finally woken up to the scale of the cyber threats we face. But in the race to snap up computer security experts, we may have started too late" (ABCRadio National 2017).

However, a rather different and contrary view of the cyber security job situation in Australia, as distinct from overseas, was given by a late 2016 survey by the Australian Information Security Association (AISA 2016) that indicates that the market demand for full and professional cyber security expertise in Australia may actually be much, much lower than elsewhere because of lack of concern within enterprises. A media report on that study claimed that it was suggesting the skills shortage could be "better characterised as a 'failure of some organisations to resource appropriately', rather than the belief that there are not enough people to fill available jobs" (Williams 2016). Indeed, there is a suggestion that, at least in Australia, the often cited problem of lack of cyber security professionals may actually not be so and that, rather, a lack of market demand for such expertise and the associated professionals is the major problem. This was an interpretation of the AISA report offered as follows:

> From the supply side, AISA says there is evidence of high levels of frustration from those looking to enter the cyber security work force, with too much focus by employers and recruiters on prior experience and detailed

knowledge of very narrow and specific areas, which it says unnecessarily narrows the pool of available candidates.

A private communication to this author from an Australian academic extolling the strengths of a recent, class-topping cyber security graduate and asking if "you are looking for a passionate, motivated and talented apprentice Penetration Tester" to contact the university, gives credence to the AISA findings about the lack of appropriate demand (M. Hale, pers. comm., 17 November 2017).

This situation of distorted demand seems to support the growth of the "nano-qualification" or "nano-certification" trend whereby some form of qualification "paper" is awarded for very specific aspects of cyber security after some usually intensive, full-time, dedicated education/training programme, often of no more than one-week's duration, and sometimes less. Industry and business seem to simply want, in many cases, a fast, specific solution to an immediate problem based on an imported cyber security add-in product, such as proper configuration of a network firewall product or configuration of antivirus scanning systems.

Of particular note and importance to how the country views any cyber security education and training programme has to be the position of Australia in relation to import/export figures for IT products and systems, as well as services based on IT, such as those offered by the "Frightful Five". Essentially Australia is almost totally just a user of information and communications technology (ICT) and its artifacts for many and varied applications. Australia may build software applications across many business areas but the components of those application programmes depend very heavily on imported software development tools and component libraries.

Australia's Department of Foreign Affairs and Trade (DFAT 2017: 23–4) has published figures that clearly enable Australia to be identified as an "information technology colony" in relation to products, systems and direct services. Its report clearly demonstrates a massive import to export imbalance in this sector. The value of exports taken by "Telecom, computer & information services" in 2015 stood at A\$3.3 billion, representing 1 per cent of total goods and services exports. Actual product/systems exports did not rate in the top 25 categories. However, import figures across such products and systems demonstrate a large disparity with export totals for goods and services in telecom, computer and information services: A\$23.2 billion, a 7.6 per cent share of imports.[6] This all points to the "technological colonisation" of Australia in ICT terms.

The Australian case suggests a lack of educated and trained cyber security professionals, as well as relevant teachers/researchers in tertiary education. It points to the urgent need for more extensive research into the overall problem of tertiary education in cyber security/ICT as well as the development and provision of the necessary academics for the area.

More recently some new centres have formed, often with private sector assistance. These include the Optus Macquarie University Cyber Security Hub, formed in 2016, with a claimed joint investment of A\$10 million. It is claimed that:

[This] investment has established a multidisciplinary network, which is providing expertise and leadership in cyber security. It offers a platform for exchange between academics and practitioners from business and government, and it aims at meeting the growing market and demand for cyber-security expertise among new graduates as well as existing employees.

*(Macquarie University 2017)*

At a national level, the Australian Federal Government announced support for Academic Centres of Cyber Security Excellence (ACCSE) in April 2016. Surprisingly, compared to both other Australian and particularly foreign efforts in this same area, the Australian Federal Government claims that it "committed $1.9 million over four years" (2016–2020) for the establishment of such centres at the University of Melbourne and Edith Cowan University to do the following:

- help build Australia's capability in cyber security by encouraging more students to undertake studies in cyber security;
- increase the number of highly skilled post-graduates with the job-ready skills needed to work in Australian business and government to tackle emerging cyber security challenges;
- provide support for research that addresses key cyber security challenges confronting the nation (DoET 2017).

The government expects that these centres will be self-sustaining, relying on student course fees and fee-for-service income, including from government agencies and other external sources.

The micro scale of this financial commitment bears little resemblance in financial policy terms to US public support for cyber security education. In what could be observed as a "Back to the Future" situation, cyber security training and education in Australia appear to be largely again relegated to the private/commercial and not-for-profit sectors away from the conventional and public tertiary education institutions, even though there has been some recent public sector support at State and Federal levels. This is clearly indicated by the recent announcement by a private entity of a planned "cyber training and technologies arena" in Melbourne to help companies prepare for and respond to cyber attacks (Arboleda 2017b). This entity, CyberGym, claims that it is "the only cyber security training and defence provider that trains organisations in three critical areas: cyber defence, events mitigation and crisis management". Indications are that a "cyber-range" of some capacity is to be used for the associated training and education activities. The associated Victorian State Government minister, the Hon. Phillip Dalidakis, particularly welcomed this Israel-based company to Melbourne. Later press reports noted that; originally established in Hadera in 2013, CyberGym is a joint venture between the Israel Electric Corporation and CyberControl, an Israeli cyber security consultancy group (Redrup 2017; Udasin 2017b). The company is also reported as clearly stating that "The company runs courses for IT professionals through to board members and mid-tier managers, placing them in a real-life cyber attack situation and coaching them on how to respond", indicating the use of cyber range facilities. This augments bilateral agreements in this area between Israel and other nations such as Japan (Udasin 2017a) as well as Australia.

Indicating the apparent and obvious requirements for government/private sector involvement and investment in cyber security education and training at a national, level with the financial capacity required, it is interesting to note that CyberGym itself is 50 per cent owned by the Israel Electric Corporation, which is a largely, 99.85 per cent, government-owned entity (IEC 2017; Press 2017) with other interests from "CyberControl, a cyber security consultancy established by veterans of Israel's National Security Authority (NISA) and other security experts" (Press 2017). CyberGym has reportedly also benefited from the involvement of the Israel Defense Forces' Unit 8200 (ibid.) and its alumni through CyberControl "founded by veterans of the Israeli National Information Security Authority (NISA)" (Hason 2017).

The Australian Computer Society (ACS) has recognised only six Australian universities as providing cyber security education at the undergraduate/Bachelor degree level and only two at the Master's degree level, as of November 2017 (ACS 2017a).

An accepted curriculum for cyber security education at the science, technology, engineering and mathematics levels has been available for over 25 years, particularly in the US. However, a curriculum suitable for the legal, policy, political and social aspects of the discipline has only emerged in the past few years, e.g. the assessment of NATO's "Tallin Manual" related to legalities and cyber warfare/conflict. Both aspects have been recognised by the Australian Computer Society (ACS) in its professional certification programme (ACS 2017b), which now clearly delineates these separate aspects of the discipline.

However, there is general agreement and overwhelming evidence in Australia, as elsewhere, that there is not only a severe shortage of educated, trained and experienced cyber security professionals but a more urgent requirement for skilled teachers and researchers in the field at tertiary institutions. This latter problem is the one that seems to require concerted government action in terms of such processes as supported PhD or Master's degree scholarships, as mentioned above and/or aggressive actions to encourage migration of overseas academics in the area to Australia. It should be noted, again, however, that the mooted shortage of cyber security professionals in Australia may not be as straightforward as it looks since there is doubt as to market demand for such professionals in Australia, particularly newly qualified entrants into the field.

### The UK as a comparator for Australia

In November 2016, Oxford University's Global Cyber Security Capacity Centre issued a report which found the education and training resources in the UK "to be at an established stage", observing that the range of offerings was "at national and local levels, ranging from primary to post-graduate", with many different types of courses (GCSCC 2016: 12). However, the review also found that few of the courses had any affiliation to industry. This suggested to the authors that the offerings do not necessarily "meet the needs of industry employers in terms of skills development, nor are educational offers measured to determine their success in meeting the skill needs of the job market".

By 2017, the National Cyber Security Centre (NCSC) of the UK GCHQ had recognised 25 Master's degree-level education programmes at universities in the UK. The rationale is stated as follows:

> It can be difficult for students and employers to assess the quality of Master's degree courses with cyber security content. NCSC certification of such degrees will give prospective students confidence that the course and its content have met strict quality standards.
>
> *(NCSC 2017b)*

At the same time, the UK initiated a programme of support for students in this area and recognition of academic centres and personnel devoted to cyber security education and research, as follows: "Working with partners in government, industry and academia, we identify and support excellence in cyber security education and research and encourage industry investment in academic research" (NCSC 2017c).

In this regard, the UK's Academic Centres of Excellence in Cyber Security Research (ACE-CSR) programme resembles the US CAE programme. This programme states:

> In February 2017, 14 universities have been recognised as ACE-CSR. These universities have met tough minimum standards and proven they have:
>
> - commitment from the university's leadership team to support and invest in the university's cyber security research capacity and capability
> - a critical mass of academic staff engaged in leading-edge cyber security research
> - a proven track record of publishing high impact cyber security research in leading journals and conferences
> - sustained funding from a variety of sources to ensure the continuing financial viability of the research team's activities.
>
> *(NCSC 2017d)*

It is further stated that "the NCSC and the Engineering and Physical Sciences Research Council (EPSRC) jointly recognise Academic Centres of Excellence in Cyber Security Research (ACE-CSR)". Importantly, the NCSC claims to support PhD students in the cyber security area at these ACE-CSR entities to "further stimulate cyber security research in the UK", and obviously to provide the necessary academic staff needed to continue education and research programmes in the UK. This aspect of both US and UK support for the development of cyber security research and education does not obviously appear in the Australian situation, e.g.

PhD student scholarships that could be potentially provided by the Australian Signals Directorate (ASD), for example, to develop new academic staff in the area, etc.

## Conclusion

Cyber security education development needs may fit into three broad categories: (1) curriculum definition; (2) the development and maintenance of educators and researchers; and (3) the fostering of students, including through provision of appropriate laboratory or similar facilities. Here are some conclusions and recommendations related to the Australia case.

### Curricula

There appears to be the need for two separate, but linked, curricula which can be broadly mapped to the separate ACS professional certification schemes in cyber security:

- technology of security
- social science of security (management, policy, regulation and law).

The first of these appears to be well developed at an international level with support of the major international professional associations, such as IEEE, the ACM and the IFIP. The second of these seems more problematic in that individual nation states often have differing regulatory and legal arrangements, such as data breach notification legislation or privacy requirements. It may be that Australia needs to work more in this area with the possibility of an emphasis on the Asia, South-East Asia environment.

### Educators

Given the acknowledged world-wide lack of educated, trained and experienced cyber security professionals for employment in both the private and public sectors, and a similar lack of expert teachers and researchers/academics in the area, it would appear that Australia urgently needs a policy to address the shortfalls. The policy of offering programmes in the United States and the UK to provide government incentives (such as postgraduate scholarships) to attract students into teaching in cyber security is one that could usefully be reviewed for Australia.

### Students and their facilities

At the same time, given the problem that appears to have emerged in Australia of slowness in student uptake of STEM subjects, including ICT, at university/TAFE levels, the evaluation of the US and UK scholarship schemes, viz. the SFS and ACE schemes, seems most appropriate, along with the need for corresponding increases in funding. Coupled with the above two imperatives is the need for relevant and appropriate laboratory facilities to enable, as for most other disciplines, students to obtain "real-world" experience in matters related to cyber security. While such laboratory systems are available, there is the associated need to increase investment in appropriate staff to install, maintain and administer such laboratories; as well as a need for the teachers to be well trained in their use and in integrating the facilities into the students' learning experience.

As pointed out in a paper (Caelli and Liu 2017) to the 21st conference of the US Colloquium for Information Systems Security Education (CISSE), in relation to cyber security education at undergraduate level in Australia:

> Cyber security studies at undergraduate/postgraduate level are offered at numerous registered universities in Australia. The level offered is extremely varied from a specific undergraduate/postgraduate coursework degree, appropriately named with the term "cyber security" or equivalent in the title, to usual IT or related degrees offering cyber security as a minor or major theme of study. A minority of universities do not offer any specific cyber security specific course while others offer such courses in association with industry organisations possibly involving industry certification.

This study, based upon close examination of publicly advertised course offerings, as would normally be assessed by any prospective student, determined that "in Australia available courses are few and are acknowledged as not meeting market demands for skilled cyber security professionals". The question is one of whether or not the Australian government, at Federal and State level, will take a lead in remedying that situation to the levels of commitment required. As of 2017, associated financial support from the public sector seemed inadequate to meet the need for educated and trained cyber security professionals over the next 5–10 years, particularly in the public sector. In addition, the market demand in Australia for cyber security professionals in the private sector needs to be studied more carefully in regard to expertise required and vacancies, as differing opinions in regard to that market demand have appeared.

## Notes

1  It was later reissued as Rand Report R-609-601 (Ware 1979).
2  Renamed the Queensland University of Technology (QUT) in 1989.
3  See https://cybersecurityventures.com/cyber security-education/#home/?view_1_page=1. The webpage is no longer accessible.
4  Association for Computing Machinery (ACM), the IEEE Computer Society (IEEE CS), the Association for Information Systems Special Interest Group on Security (AIS SIGSEC), and the International Federation for Information Processing Technical Committee on Information Security Education (IFIP WG 11.8).
5  See www.csec2017.org/about.
6  This is the total for telecoms products, computer products and related services.

# References

ABCRadio National. 2017. Cyber Insecurity: The Skills Shortage Exposing Australia to Attack. Available at: www.abc.net.au/radionational/programs/backgroundbriefing/2017-06-11/8597214.

ACM. 2017. Cybersecurity Curricula 2017 Curriculum Guidelines for Post-Secondary Degree Programs in Cybersecurity. Available at: https://cybered.hosting.acm.org/wp/about/.

ACS. (Australian Computer Society). 2017a. Courses with Cyber Security. Available at: www.acs.org.au/cpd-education/cyber security-courses.html.

ACS. (Australian Computer Society). 2017b. Certification. Available at: www.acs.org.au/professionalrecognition/certification-landing-page.html (accessed 14 November 2017).

AISA. (Australian Information Security Association). 2016. The Australian Cyber Security Skills Shortage Study 2016.. Available at: www.aisa.org.au/Public/Training_Pages/Research/AISA%20Cyber%20security%20skills%20shortage%20research.aspx.

Arboleda, N. 2017a. Quarter of a Million Australians Now Work in IT: Census. *CRN*, 13 November. Available at: www.crn.com.au/news/quarter-of-a-million-australians-now-work-in-it-census-477476?eid=4&edate=20171114&utm_source=20171114&utm_medium=newsletter&utm_c ampaign=daily_newsletter.

Arboleda, N. 2017b. Security Training Provider Cybergym Opens 'Cyber Training Arena' in Melbourne, *CRN*, 13 November. Available at: www.crn.com.au/news/security- training-provider-cybergym-opens-cyber-training-arena-in-melbourne-477371?eid=4&edate=20171113&utm_source=20171113&utm_medium=newsletter&utm_campaign=daily_newsletter.

Bishop, M. and L. Snyder. 1979. The Transfer of Information and Authority in a Protection System. In *Proceedings of the Seventh ACM Symposium on Operating Systems Principles*, 45–54.

CAE Community. 2017. CAE in Cyber Security Community. Available at: www.caecommunity.org/about-us/what-cae#.

Caelli, W. and V. Liu. 2017. *Cyber Security Education at Formal University Level: An Australian Perspective*. Paper presented at the 21st Annual Colloquium for Information Systems Security Education (CISSE), Las Vegas, June.

Caelli, W., V. Liu and D. Longley. 2013. Background to the Development of a Curriculum for the History of "Cyber" and "Communications" Security. In R.C. Dodge Jr and L. Futcher (eds), *Proceedings of Information Assurance and Security Education and Training: 8th IFIP WG 11.8 World Conference on Information Security Education, WISE 8*, 39–47.

CERIAS. (Center for Education and Research in Information Assurance). 2017a. CERIAS-COAST. Available at: www.cerias.purdue.edu/site/about/history/coast/.

CERIAS. (Center for Education and Research in Information Assurance and Security). 2017b. About Us. Available at: www.cerias.purdue.edu/site/about.

CISSE. (Colloquium for Information Systems Security Education). 2017. About Us. Available at: www.cisse.info/about.

CSA. (Cyber Security Academy). 2017. Available at: www.cyber securityacademy.com/.

CSPRI. 2017. CSPRI's History. Available at: https://cspri.seas.gwu.edu/cspris-history.

DFAT. (Department of Foreign Affairs and Trade). 2017. Composition of Trade, Australia 2015–16. January. Available at: https://dfat.gov.au/about-us/publications/Documents/cot-fy-2015-16.pdf.

DoET. (Department of Education and Training). 2017. Academic Centres of Cyber Security Excellence (ACCSE). Canberra: Australian Government. Available at: www.education.gov.au/academic-centres-cyber-security-excellence-accse.

Donovan, S., B. Cobert and T. Scott. 2016. Federal Cyber Security Workforce Strategy. Memorandum M-16–15. Washington, DC: Office of Management and Budget,

Executive Office of the President. 12 July. Available at: www.chcoc.gov/content/federa
l-cyber security-workforce-strategy.

DSB. (Defense Science Board). 1970. Security Controls for Computer Systems: Report of
Defense Science Board Task Force on Computer Security. Available at: https://nsarchive2.
gwu.edu//dc.html?doc=2800105-Document-01-Defense-Science-Board-Task-Force-on.

FIT. 1989. *1989 Handbook of the Faculty of Information Technology: Computing Science, Information Systems*. Queensland, Australia: Queensland University of Technology.

GCSCC. (Global Cyber Security Capacity Centre). 2016. *Cyber Security Capacity Review of
the United Kingdom*. University of Oxford. November. Available at : www.sbs.ox.ac.uk/
cybersecurity-capacity/system/files/Cybersecurity%20Capacity%20Review%20of%20the
%20United%20Kingdom.pdf.

Harvard Kennedy School. 2017. Cyber Security: The Intersection of Policy and Technology. Notes for Course, 14–19 January 2018. Available at: www.hks.harvard.edu/educa
tional-programs/executive-education/cyber security.

Hason, O. 2017. Curriculum vitae. Available at: www.linkedin.com/in/ofir-hason-a
802b229/.

Hoffman, L. 2017. Computer Science. School of Engineering, George Washington University.
Available at: www.cs.seas.gwu.edu/lance-j-hoffman.

IEC. (Israel Electric Corporation). 2017. Available at: www.iec.co.il/en/ir/pages/default.aspx.

ITPA. (Information Technology Professionals Association). 2017. Available at: www.itpa.
org.au/.

JTF. (Joint Task Force on Cyber Security Education). 2017. Available at: www.cesc2017.org.

Macquarie University. 2017. Optus Macquarie University Cyber Security Hub. Available at:
www.mq.edu.au/about/about-the-university/offices-and-units/optus-macqua
rie-university-cyber-hub.

Manjoo, F. 2017. Tech's Frightful Five: They've Got Us. *New York Times*. 10 May. Available at:
www.nytimes.com/2017/05/10/technology/techs-frightful-five-theyve-got-us.html.

Martin, K. 2013. Introduction to the Information Security Group, Royal Holloway College,
University of London. Video overview. 14 February. Available at: www.youtube.com/
watch?v=UbEUVJ5GdMM.

NCSC. ( National Cyber Security Centre (UK)). 2016. Gain Recognition as an Academic
Centre of Excellence in Cyber Security Research. 10 October. Available at: www.ncsc.gov.
uk/information/gain-recognition-academic-centre-excellence-cyber-security-research.

NCSC. (National Cyber Security Centre (UK)). 2017a. NCSC-certified Degrees. Update.
12 October. Available at: www.ncsc.gov.uk/information/ncsc-certified-degrees.

NCSC. (National Cyber Security Centre (UK)). 2017b. Education and Research. Available
at: www.ncsc.gov.uk/education-research.

NCSC. (National Cyber Security Centre (UK)). 2017c. Academics and Researchers..
Available at: www.ncsc.gov.uk/Academics-and-researchers.

NCSC. (National Cyber Security Centre (UK)). 2017d. Academic Centres of Excellence in
Cyber Security Research. www.ncsc.gov.uk/articles/academic-centres-excellence-cyber-sec
urity-research.

Newhouse, W., S. Keith, B. Scribner and G. Witte. 2017. National Initiative for Cyber
Security Education (NICE) Cyber Security Workforce Framework. NIST Special Publication 800–818. https://doi.org/10.6028/NIST.SP.800-181.

NICE. 2017. A Path to Obtaining Cybersecurity Work Experience: Internships, Cooperative Education, and Apprenticeships, NICE Webinar. Available at: www.nist.gov/
news-events/events/2017/11/nice-webinar-path-obtaining-cybersecurity-work-experien
ce-internships.

NIST. 2017a. National Cyber Security Career Awareness Week. Available at: www.nist.gov/itl/applied-cyber security/nice/national-cyber security-career-awareness-week.

NIST. 2017b. Center of Academic Excellence Resource Centers. Available at: www.nist.gov/news-events/news/2017/04/center-academic-excellence-resource-centers.

NIST. 2017c. National Centers of Academic Excellence in Cyber Defense (CAE-CD). NIST- NICE. Available at: www.nist.gov/document/cae-cdpdf-0.

OPM. (Office of Personnel Management (US)). 2017a. CyberCorps: Scholarship for Service. Available at: www.sfs.opm.gov/.

OPM. (Office of Personnel Management (US)). 2017b. Students: Frequently Asked Questions (FAQs). CyberCorps: Scholarship for Service. Available at: www.sfs.opm.gov/Stud FAQ.aspx#num14.

PCCIP. 1997. Critical Foundations: Protecting America's Infrastructures: The Report of the President's Commission on Critical Infrastructure Protection. October. Available at: www.pccip.gov.

Press, G. 2017. CyberGym Makes Sure You Know What It Really Feels to Get Hit by a Cyberattack. *Forbes*. 27 June. Available at: www.forbes.com/sites/gilpress/2017/06/27/cybergym-makes-sure-you-know-what-it-really-feels-to-get-hit-by-a-cyberattack/#5503ca365cbe.

QUT. 1991. *1991 Handbook*. Queensland, Australia: Queensland University of Technology.

QUT. 2017a. QUT Institute for Future Environments (IFE). Available at: www.qut.edu.au/institute-for-future-environments (accessed 12 November 2017).

QUT. 2017b. Available at: www.qut.edu.au/science-engineering/research/research-strengths#h2–6.

Redrup, Y. 2017. States Vie for Israeli Cyber Security Investment as CyberGym Heads Downunder, *Australian Financial Review*. 20 February 2017. Available at: www.afr.com/technology/web/security/states-vie-for-israeli-cyber-security-investment-as-cybergym-heads-downunder-20170217-guftj1 (accessed 13 November 2017).

RH. (Royal Holloway). 2017. Information Security Group website. Available at: www.royalholloway.ac.uk/isg/home.aspx.

Udasin, S. 2017a. Israel, Japan Sign Economic, Cyber Cooperation Agreements. *The Jerusalem Post*. 3 May. Available at: www.jpost.com/Israel-News/Israel-Japan-sign-economic-cyber-cooperation-agreements-489647.

Udasin, S. 2017b. American Firm CyberReadyUSA Acquires Practice Arena from Israel's CyberGym. *The Jerusalem Post*. 1 August. Available at: www.jpost.com/Israel-News/American-firm-CyberReadyUSA-acquires-practice-arena-from-Israels-CyberGym-501328.

University of Washington. 2017. Essentials of Cyber Security, edX for University of Washington. Available at: www.edx.org/professional-certificate/uwashingtonx-essentials-cyber security.

Ware, W.H. (ed.). 1970. Security Controls for Computer Systems: Report of Defense Science Board Task Force on Computer Security. Washington, DC: Office of the Secretary of Defense. Available at: www.rand.org/pubs/reports/R609-1/index2.html.

Williams, S. 2016. Aussie Organisations Unknowingly Contributing to Cyber Security Skills Shortage. Security Brief. 29 November. Available at: https://securitybrief.com.au/story/aussie-organisations-unknowingly-contributing-cyber-security-skills-shortage.

# 2

# MASTERING THE CYBER SECURITY SKILLS CRISIS

*Adam P. Henry*

The cyber security skills and education crisis is a key issue affecting all countries. Governments are currently looking more and more to universities to help solve the problem. This chapter looks at one key area of the problem: are current Master of Cyber Security programmes in Australia preparing students for the country's workforce?

Cyber security education has become a new field of study across the world as a result of the rapid transformation of platforms, vulnerabilities and threats in the past decade. There is currently a lag effect between education research and emerging needs in most countries. As governments release cyber security strategies, education is always mentioned, though, as cyberspace education is still in its infancy, there has been a certain lack of understanding of the field as a public policy problem and even as a pedagogic challenge (Austin 2017). In the case of Australia, no university scholar is undertaking full-time research into pedagogies and/or public policy for cyber security education. As Slay (2016) observed, there is a lack of people, there is no clear understanding of what cyber security means, what a cyber security professional is, or how they should be trained.

The Australian Cyber Security Growth Network's Cyber Security Sector Competitiveness Plan (SCP) (2017: 2), states:

> Australia has difficulty attracting and retaining cyber security talents. While the skills shortage is affecting the cyber security industry globally, there are signs that the lack of cyber talent in Australia is among the worst in the world. Australian firms struggle to find job-ready cyber security workers despite offering high wage premiums.

The government's 2016 Cyber Security Strategy (PM&C 2016) and the 2017 First Annual Update (PM&C 2017) report that "the scale and reach of malicious cyber activity affecting Australian public and private sector organisations and individuals [are] unprecedented" (PM&C 2016: 2). These sentiments are supported by Austin (2016) and Austin and Slay (2016) who point out that while technical solutions are important, it will be institutional, cultural and social changes that will be most effective in mitigating cyber insecurity. As this field is complex and multidisciplinary, educational responses must focus not only on technical solutions but also must incorporate the myriad of other topics such as national defence, economics, sociology, political science, diplomacy, history, and psychology (Kessler and Ramsay 2013: 36).

Against this background, Australia's cyberspace education sector is currently in its infancy. The Council of Australian Governments (COAG), at its December 2016 meeting, identified cyber security education as an important area of future cooperation (Council of Australian Governments 2017). As the 2016 Australian strategy and 2017 update conclude: "it is critical that we build our nation's stock of cyber security skills, which are becoming increasingly essential for life and work in our connected world" (PM&C 2016: 4). There is wide consensus that a considered multidisciplinary pedagogical focus appropriate to the more complex cyber threat scenarios affecting national public policy is required.

This chapter argues for yet another step beyond recognition of the multidisciplinary challenge. It argues for an approach that is not only multidisciplinary but one that more explicitly recognises cyber security as comprising fundamentally distinctive specialisations at the outset, where different mission-specific sets (countering crime versus fighting cyber war, or child protection versus enterprise protection) define the learning objectives, the content, the level of expertise and the value of various programmes to future employers.

This sharpening of focus could then usefully be combined with mission-specific workplace-integrated learning programmes, similar to those in medical education. But these workplace programmes would not be for "general practice". Currently, at the tertiary level at least, cyber security education prepares its graduates for some sort of general practice, whereby courses cover the large base which is captured in the term cyber security. This may include network security, forensic studies, information assurance, programming and data analytics. Educational responses for cyber security may need to incorporate much earlier approaches that lie well outside the software and hardware aspects. In cyber security education policy and research on pedagogy, no convincing way has yet been found to incorporate the myriad of other topics (Cooper et al. 2010).

Cyber security should be viewed more like engineering with distinct differentiating sub-fields at a very early stage, such as electrical, mechanical, civil, aeronautical and bio-medical. A simple example that illustrates the aim of this chapter is the proposition that the educational needs of someone developing government policy on international cyber relations is very different from the educational needs of someone working in a financial institution protecting their networks from cyber fraud. To extend the argument, neither of those professions requires any significant knowledge of cyber forensics on a scale that police authorities would need to be able to gain convictions for most forms of cyber crime.

## Literature review

There are few clear national visions and little consensus on how to solve the shortfalls in cyber security education and the subsequent skills crisis. In Australia, the Sector Competitiveness Plan supports this further by stating that there are signs that the formal education system is failing to produce enough job-ready cyber security graduates (Australian Cyber Security Growth Network 2017: 35). The skills gap is important and this has been widely acknowledged, but there is still the "critical need to address the talent shortage by increasing the number of individuals who have cybersecurity skills" (Vogel 2016). This is compounded by a large amount of research focusing on the technologies and techniques of cyber security at the enterprise level, which contrasts with a distinct lack of research into cyber security education and pedagogical methods. There is some research into the field of system models for cyber security education in general terms, but it still does not go far enough. McGettrick (2013: 23) reiterates this point, stating that cyber security is still an immature field lacking a cohesive intellectual body of activity and clear underlying science.

To ensure that cyber security education continues to mature, Kessler and Ramsay (2013: 36) propose that academia needs to apply "new ways of thinking, new understanding, and new strategies" to a nation's response to this new digital information age. This proposition aligns with the current emphasis on multi-disciplinary approaches to cyber security education. Cyber security is about process as much as it is about technology, the response to cyber-related security challenges today is not solely about technical solutions, but requires a multi-faceted and multidisciplinary focus (ibid.: 36).

There are currently few agreed metrics or baselines by which stakeholders can evaluate progress towards meeting the cyber security educational requirements. The United States has an overarching higher education mechanism with the Centers of Excellence and the models linking workforce needs to higher education outcomes (Kessler and Ramsay 2013; Conklin et al. 2014). There is also the newly announced Australian Government Academic Centres for Cyber Security Excellence (ACCSE), which aim to "increase the number of highly skilled post-graduates with the job-ready skills needed to work in Australian business and government to tackle emerging cyber security challenges". If universities do not adapt and modify their current methodology and course structure, they will fall short, though it must be noted that the Australian government has not published any comprehensive baseline studies of the current outputs.

The key messages coming out of current research reiterate the importance of the purpose for the education (outlined below in the framework) and the importance of frameworks (models) in enhancing cyber security education and awareness (Amankwa et al. 2014: 250; 2015: 76). Typically, these works offer a critical view of the current curricula and the input/output method of education for cyber security which is universally regarded as inadequate (Conklin et al. 2014; Austin 2017: 1). There is a major gap in the alignment between the education of a student and the hands-on skills required to make them job-ready: the training versus education dilemma. Training focuses more on how and deals with "current technology and methods". Education focuses more on why ("theory and mechanisms") behind the professional activity. Linking theory and practice is vital for cohorts of Master of Cyber Security courses to be effective in the workforce. Cyber security is constantly evolving, making it challenging to acquire and maintain the skills necessary to act as a responsible cyber security professional (Martin 2015).

This is not a new issue, as Hentea and Dhillon (2006: 226), observed a decade ago: "the adoption of courses that link theory and practice is vital for some courses offered for information security education, such that, the individual acquires the ability to put theories into practice". These scholars observed the large "discrepancy between the levels of skills expected by employers and those the graduates have after completing their studies". In order to address these problems, the academic community probably needs to restructure the curricula. Lehto (2016: 28) gives a grim view whereby universities only provide cyber security education from the university perspective. This is true for many universities, but there are some who are moving towards industry partnerships to enhance the effectiveness of their programmes as a differential for potential students. This type of cooperation and collaboration is vital for the effectiveness of cyber security programmes.

The key points that are necessary for cyber security courses to be relevant in the workplace are:

- depth over breadth (purpose-driven) (Manson and Pike 2014);
- work-integrated placements (Koppi et al. 2008);
- practical skillset development – real-world scenarios and simulations (Koppi et al. 2010);
- the avoidance of an "all-in-one" approach (general practice versus mission-specific) (Conklin et al. 2014).

Planners should not focus on the development of a single foundational curriculum. It would be a mistake to imagine that there is one curriculum that can meet all the major requirements for the diverse field of cyber security. Graduates from any cybersecurity programme cannot simply be interchangeable, and thinking like that can be as bad for cyber security as for other specialised professions (Conklin et al. 2014). A key requirement for courses to remain relevant is to continually update the teaching and learning methods and ensure the content is in line with new directions in industries. Koppi et al. (2010) put forward that the relationship between industry and universities needs to be improved, particularly with respect to the development of industry-integrated curricula. This requires an understanding not only of the purpose of the course for the university, but also of the purpose and relevance to the student undertaking the course (Armstrong et al. 2013). High-quality cyber security programmes need to differentiate between the multi-disciplinary aspects of courses and the unique requirements of each course. A strong technical-based curriculum requires hands-on activities, including the use of cyber ranges, simulations and war games. This approach with purpose-designed work-place-integrated learning strengthens the knowledge and skill sets of the students and improves employability. The Sector Competitiveness Plan supports this as it refers to a survey result which sees 77 per cent of cyber security professionals believing that the "current training and education programs are not fully preparing professionals for the workplace reality leading to calls for academic programs to incorporate more practical learning". Thus, any hybrid technical cyber security education programme should still be purpose-driven and mission-specific.

It should be noted that it is common practice in other academic programmes to have a strong focus on practical skills acquired during work placements. A report on work experience in Australia stated that 71 per cent of respondents were satisfied or very satisfied with the work experience and that they had developed relevant skills and knowledge. Nearly 30 per cent of respondents were offered an employment opportunity after completing their placement (Australian Government Department of Employment 2017). Koppi et al. (2010) state that while fundamental theories were seen as providing a firm foundation for a dynamic and changing discipline, there is an unfulfilled need for their practical relevance and application to the real world. It will always be a challenge to academia to bridge the gap between theory and the real needs of industry. These performance measurements through real-world scenarios are critical to being effective in the workplace. This is prominent in the field of medicine. Large amounts of workplace-integrated learning are found in the medical field. This is also dependent on knowledge, skill levels and specialist training/workplace development. Direct experience of the task which the person will be required to undertake is essential (Manson and Pike 2014). For cyber security education, especially in the technical areas, there should be a requirement for this type of complex practical tasking that requires a "high degree of mastery to gain success".

## Methodology

The chapter begins with an original characterisation of education needs in cyber security according to five broad headings, each with distinct sub-sets which can be arranged in a complex matrix, as outlined in following sections. The chapter then demonstrates the potential value of that matrix by analysing just one slice through more than several hundred possible combinations. That slice is based on tertiary education (Master's level) as the departure point. The related qualitative investigation has been based primarily on a survey of Master's students or recent graduates at the University of New South Wales Canberra, Australia. The data was then analysed in the context of other information about the expectations of employers and universities in order to begin to identify gaps in the expectations of the stakeholders. To establish a clear opinion of current students, the survey explored their expectations regarding their different Master's programmes. Comparing the work roles of these students to individual courses taught in the Master's programmes also enabled gaps to be identified. Further to this, the Cyber Security Education

**FIGURE 2.1** The Cyberspace Education Framework

Framework enables a clear and consistent comparison for the current offerings. Both international and national employer survey results were compared with the students' opinions. Discussions with a recruitment firm were undertaken to ensure the results were consistent with current views in industry and with the recommendations of the chapter. Discussions with key personnel in several universities were also undertaken to explore the results and individual expectations of their courses.

## The Cyberspace Education Framework

The Cyberspace Education Framework focuses on the broad high-level education objectives, which can then be narrowed down to show key outcomes for mission-specific activities. This approach reminds us that there can be no single universal approach to cyber security education. It is multi-faceted, multi-dimensional and purpose-specific. At the same time, the framework allows us to see relationships between different education activities and outcomes. When it comes to baselines and benchmarks for cyber security education, it is a basic contention of this model, that these can only be established by reference to particular slices through this framework. The purpose of the framework reiterates the requirement for nations to pursue cyber education maturity (Austin 2017). Within the framework, five elements make up the matrix which leads to a very large number of quite distinct cyberspace education outcomes (Figure 2.1).

### Education type

There are nine key categories of education type. This captures the different formal and informal types of education a student may pursue. This model identifies that an individual may undertake one or more different levels of education. The education undertaken is not defined by a sequence, but rather it is assumed that the education patterns undertaken differ from individual to individual and that each type can be undertaken more than once (that is, revisited).

The categories of types of education are:

- on the job training
- self-taught
- primary school

- secondary school
- vocational
- higher education
- industry certifications
- adult education
- University of the Third Age.

## Level of expertise

The model proposes five key levels of expertise, but this is only a departure point. These range from Basic through to an Advanced Expert. The majority of formal courses available are within the basic through to expert levels. Each level of expertise needs to be viewed against each element of the framework as there are many different streams within cyberspace. Examples against each level are shown in Table 2.1, while also reflecting the fundamental point that, within even one level of cyberspace education, there are multidisciplinary fields and purposes. Having technical expertise can be considered as important as having international relations expertise. While the two are very different fields of education and specialisation, both need to be ranked against the five levels of expertise.

**TABLE 2.1** Examples of levels of expertise

| Level | Definition |
| --- | --- |
| Basic | A student within a primary school who completes a course regarding eSafety to a high standard; a CEO who knows cyber security is essential for profitability but does nothing about it; a criminal using stolen credit card details |
| Intermediate | A Vocational Education and Training (VET) student who successfully completes a Certificate in Information Security; a lawyer who makes an effort to segregate sensitive data sets relating to an individual high value client; a criminal using phishing scams to capture people's log-on details |
| Advanced | A PhD graduate specialising in system defence and cyber resilience for an organisation, whose research includes practical studies and scenario-related exercises; a graduate of several professional certifications (such as CISM, CISSP), who also has significant experience in threat mitigation and system resilience; an individual who develops ransomware and initiates major attacks for financial gain |
| Expert | A cyber security professional who has completed the Certified Cyber Security Expert (CSX) course offered by ISACA; an individual who through accessing third party vendors gains access to and steals intellectual property from a major multinational organisation for a nation state |
| Advanced Expert | An individual who has Certification as a Cyber Guardian offered by System Administration, Networking, and Security Institute (SANS). The institute has issued 86,000 certifications to computer professionals, of which only 35 are Guardians; Members of the teams who invented and evaluated the Stuxnet worm. |

## Field of education

The following list shows the broad fields of education in regard to cyberspace. It is important to note that only one field focuses on technical aspects and this demonstrates the multidisciplinary nature of cyber security. Using this type of multidisciplinary model in the framework enables a broader view of cyberspace. This is a key aspect of the framework and the baselining process.

The five key fields of education are:

- Political
- Social
- Legal
- Technical
- People.

## Purpose

To develop more effective and more focused education policies, there is a requirement to address why specifically we need these skills. Each country requires a cyber-educated workforce. This not just for national security agencies and police agencies, but all industries, ensuring continued economic growth. It is, therefore, important within the framework to identify the reason or purpose (the mission set) for undertaking the cyberspace education.

The broad types of purpose (mission sets) are many, and this framework proposes 13 distinct mission sets:

- espionage/counter-espionage
- counter-terrorism
- countering crime (police)
- cyber-enabled war
- protection of the financial services sector
- protection of other critical infrastructure
- protection of children
- intellectual property protection
- privacy protection
- legislation development and legal practice
- SME and enterprise cyber security (resilience)
- non-government organisations and political party cyber security
- home user cyber security.

## Application

We can also identify quite different aspects of cyber security education depending on the process the student will adopt to apply the knowledge/skills or the institutional circumstances. The broad types of application are:

- individual action
- team member
- team leader
- mid-level management
- executive management
- national policy leadership (government or private sector)
- community policy leadership.

The Cyberspace Education Framework enables comparisons between cyberspace education activities and shows what the outcome of each activity is. This framework helps establish baselines for future comparison. The results of the comparison show the effectiveness of the framework for cyberspace education policy development.

## *Matrix*

These five elements, each with five or more distinct categories, allow us to postulate a very large number of education types and outcomes. While we may not expect all possible elements to be meaningful (e.g. primary school/advanced/technical/cyber war/team leader), the matrix allows us to understand the potential of much sharper focus. In particular, primary school children need to know child protection, before they need to know technical issues such as coding. The matrix also allows us to situate existing programmes and align them with specialisations, mission sets, roles and outcomes. This is a very different approach to that of core competencies which has been the focus of much public policy discussion and which is important work. It is, however, far from being the whole story, and may not even be the main story. Table 2.2 brings together the sub-elements of each of the five main elements. The bold sub-elements represent the "slice" of the education problem this chapter is looking at.

It is against the consideration raised by elaborating the matrix, that the author believes we can better evaluate any existing programmes. This chapter chooses just one slice of the matrix (Higher education) and one subset of it (Master's degrees) to understand better the state of cyber security education in Australia. It is a basic corollary of the matrix that all slices need to be evaluated, in broad terms at least, against the criteria listed.

## Research results

To appropriately answer the question "Are Master of Cyber Security programmes preparing students for the workforce?", this project explored the viewpoints of students, employers and universities, comparing key data points and information to ensure a solid comparative base for the research. The 2016 NIST Framework of work roles in cyber security linking the knowledge, skills and abilities (KSA) to educational outputs also enables a further comparison between the current Master's programmes and the top five skills crisis work role requirements (NIST 2016).[1]

**TABLE 2.2** Matrix view of the Cyberspace Education Framework

| Type | Expertise | Field | Purpose | Application |
|---|---|---|---|---|
| On the job training | **Basic** | **Political** | **Generalist** | **Individual action** |
| Self-taught | **Intermediate** | **Social** | Espionage/counter-espionage | **Team member** |
| Primary school | Advanced | Legal | Counter-terrorism | Team leader |
| Secondary school | Expert | **Technical** | Countering crime (police) | Mid-level management |
| Vocational | Advanced expert | People | Cyber-enabled war | Executive management |
| **Higher education** | | | Protection of the financial services sector | National policy leadership |
| Industry certifications | | | Protection of other critical infrastructure | (government or private sector) |
| Adult education | | | Protection of children | Community policy leadership |
| University of the Third Age | | | Intellectual property protection | |
| | | | Privacy protection | |
| | | | Legislation development and legal practice | |
| | | | SME and enterprise cyber security (resilience) | |
| | | | Non-government organisations and political party cyber security | |
| | | | Home user cyber security | |

Further to this, the Cyberspace Education Framework was used to compare current generalist cyber security degrees to the more mission-specific Master of Science in Computer Forensics and Cybercrime Investigation course, to demonstrate how a mission-specific programme can more adequately address a specific industry requirement. This holistic analysis provides a deeper view into the skills crisis and how universities can work towards ensuring their students are ready for the workplace.

## Student expectations survey

The project surveyed current students and alumni of Master's programmes at the University of New South Wales (UNSW), Canberra, Australia. The campus has five Master of Cyber Security offerings, mostly through distance learning, with some individual courses offered in one-week intensive mode on campus. The survey obtained responses from 22 per cent of the 325 student cohort. Each course offered through the UNSW Canberra is represented in the survey but the majority of the cohort were undertaking Master of Cyber Security Operations (35 per cent), Master of Cyber Security, Strategy and Diplomacy (28 per cent) and Master of Cyber Security (24 per cent). This demonstrates the multidisciplinary nature of the cyber security programmes with students pursuing policy, international relations and strategy components as well as the traditional technical streams. Some 87 per cent of the cohort were current students, with 93 per cent of respondents studying in Australia.

A range of current occupations were being undertaken by the cohort, including a third from the Defence Force, 38 per cent from private industry and 24 per cent from state and federal public service. This reinforces the multi-faceted nature of cyber security and how broadly the requirements for a skilled workforce truly are. Some 56 per cent of all participants were undertaking the course to gain a new role in a new workplace; 24 per cent were undertaking the course to better equip them for their current position; and 15 per cent were undertaking the course as they were interested in the topic.

Interestingly, 60 per cent believe they will be able to use the knowledge and skill sets acquired in the course at their current workplace or appear to currently work in a cyber security role. A large portion (40 per cent) do not work in the cyber security industry. Some 92.5 per cent believe that they would be able to use the knowledge and skill sets acquired in the course at a future workplace; 65 per cent agreed that a work placement would be useful; 88 per cent said that the course has given them further knowledge and skill sets they considered useful in either their existing workplace or future career goals. Of the 11.5 per cent who said no, a large portion suggested that no practical skills or real-world applications were taught. Of the 37 per cent of students who had undertaken courses that provided cyber range simulations, i.e., cyber operations including threat assessment, detection and prevention, 87.5 per cent agreed that the simulations had strengthened their knowledge and skill sets for their future career ambitions. Some 83 per cent of respondents rated the course satisfactory (slightly satisfied through to extremely satisfied) and said it was effective in meeting their expectations.

Interestingly, 34 per cent of respondents said they would undertake postgraduate research, such as a PhD, and a further 45 per cent would undertake an industry-based certification. Three-quarters of respondents had not undertaken an industry certification. Of the respondents who had undertaken an industry certification, 53 per cent agreed that it was effective in preparing them for their future ambitions and a further 42 per cent neither agreed nor disagreed. The high rate of neither agree nor disagree could indicate respondents might have undertaken the course to fulfil a requirement for their resume.

These results show that a large portion of the cohort work in areas associated with cyber security, but a large number would attempt to enter the cyber security workforce. The cohort is seeking new roles and has undertaken the course to improve their knowledge and skill sets. A high proportion of the cohort both supported the requirement for workplace-integrated learning and the use of specific real-world practical skills, using scenarios and hands-on labs.

## Industry viewpoints

In contrast to the student cohort, there have been many surveys (national and international) conducted at the enterprise level regarding the skills crisis and skill sets required to fill cyber security positions. Recent studies by the Information Systems Audit and Control Association (ISACA) and the Australian Information Security Association (AISA) reveal some interesting trends. The ISACA report stated that "practical hands-on experience is the most important cyber security candidate qualification to 55 percent of enterprises". This is in stark contrast to formal education and personal endorsements ranked equally as least important (ISACA 2017). This shows that current education and pedagogical methods are not hitting the mark. There is a high degree of focus on industry certifications with nearly 70 per cent of businesses asking for an industry security certification of some sort for job candidates. This is in line with the findings of the AISA report, whereby "many respondents did not think that current academic qualifications adequately prepared cyber security graduates for the workplace" (AISA 2017). The report states that "experience is more important to recruiters than knowledge, certifications or education". It goes on further to state that respondents "were critical of the academic qualifications available for cyber security workers". Interestingly the report says that it may be because "recruiters and employers do not understand the different academic qualifications that are available and the knowledge and capabilities of the graduates" from those programmes. As 40 per cent of the student cohort surveyed are not currently in a cyber security role, they may have difficulty finding an appropriate position after their course.

This further demonstrates the requirement for courses to be aligned to workforce requirements. Universities should actively work with industry to ensure their programmes are not only known to employers and recruiters, but are relevant. An interesting trait the survey reported, was the requirement for five years of experience with 90 per cent of advertised positions ("including junior positions such as security analysts") requiring this. The survey reported that architects, technical security consultants, forensic examiners, incident handlers or investigators and security analysts or advisors were the most in demand.

## Educational outcome to work role comparison

The survey results indicate different expectations between students and employers and a low level of industry confidence in the current programmes. It is beneficial to compare how aligned current Master's programme offerings are to the workplace knowledge, skills and abilities (KSA) requirements, of the above roles most in demand to establish if there are major gaps or alignment. Using the NIST Framework for knowledge, skills and abilities related to work roles and comparing it to the units offered in the Master's programmes establishes a clear picture of what industry has stipulated. This was done by comparing the course information provided on their websites to the KSAs outlined in the NIST to create the matrix in Table 2.3.

The total alignment of generalist Master's programmes to work role KSAs indicate an overall alignment of 51 per cent. To accurately address the skills crisis, universities would need to amend their courses to better cover the required KSAs. Currently all universities courses align best with the Cyber Defence Incident Investigator work role. This could be a starting point for enabling greater consistency with work roles and actively working with industry on further alignment. The Technical Security Consultant (Information Systems Security Operations) role was the most poorly aligned. This course could also benefit from industries' input into core requirements

**TABLE 2.3** Generalist course alignment to work role KSA

| Institution | Systems security analyst (%) | Systems architect (%) | Cyber defence incident investigator (%) | Forensic analyst (%) | Technical security consultant (systems security operations) (%) | Overall alignment with work role KSAs, numbers of surveys (%) |
|---|---|---|---|---|---|---|
| Deakin* | 46 | 32 | 50 | 47 | 37 | 97/225 (43) |
| ECU* | 43 | 47 | 67 | 53 | 37 | 113/225 (50) |
| UNSW Canberra | 57 | 58 | 77 | 57 | 43 | 131/225 (58) |
| Total number and (%) | 79/162 (49) | 78/171 (46) | 58/90 (64) | 91/180 (51) | 35/90 (39) | 341/675 (51) |

*It should be noted that Deakin University offers a unit specifically based on a Practical Project and Edith Cowen University offers a Work Integrated Learning unit which could increase their alignment with the work roles. These results offer a viewpoint into how the courses align and is offered for the purposes of discussion rather than as a definitive assessment. Future research could be undertaken to compare exact learning outcomes and criteria offered in the courses.

and active internships/work-integrated learning opportunities. Universities could partner with consultancy organisations to provide options like an "earn and learn", whereby students enter at a low level in the consultancy and as they develop and complete the course, rise up the ranks. This would be useful for students who have no experience or no current role in cyber security. From these results it would be fair to say that the courses do not currently align with the top five skills crisis work roles. This reinforces and supports the industry surveys' results.

This demonstrates the need to develop the type of capability required for both students and employers. New approaches focused on the growing and changing demands of the cyber security field should be followed.

### Comparative view of generalist versus mission-specific Master's programmes

To put this into perspective, this chapter compares and contrasts three separate Master of Cyber Security courses (general practice) against a more mission-specific Master of Science – Forensic Computing and Cybercrime Investigation from University College Dublin, Ireland, using the Cyberspace Education Framework. These courses provide a level of expertise within separate subsets of the cyber security field. The example looks at the generic cyber security (technical) degree compared to a course offered with a mission-specific law enforcement focus specifically for law enforcement officers only. The example highlights the value of the mission-specific requirement for a degree when compared to the general practice Master's degree. This focus enables a view of who must bear the responsibility for the specific purpose. In this example, it would be law enforcement agencies and the government's appropriate policy areas for law enforcement, driving the course and providing relevant expertise and material. This could be at the state, national or international level. This mission-specific curriculum enables institutions to partner with relevant stakeholders and develop courses that fit a purpose or public policy requirement. Since we look to the private sector to provide relevant technologies and expertise to new cyber security education programmes, we do need to note that private sector underpinnings of cyber crime prevention are very different from those of other missions, such as cyber offensive and defensive operations for national security. Table 2.4 demonstrates how the mission-specific education method compares to traditional curriculum.

It is interesting to note that all three Master of Cyber Security programmes state law enforcement within the purpose. There are clear differences between the effectiveness and the knowledge/skill sets acquired from undertaking the general practice Master of Cyber Security compared to the Master of Science – Forensic Computing and Cybercrime Investigation. In performing the same analysis between the work role KSAs for a Forensic Analyst to the learning outcomes of the UCD course, there was a 97 per cent match between the educational outcomes and the work role KSAs. This is a stark difference to the generalist courses. This clearly demonstrates the effectiveness of and requirement for mission-specific cyber security education.

**TABLE 2.4** Comparison of generalist to mission-specific Master's course

| | Classic curriculum approach to Cyber Security (Technical) degrees | Master of Science – Forensic Computing and Cybercrime Investigation |
|---|---|---|
| Education type | Tertiary (postgraduate) | Tertiary (postgraduate) |
| Level of expertise | Intermediate This depends largely on the specific institution and could only be considered at a higher level if they offer a hybrid model of learning including major work-integrated learning opportunities and practical simulations using cyber ranges | Expert A law enforcement specific stream. This enables an advanced course specifically on the KSAs required, including collaboration with key law enforcement agencies |
| Field of education | Focus – Technical (General Practice) broadly focusing on Computer Forensics, Network Security, Information Security, Programming, Wireless Security | Focus – Technical (Computer and Cybercrime investigations) |
| Purpose | None of the key purposes on that axis of the matrix are specifically addressed by most Master's-level cyber security programmes. Most are designed to meet the demand for technical experts who can implement (not lead) low to mid-level technical cyber security functions, "general practice" in government, industry or law enforcement. *Objective* Each university states different objectives in a broad statement: Expert cyber security professionals who can protect organisations from these threats are in high demand and this course can prepare you for a successful career anywhere in the world (Deakin University). It is designed for postgraduate scholars and professional managers with appropriate undergraduate qualifications in IT, computer science, electrical computer or systems engineering or a related discipline and/or extensive relevant professional experience who wish to gain a more detailed understanding of the technical skills and expertise relevant to the technical implementation and leadership of the cyber security function (UNSW). | Designed to meet only one purpose: education and training for law enforcement officers in cyber crime *Objective* To provide high quality forensic computing and cybercrime investigation training and formal education. It is also designed to deliver cutting-edge, up-to-date cyber crime investigation techniques, strategies and tactics that allow students to understand and tackle emerging trends in cyber crime. To teach existing law enforcement officials to be able to operate effectively and think critically in analysing and preforming cybercrime investigation through practical studies and scenario-related exercises to detect and secure prosecutions. |

*(Continued)*

**Table 2.4** (Cont.)

| Classic curriculum approach to Cyber Security (Technical) degrees | Master of Science – Forensic Computing and Cybercrime Investigation |
| --- | --- |
| This coursework degree is designed to meet the demand for cyber security professionals within government, law enforcement and industry. The course provides a pathway for existing information technology professionals seeking to commence or further progress their careers in the cyber security domain. It is also relevant to those seeking to enter the IT profession who have no previous experience in the cyber discipline (ECU).<br><br>*Units of Study*<br>Computer Forensics<br>Network Security<br>Information Security<br>Programming<br>Project Management<br>Wireless Security<br>Data Analytics<br>General practitioner | *Units of Study*<br>Computer Forensics<br>Network Investigations<br>Malware Investigations<br>Mobile Devices Investigation<br>Linux for Investigators<br>Live Data Forensics<br>Data and Database Forensics<br>Online Fraud Investigations<br>Legislation<br>Financial Fraud Investigation<br>Case Study<br>Research Project<br>Law enforcement officer |
| Application | Become a team member in a cyber security team and enhance career with new workplace options operating within a range of often disconnected technical operations areas | Countering cyber crime as an advanced technical specialist within a digital crimes law enforcement unit |

## Framework implications

The framework enables a high-level comprehensive view of cyberspace education. This information is then collated to enable benchmarks and baselines to be developed into metrics. From this information, the purpose for the education can be identified. The purpose can also be identified as "the why". Why is the education being undertaken or why is the education programme being delivered? This is a very important aspect of the framework and goes towards successful educational policy and programme development and implementation. This approach leads to purpose-driven or mission-specific education. For example, is a programme being delivered to teach students about national security, create base-level enterprise security officers or just because cyber security seems popular at the moment?

The educational outcomes need to be purpose-driven, not driven by institutions that may not have any tangible links to relevant workplaces. Institutions are not the only piece in the puzzle, the same way governments/industry are not, and neither can solve all the cyber security educational requirements. These are broad and require multiple stakeholders working together. A purpose-driven focus enables stakeholders to look at the why and, from that, develop appropriate solutions, i.e., new curricula for Master of Cyber Security courses. Updating and realigning the general practice approach with a more mission-specific purpose-driven method, including workplace-integrated learning and engaging with industry to optimise the Master's programmes.

Having a course specifically for students who are already in law enforcement enables students to apply their learning straight away. They are not required to undertake basic investigative or evidence gathering courses as they have already acquired that knowledge. This enables the course to be more in-depth and focused on more expert-level outcomes.

As observed by Parrish et al. (2018), governments often aim for a single curriculum to address their country's cyber security skills deficit. They warn that such an approach will fall short, as mentioned above, because the "multidisciplinary nature of cyber security requires different streams". One can sympathise with this approach as a first departure point, but a broader scope is needed, as these authors argue, particularly one that can address the purpose of the cyber security education and that can cater to the needs of the "different public policy requirements, career paths and education levels required".

## Further investigation with informants

Two universities (University of Melbourne and University College Dublin) and Hays Recruitment were invited to provide their views on the research and more broadly on the cyber security industry. Overall, their views reinforce the distinct gap between educators and industry and the requirements for both. The University of Melbourne stated that "specialist cyber security courses undoubtedly have a role to play in the overall education framework". While a gap in specialist skills is an issue, it is one that can be addressed both quickly and effectively through dedicated training, whether that be through mission-specific Master's programmes, like the one offered by University College Dublin, or commercial training courses. Hays Recruitment, on the other hand noted that "experience is the biggest requirement for employers and both industry certifications and academic qualifications do not rank as highly and are not considered nearly as relevant".

The University of Melbourne stated that "specialist cyber security courses undoubtedly have a role to play in the overall education framework". This aligns with comments from Hays Recruitment whereby "technical cyber security roles are specialised and require specific skillsets for each individual work roles. Generalist programmes, while providing an overview into multiple areas, don't address the requirements for specialised work roles." Hays Recruitment went further, saying that they "actively work with industry in developing recruitment requirements for cyber security roles as the field is still immature".

All informants agreed that work placements can be extremely valuable, in both the student's education and their subsequent employability. As experience is seen by industry as the most valuable recruitment trait, there is a requirement for universities to consider this further. Hays Recruitment supported the viewpoint of students/employees starting in low-level positions and moving into the relevant roles as their experience grew. UCD "works very hard officially through partnerships and through indirect industry contacts to assist students in finding work, either during (internships) or after finishing their courses". This type of interaction assists in establishing the value of these programmes to potential employers or recruitment agencies.

It is interesting to note that the University of Melbourne stipulates that

> the evolution of cyber security threats outpaces that of the corresponding training. It is important that we instil in our graduates the skills necessary to be able to independently undertake the constant education needed to perform well in the field.

All informants agreed that practical simulations and cyber ranges play an important part in developing the necessary leadership skills to evaluate and respond to an emerging threat. These skill sets are required to ensure there is a level of work-based experience. University College Dublin stay relevant through working closely with industry and subject matter experts. This provides courses that are specific, in-depth and work role-relevant, ensuring the course materials are up to date. This also ensures that students who have participated in the course are recognised by employers and understand the KSAs they have acquired in undertaking the course.

There are currently high expectations on employees to have five plus years' experience and have KSAs in multiple areas. There could be a base level for lower-skilled employees and training them in certain areas to fill a role due to the cyber security skills crisis. The requirement for practical skills and work-integrated learning in courses and further industry-university collaboration will ensure programmes are aligned with work role requirements and relevant. It benefits neither industry nor universities if students undertaking these types of courses cannot find employment.

Other aspects affecting the employers is that not all roles require specific cyber security qualifications. There are courses that prepare technical students to undertake required work roles and have appropriate KSAs. An example of this is software engineering; this is not specifically cyber security-based but builds on large amounts of cyber security KSAs. This is an area that requires further investigation into the benefit of establishing them as either specific cyber security-named courses or reinforcing the multi-faceted and multidisciplinary nature of cyber security. The final point of interest was that Hays Recruitment stated that they did not have major difficulty in filling the cyber security roles for employers in Canberra. This goes against the current trend of a skills crisis, if the roles are actively being filled. Though it should be noted that as the nation's capital, Canberra has large numbers of workers from interstate and internationally who come to specifically work for the Australian Public Service or industries that contract with government.

## Discussion

Universities are places of higher learning that can both lag behind industry or be at the forefront of advances and innovation, and many scholars simply choose to have nothing to do with industry since they are pursuing less applied subjects. Universities must continue the vision of excellence in research and higher education, while pursuing beneficial partnerships with industry. Moreover, as this field of cyber security is still in its infancy, it could be case that many decision-makers in Australian industry currently do not know what they need in terms of employee training and education in this domain.

The initial survey of the student cohort, the results from both the comparison of work role KSAs and the mission-specific course examples demonstrate there is a gap in student expectations when undertaking the Master of Cyber Security and the future possibilities for employment. While students who already have a role in a cyber security position found they should be able to use their acquired KSAs, the students who are not employed thus may find it difficult to find future employment. These assumptions only look at the overall picture and not the other skill sets the students have relevant to potential employment. The comparison in work role KSAs and outputs of the generalist Master's programmes reinforce the message that industry reported in the ISACA and AISA surveys, whereby academic qualifications were not highly regarded. Moreover, it should be noted that Master's degrees can be vocational, but they can also be preparatory for further studies and research, such as a PhD, and can focus on the technical aspect of cyber security, as much as on applied activities.

It would be beneficial for universities, as the research asserts, to partner further with industry to establish career pathways for students, offering practical and work-integrated learning opportunities and ensuring the programmes are meeting key skills crisis work roles. Universities could investigate industry partnerships in ensuring career paths for students while studying and after graduation.

This last point is especially important for the universities who were awarded the ACSSE, as one of the key goals is to increase the number of highly skilled post-graduates who can deal with the emerging cyber security challenges.

## Key research outcomes

The following key research outcomes should be considered by universities and industry to promote effective alignment between the educational outcomes and industry requirements:

- The Cyberspace Education Framework provides a valuable tool for analysis of education and training programmes.
- The industry survey results demonstrate a gap between university offerings and industry's requirements from them as education institutions. Universities have the potential to expand and amend their programmes to meet industry's needs.
- A move away from the "all-in-one" generalist curricula and instead offering distinct multi-faceted and multidisciplinary course streams would enable courses to be individually tailored to meet specific mission-specific requirements.
- Aligning programme streams to industry vacancies could add value to Master of Cyber Security programmes.
- Practical skill sets application and development are vital for technical-based programmes.
- Workplace-integrated learning is essential (if implemented correctly) and can provide valuable experience to students who are not in the industry or want to actively expand new skill sets.
- Universities working with industry to provide internships/work placements could be a valuable promotion tool for universities.

## Applying this research

Adapting current cyber security education to a necessary workplace-integrated learning programme involves applying the methods and findings outlined above to mission-specific and role-specific programmes. The discussion below around possible planning for a new mid-career or early career Master's degree illustrates what that might look like if UNSW Canberra were to undertake to prepare team leaders in advanced cyber operations for military and national security purposes. The proposal would involve consultation with the sectors and industries that the courses are intended to support, principally but not exclusively Defence (the Australian Defence Force and Department of Defence), other national security agencies, and the private sector. Additional development of new courses may depend on additional funding, if only for the government to incentivise fully integrated learning programmes. Here is how a new process might unfold.

Mapping of the key KSAs and attitudes for such a degree might ascertain, based in part on this chapter, that the main gaps in current UNSW Canberra programmes were:

1.  *Knowledge*: understanding of legal aspects of cyber security, as applied to rules-of-engagement for attributing sources of cyber threat, mechanisms for referral to authorities of suspected criminality encountered in intelligence work, and techniques of offensive deterrence (active defence).
2.  *Skills and abilities*: mentored investigative or research skills in applying the techniques used on both unclassified and real cyber ranges in medium complexity red v. blue exercises.
3.  *Attitudes*: practicums to develop successful attitudes to deal with the uncertainty prevalent in cyber attribution, the pervasiveness of cyber operations, invasiveness of malicious intent and probing, and the deleterious effects of the mostly indecisive outcomes (i.e. no win/lose or reward).

UNSW Canberra with representation from the Defence Force and the government could negotiate with cybersecurity industries with the necessary experience and security clearances to help develop and oversee three different integrated workplace learning programmes: (1) for Defence; (2) for government departments (State/Territory or Federal); and (3) for industries that provide essential national services such as finance, transportation and utilities. Private sector companies could agree to partner in developing the practicums, e.g., US Company A and UK Company B.

Stakeholders could work towards developing a formal degree programme that would extend current cyber security Master's programmes for one year (full-time equivalent) by including specialised integrated workplace learning programmes into a second year, each of which leverages common existing subjects into more specialised purpose-specific outcomes (defence, other government, industry – all of which have roles in cyber military operations). To raise the standard of education with high-level academic input, a new funding model could include two industry chairs (US Industry A and UK Industry B) and two academic chairs (applied cyber security law and cyber range research operations). The academic subjects for the intensive knowledge component and practicum might be:

- Semester 1 (Year 1):

    a   Cyber law (Applied Legal Chair/Industry Chair B)
    b   Cyber acquisition governance (Current Academic/Industry Chair A)
    c   Advanced cyber security test and evaluation techniques (Current Academic/Industry Chair A)
    d   Cyber network architectures (Current Academic/Industry Chair B)

- Semester 2 (Year 1):

    a   Cyber network protections and attributional tools (Current Academic/Industry Chair B) b   Cyber-defensive techniques, including cooperative vulnerability testing (Cyber Range Operations Chair/Industry Chair A)

    c   Cyber-offensive techniques, including penetration testing) (Cyber Range Operations Chair/Industry Chair A)

    d   Cyber warfare strategic dimensions (international factors, hybrid warfare, hacker profiles, cyber crime, etc.) (Applied Legal Chair/Industry Chair B)

- Practicum Year (Year 2)

    a   Research project (All)

The new programmes could commence with new external funding for 25 students in each programme per year (75 in total), growing by a further 25 positions in each programme each year over three years to a total of 225 per year. As the funding is provided by the government, only Australian citizens with a minimum security clearance would be allowed, while Defence students are subjected to additional clearances before the practicum phase. The delivery of classified Australian-only education programmes in a university setting would be problematic and would be seen by many as contrary to the ethos of Australian universities. A cyber security institute and the Australian Government Department of Education and Training could partner to accredit the new integrated workplace learning programme with reviews every two years. The first graduates are presented with both a Master of Cyber Security and a cyber security institute accreditation as high-level practitioners. The programme becomes both an important feeder of graduates with recognised KSA in cybersecurity that are sufficiently experienced more quickly than current industry norms (i.e. 2.5 years compared to 5 years), but could spawn replication in other cyber security education programmes within Australia and abroad.

## Areas for future research

There are five key areas for future research which should be undertaken to further investigate the educational outcomes and industry requirements.

- What the Australian cyber security industry wants and requires from education institutions.
- Educational outcomes and industry work roles required to accurately map the broad requirements of the skills and education crisis.
- There is a key lack of relevant data on baselines and benchmarks on the effectiveness of cyber security education programmes. More investigation of the relevance of all current programmes focusing on cyber security and the true requirements of industry.
- Should there be a more hybrid model for cyber security education (a cyber security college) incorporating aspects of higher education, vocational education and training (VET) and industry certifications?
- Further research into establishing trainee or cadetship programmes or similar would be beneficial for students to gain the necessary experience.

This research demonstrates that investigation of university courses and their alignment to work role KSAs will provide a valuable picture for universities, industry and policy-makers alike. Further investigation is required to ensure that all aspects, including KSA outcomes, skills acquired from practical projects, workplace-integrated learning and the course learning outcomes are more fully addressed. This focus could ultimately shape public policy on key cyber security issues. It is essential for a nation to be cyber-resilient in order to truly prosper in the digital information age.

## Conclusion

The aim of this research was to investigate if the current Master of Cyber Security programmes were preparing students for the workforce. The results note that more needs to be done in this space, but disruption is often hard to implement in large organisations such as universities. The results show that while student experiences are positive, alignment of courses offered with work role KSAs is low. Overall, a course that moves more towards being mission-specific, purpose-driven and closely aligned with the work role KSAs would greatly improve the success of students moving into the workforce and the effectiveness of the courses offered. Universities need to promote their programmes more broadly with industry to break the current viewpoints and perceptions. It is fair to say that in general, the relationship between industry and universities needs to be improved particularly with respect to the development of industry-integrated curricula, as has been argued for a decade (Koppi et al. 2008).

The requirement for purpose-driven and mission-specific cyber security education is increasing and will continue to become more relevant. This focus enables stakeholders to establish key educational programmes and policies relevant to the particular requirement. The Cyberspace Education Framework provides a model to view cyber security education holistically within the public policy context. This method aims to ensure relevant pedagogical aspects are covered and identified. This enables baselines and benchmarks to be used. The chapter tested the model against higher education examples and demonstrated that the model can be used for future reviews, encompassing the alignment with work role KSAs. This can then be used to create a cyberspace education maturity index that can be reviewed each year. Ongoing evaluation is critical to identifying strengths and weaknesses in existing programmes and specific areas that need to be addressed.

In response to the initial question posed (Are current Master of Cyber Security programmes preparing students for the workforce?), this chapter demonstrates a requirement for the realignment of courses to enable relevant work role KSAs to be acquired by students during their studies. The government's strong focus on cyber resilience must be understood. Australia has the opportunity to be a leader in cyber security education globally. This potential needs to be viewed with disruption in mind, with universities being open to new ways of operating in partnerships with industry. The requirement for universities to produce highly skilled postgraduates with the job-ready skills needed should be viewed as an opportunity and the way forward.

## Note

1   The US Government's National Institute of Standards and Technology (NIST) developed the Framework in response to Presidential Executive Order (EO) 13636, *Improving Critical Infrastructure Cybersecurity*, issued in 2013. The Framework is voluntary guidance, based on existing standards, guidelines, and practices.

## Acknowledgements

The author is grateful to Dr Keith Joiner, CSC, for his assistance in compiling an example to envisage how the research findings might be applied and with what consequences.

## References

AISA. (Australian Information Security Association). 2017. The Australian Cyber Security Skills Shortage Study 2016. AISA Research Report. Available at: www.aisa.org.au/Public/Training_Pages/Research/AISA%20Cyber%20security%20skills%20shortage%20research.aspx?New_ContentCollectionOrganizerCommon=3#New_ContentCollectionOrganizerCommon.

Amankwa, E., M. Loock and E. Kritzinger. 2014. *A Conceptual Analysis of Information Security Education, Information Security Training and Information Security Awareness Definitions*. Paper presented at The 9th International Conference for Internet Technology and Secured Transactions (ICITST-2014).

Amankwa, E., M. Loock and E. Kritzinger. 2015. *Enhancing Information Security Education and Awareness: Proposed Characteristics for a Model*. Paper presented at 2015 Second International Conference on Information Security and Cyber Forensics (InfoSec).

Armstrong, H., R. Dodge and C. Armstrong. 2013. Reaching Today's Information Security Students. In R. C. Dodge and L. Futcher (eds), *Information Assurance and Security Education and Training*. New York: Springer, pp. 218–225.

Austin, G. 2016. Australia Rearmed! Future Needs for Cyber-Enabled Warfare. Discussion Paper 1. Australian Centre for Cyber Security, UNSW Canberra. Available at: www.unsw.adfa.edu.au/unsw-canberra-cyber/sites/accs/files/uploads/DISCUSSION%20PAPER%20AUSTRALIA%20REARMED.pdf.

Austin, G. 2017. Cyber Security Formation: An Educational Maturity Model for Australia. Unpublished note.

Austin, G. and J. Slay. 2016. Australia's Response to Advanced Technology Threats: An Agenda for the Next Government. Discussion Paper 3, Australian Centre for Cyber Security, UNSW Canberra. Available at: www.unsw.adfa.edu.au/unsw-canberra-cyber/news/discussion-paper-australias-response-advanced-technology-threats-agenda-next-government.

Australian Cyber Security Growth Network. (2017). Cyber Security Sector Competitiveness Plan. Available at: www.acsgn.com/cyber-security-sector-competitiveness-plan/ (accessed 1 June 2017).

Australian Government Department of Employment. 2017. Unpaid Work Experience in Australia: Prevalence, Nature and Impact. Australian Government. Available at: https://docs.employment.gov.au/system/files/doc/other/unpaid_work_experience_report_-_december_2016.pdf.

Conklin ,W., R. Cline and T. Roosa. 2014. *Re-engineering Cybersecurity Education in the US: An Analysis of the Critical Factors*. Paper presented at 2014 47th Hawaii International

Conference on System Sciences. Available at: http://ieeexplore.ieee.org/stamp/stamp.jsp?reload=true&arnumber=6758852.

Cooper, S., L. Hoffman, L. Pérez, C. Pfleeger, R. Raines, et al. 2010. An Exploration of the Current State of Information Assurance Education. *ACM SIGCSE Bulletin* 41(4): 109.

Council of Australian Governments. 2017. COAG meeting Communiqué, 9 December 2016. Available at: www.coag.gov.au/meeting-outcomes/coag-meeting-communiqué-9-december-2016.

Hentea, M. and H. Dhillon. 2006. Towards Changes in Information Security Education. *Journal of Information Technology Education*, 5, 221–233. Available at: http://jite.informingscience.org/documents/Vol5/v5p221-233Hentea148.pdf.

ISACA. 2017. State of Cyber Security 2017. Part 1: Current Trends in Workforce Development. Available at: www.cybersecobservatory.com/wp-content/uploads/2017/06/state-of-cybersecurity-2017_res_eng_0217.pdf.

Kessler, G. and J. Ramsay. 2013. Paradigms for Cybersecurity Education in a Homeland Security Program. *Journal of Homeland Security Education*, 2, 35–44. Available at: www.journalhse.org/sft710/kesslerramsayjhsearticlefinal.pdf.

Koppi, A., F. Naghdy, J. Chicharo, J. Sheard, S. Edwards and D. Wilson. 2008. *The Crisis in ICT Education: An Academic Perspective.* Paper presented at Annual Conference of the Australasian Society for Computers in Learning in Tertiary Education. Available at: http://ro.uow.edu.au/infopapers/901/.

Koppi, T., S. Edwards, J. Sheard, W. Brooke and F. Naghdy. 2010. *The Case for ICT Work-Integrated Learning from Graduates in the Workplace.* Paper presented at 12th Australasian Computing Education Conference. Available at: https://opus.lib.uts.edu.au/bitstream/10453/19326/1/2011001487.pdf.

Lehto, M. 2016. Cyber Security Education and Research in Finland's Universities and Universities of Applied Sciences. *International Journal of Cyber Warfare and Terrorism (IJCWT)* 6(2): 15–31. Available at: www-igi-global-com.wwwproxy1.library.unsw.edu.au/gateway/article/full-text-html/152645pdf.

Manson, D. and R. Pike. 2014. The Case for Depth in Cybersecurity Education. *ACM Inroads*, 5(1): 47–52. doi:10.1145/2568195.2568212.

Martin, P. 2015. Cyber Security Education, Qualifications and Training. *Engineering & Technology.* Available at: https://pure.royalholloway.ac.uk/portal/files/25218802/IETEducationTraining.pdf.

McGettrick, A. 2013. Toward Curricular Guidelines for Cybersecurity. Report of a Workshop on Cybersecurity. Association for Computing Machinery. Available at: www.acm.org/education/TowardCurricularGuidelinesCybersec.pdf.

NIST. 2016. NICE Framework Provides Resource for a Strong Cybersecurity Workforce. Available at: www.nist.gov/news-events/news/2016/11/nice-framework-provides-resource-strong-cybersecurity-workforce.

Parrish, A., J. Impagliazzo, R.K. Raj, H. Santos, M.R. Asghar, *et al.* 2018. Global perspectives on cybersecurity education for 2030: a case for a meta-discipline. In *Proceedings of the 23rd Annual ACM Conference on Innovation and Technology in Computer Science Education*, pp. 36–54.

PM&C. (Department of the Prime Minister and Cabinet (Australia)). 2016. Australia's Cybersecurity Strategy. Available at: https://cybersecuritystrategy.dpmc.gov.au/resources/index.html.

PM&C. (Department of the Prime Minister and Cabinet (Australia)). 2017. Australia's Cybersecurity Strategy First Annual Update. Available at: https://cybersecuritystrategy.pmc.gov.au/first-annual-update/.

Slay, J. 2016. Training and Education for Cyber Security, Cyber Defence and Cyber Warfare. *United Service* 67(3): 24–26, 31. Available at: search.informit.com.au/docum
entSummary;dn=301424020269498;res=IELHSS.

Vogel, R. 2016. Closing the Cybersecurity Skills Gap. *Salus Journal*, 4(2): 32–46. Available at:
www.salusjournal.com/wp-content/uploads/sites/29/2016/05/Vogel_Salus_Journal_
Volume_4_Number_2_2016_pp_32-46.pdf.

# 3

# BEYOND AWARENESS

## Reflections on meeting the inter-disciplinary cyber skills demand

*Andrew Martin and Jamie Collier*

The WannaCry ransomware which crippled large parts of the UK National Health Service (NHS), and dozens of organisations around the world, in May 2017, eloquently – if alarmingly – illustrates the complex *ecology* of today's cyber security challenges. The malware itself used a number of detailed technical vulnerabilities, which had been present in Microsoft products for many years, but went unnoticed or unexploited by most people. The exploits used were seemingly derived from the work of intelligence agencies and those in their orbits. The spread of the malware happened to be halted (accidentally) by a single individual – who was later arrested (rightly or wrongly) for alleged earlier cyber crime. There was considerable misdirection or misreporting of the particular operating systems versions which were vulnerable and led to propagation, and this served to distract malware analysts and their respective organisations, so that it was difficult to look quickly and provide detection and/or insight. Some affected networks were cutting access to the Internet, and in some cases, this actually served to prolong the internal propagation of the encryption (since the malware on an isolated network could not observe the activation of the domain name "kill-switch"). The ransomware entailed a considerable challenge in attribution (an important aspect in international relations, particularly where government systems were involved) so that the overall motive for WannaCry is far from clear, given imprecise (or non-existent) targeting, and poor design from the perspective of raising money from the payment of ransoms. The malware had decidedly unpredictable impacts – due in part to local circumstances, and different prioritisation of technical investment/time (under significant resource constraints): the clinical impacts upon the NHS have not yet been quantified.[1]

A rounded insight into this high-profile incident can only be achieved through a synthesis of these many factors, and a range of skills and knowledge not assembled in any traditionally educated individual or conventionally constructed team.

Cyber security has become such a pressing concern for businesses and organisations – as well as individuals – that there is a widely reported shortage of "cyber security professionals" (Megaw 2015; Hancock 2017; Nunns 2017). And yet the description of the skills needed by such professionals is often narrowly drawn – skills centred around risk assessment, or around technical familiarity with a particular product or standard. In fact, the challenge for society is surely much broader than this. The cyber security skill shortage extends to other disciplines and areas of expertise, such as law, business strategy and public policy. Moreover, there is a dearth of talented individuals who can understand and communicate across different domains. For example, anecdotally it seems hard to find professionals who not only can speak the language of a technical cyber security team but also can articulate concerns to a board or ministerial level in an accessible manner.

Such a breadth of concern is clearly seen in the routine requirement for staff in many sectors to undergo training in "cyber security awareness" despite evidence that such training has at best a negligible effect on overall cyber security outcomes (Bada et al. 2015). Such awareness may be a desirable baseline, but it is not itself adequate to equip professionals with the skills they need to make decisions cognisant of their security implications. It is often recognised that responsibility for cyber security extends far outside the "IT department" – ideally, all the way to the boardroom – yet paradoxically key decisions about the design of products, services and operations are necessarily made by professionals with no particular cyber security expertise.

Such disconnections inevitably lead to bad cyber security choices being made. Without proper communication and input from a variety of perspectives, security policies often result in requirements and procedures that pit security against utility and usability. Users typically find ways to circumvent overly stringent and inconvenient security policies. Faced with unreasonable demands (i.e., "change your password now, and ensure these rules are followed"), users will typically follow a path that involves the minimum effort (changing password qwerty1 into qwerty2) without truly engaging with the risks and reasoning behind the policy. Likewise, civil servants may bypass encrypted work computers that include awkward and disruptive security protocols by using their personal devices for professional work instead. In other instances, sensible security policies are ignored.

Sometimes, a complex technical analysis is necessarily reduced to a simple answer, in order that a senior executive may take an apparently informed decision. We are aware of one company which in the early days of "bring your own device"[2] was faced with a decision about which employees' devices were sufficiently secure to be allowed to connect to the corporate infrastructure. Executives asked for a technical analysis, and received the distilled answer "Android: No; iPhone: Yes". The CTO was amused (but confused) to meet his opposite number in a similar firm a few weeks later, and learn that the second firm had asked the same question within its own organisation, and received back the answer "Android: Yes; iPhone: No". It is hard to avoid the conclusion that an apparently scientific process was in fact nothing of the sort. How is the Board to make meaningful decisions about managing risk to the business in this context?

Issues of cyber security are confounding because they touch many parts of the enterprise, including product development, email communications and the storage of intellectual property, yet often have no easy default answer. Buying the newest solution may expose one to unforeseen risks; retaining an old solution may also be far from risk-free, especially when it falls into the "legacy" category and ceases to be supported by its designer or manufacturer.

Perhaps there is a deeper tension at work. It is often said that the security analyst or systems designer must have a sceptical or devious mind – the kind of mindset that enables one to think like the attacker or adversary – as well as the skills necessary to envisage the attacks which might be perpetrated. By contrast, the entrepreneur thrives in taking risks, and tends to be optimistic about outcomes. Constant exposure to the worst of human nature may render one cynical; a customer-centric, service-oriented mentality might tend to make one think the best of people, or to be optimistic about the opportunities provided by the market.

It has also long been said that this tension is best resolved through multi-disciplinary teams. Yet, such efforts can easily be poorly executed. Executives may initially get involved in the formulation of a broad strategic plan, yet the execution is often left to technical security teams to implement with Boards reluctant to revisit the issue or to refresh themselves on security protocols thereafter.

This tension is also seen on the national and international stage when politicians discuss cyber security. Here, an increasingly technically literate press is quick to expose flaws in government pronouncements. For example, the (then) UK Home Secretary Amber Rudd was widely criticised for writing a newspaper article (Rudd 2017) on encryption where she both acknowledged the benefits of encryption while also implying that it was not necessary for "real people". Likewise, when the German and French Ministers of the Interior sent a joint letter to the European Commission calling for measures to stem recent terrorist incidents, their demands for technology companies to develop encryption systems that are secure yet easily crackable by law enforcement were criticised by the technical press, given the impossibility of developing such a system (Thomson 2017). Here, other issues are at play: the politician may not be an expert on the technical details of the policy he or she espouses, but will have a large group of advisors, all of whom have their own agendas. The details of the argument being espoused may be obscured by a need – or perceived need – for secrecy (from law enforcement and intelligence agencies). Alternatively, cyber security issues are increasingly becoming politicised: statements that promise a tough line on encryption regularly follow terrorist attacks to signal (albeit perhaps in a superficial and ineffective manner) a response to the attack at hand. All of this becomes particularly contentious when regulation and spending are justified by a response to the danger of cyber terrorism – since to date the actual harm from cyber terrorism seems minimal (grugq 2016). However, whatever the incentive, the result is often a failure to communicate – and hence, we might say, a failure of democracy.

These are large and complex issues: our analysis here is at a high level, seasoned with personal experiences. Therefore, this chapter is offered in the spirit of *reflective practice*: we make a few observations about the nature of the challenge, and draw on the authors' experience of activities and programmes which address parts of this.

## The need for an interdisciplinary approach

Because the technologies and practices of cyberspace are common to so many aspects of society, each group of professionals sees the challenges of cyber security through its own disciplinary lens. Yet, it may be generally observed that without the integration of these perspectives, meeting the security challenge tends to be forever out of reach. This is in large part because security is not about analysing and gaining control over some physical process, but about frustrating the aims of one or more adversaries. If the thinking of those adversaries is more agile or integrated than that of the defenders, they will tend to have the upper hand. There is a strong alignment between some academic and professional disciplines of relevance – but also much divergence. Since we are considering primarily questions of education, research and practice, all of these realms are relevant to our study.

### *Professional silos*

We may identify a number of disciplines (in both professional and academic spheres) which naturally and – unhappily perhaps – form "thought silos" containing welcome wisdom but failing to connect to necessary insights in other fields.

Clearly, in almost all areas of human endeavour, there are points of contact between different disciplines and specialisms; this is the basis of civilisation and society. A well-understood example of this context is seen in developing an understanding of climate change and its impacts. This is an issue requiring contributions from climate physicists, oceanographers, economic geographers, alternative energy providers, policy and regulation experts, and more – even perhaps historians of science. All of these skill sets are fundamental in confronting the problem, albeit from entirely different approaches and perspectives. Yet, while the need for such an eclectic approach to climate change is now accepted as conventional wisdom, there appears to remain a widespread perception that the cyber security challenge, by contrast, is largely a technical challenge. Moreover, some analyses seem to imagine the technical challenges or adversary behaviour leading to security incidents as akin to being a force of nature: this is surely a mistake, too: technology can be improved; adversaries can have their incentives diminished.

The need for improved connections between silos is profound. The narrow view of cyber security is at least in part due to the relative immaturity of the discipline, and its present state of flux. Indeed, it remains to be seen whether cyber security can be characterised as a discipline, or as something else (a meta-discipline?). It may be that at some future time, there will be a common understanding of the elements of disciplines $X$ and $Y$ which must be understood in discipline $Z$ in order to build an understanding of cyber security. Such a distillation of views is certainly not available now; it is a matter of debate whether it will become evident in the foreseeable future.

The outmoded distinctions that have been historically established between various academic and professional disciplines fail to reflect contemporary reality. Indeed, if disciplinary boundaries were drawn again today, topics such as cyber security demonstrate that issues as disparate as software engineering, cryptography and system design can overlap with non-technical questions of privacy, philosophy and deterrence. Yet, the majority of current thought silos were formed before the issue of cyber security emerged. The relationships between various thought silos are based, therefore, not on the needs of today but on historical precedent. There is established cross-over between international relations and law since both disciplines have long examined war. Similarly, the intelligence community has an established (though sometimes tenuous) link with cryptography academics, sharing an interest in encryption. Yet, for the most part, the cross-overs that are needed to examine cyber security effectively do not exist: international relations academics have not needed to collaborate with system engineers in the past; policy experts have not been required to consult software engineers and cryptographers. Often, even the subdivisions within two separate discipline are wildly misaligned. An example is the issue of privacy. For the technical community, both privacy protection and digital rights protection are examined together with the material differences in processes insignificant. Within the legal discipline, however, the distinction is markedly more significant, with one related to criminal law and the other related to the private law of contracts.

The lack of disciplinary overlap, and therefore the lack of communication between disciplines, has meant that many thought silos have proceeded in isolation without the necessary consultation and communication. The policy community (in both an academic and professional capacity) has been guilty of producing theories and agreements that are not grounded in technical realities. International efforts such as the UN Group of Governmental Experts (a UN-mandated Working Group in the field of cyber security) and the production of the *Tallinn Manual* (a non-binding, scholarly effort to apply international law to the issue of cyber security) have been criticised by those in technical and operational communities for failing to adequately understand technical details related to the topic at hand (Aitel 2017a; 2017b; Sukumar 2017). By contrast, in proposing political responses to some of the most significant incidents in recent years, those from more technical backgrounds have often proposed solutions that, while sensible in practice, are wholly inconceivable due to the reality of politics, bureaucratic interests and negotiations.

We might take the view that *all* of our disciplines have failed to prepare us adequately for the cyber security challenge that now faces us.

- *Computer science* (and allied disciplines, such as computer engineering, electronics and software engineering) has helped us to build massively capable, fast, interconnected systems, but these are systems with no "safety net" where security is concerned. Most software could justifiably be called shoddy in at least some of its aspects: the economic imperative drives this, but so does a mismatch of tools and skills with the practitioner community. Incidentally this is a situation made even worse by educational programmes which imply that everyone can write code. Maybe everyone *can*, very clearly not everyone *should*.

- Notwithstanding contemporary interest in security economics, the field of *economics* has not given us good tools to understand how to build incentives for good software and security practices. Nor, allied with criminology, did it foresee or particularly help to disrupt the dark markets in vulnerabilities, compromised systems, and personal data – nor the complex symbiosis in which these exist with the developers of technology.
- It is often said that the *law* struggles to keep pace with technological development: this is almost necessarily true with respect to many technologies but the technologies of cyberspace give rise to many conundrums with genuine novelty.
- *International relations* understood only very late the strategic importance of the construction of cyberspace, following the 2008 attacks which severely disrupted systems in Estonia, with seemingly a strong underlying political motive (Kello 2017).
- The study of *business* has only very recently seen MBA programmes introducing core modules on cyber security, despite it already being high on every company's risk register, and a topic of considerable complexity which Company Boards fail to understand at their peril.
- *Ethics and philosophy* have struggled to keep pace with some of the issues surrounding management of personal data – and, tellingly to provide a generally accepted framework for considering the competing demands of encryption (in both data communications, and in protecting data at rest) for personal privacy and security, weighed against the interests of the state in protecting citizens (or the state) through surveillance – or even in balancing those personal rights with the interests of companies and service providers.

Instead, we draw almost as much inspiration from science fiction as we do from the disciplines which seemingly should inform our discourse (Mellor 2017).

There is of course no shortage of professional accreditations in the information security field. They overlap, and some are widely held to have more value than others – but there is relatively little consensus. Most are at the level of certifying the "specialist" – in technical computing fields, and in risk management.

As observed by Henry (2017), cyber security has much in common with engineering – as properly understood, a profession encompassing many distinct fields from civil and mechanical through to software, chemical and biochemical engineering. More might be made of this observation – and yet, as we have noted above, the range of disciplines contributing to cyber security is perhaps even broader: the architect or civil engineer may occasionally need to consider and anticipate the actions of a hostile foreign power, but this will not be an uppermost design consideration generally. By contrast, the creator of any mid-range database or online service needs to consider its security against the well-funded adversary at the scale of the nation state.

## *Example domain: privacy*

An illustrative example of this problem exists in the protection of individual privacy. Drivers for this concern come in part from business goals (some vendors make privacy a positive distinctive for their product), in part from ethics, in part from politics (a desire to avoid emulation of repressive regimes of past and present). These goals are made precise in law and regulation – topically including, at the time of writing, the European General Data Protection Regulation (European Union 2016). That this regulation is a considerable evolution of the two decades-old EU Data Protection Directive (95/46/EC) is an indication that privacy represents something of a moving target, driven in part by the evolution of technology, and in part by a developing understanding of how privacy may be violated or abused.

The appropriate technical implementation of such regulations is of course a contentious area with no simple solutions. The "Privacy by Design" movement (Fischer-Hübner 2001; Cavoukian 2009) begins to make the bridge, albeit driven by a more abstract notion of privacy than that embodied in legislation. As an initiative of the Information and Privacy commissioners in various jurisdictions, it remains quite high level. Its interpretation within a particular software or systems design is a matter of a separate professional judgement – and it is worth noting that here (as in many areas of security), good design may be undermined by unthinking implementation. For example, in collecting, processing and presenting data from the *Streetview* program, Google claims to have followed good practice. But according to some accounts, someone tasked with building the system collected far more data from nearby WiFi access points and their users than was necessary, thereby potentially undermining a careful considered privacy policy (Kiss 2010).

## *Example domain: HCISec*

The area of human-computer interaction has long been a stand-out area of computer science: making computer systems which people can use easily and productively requires quite a different skill set from the task of designing and implementing software. Critically, this draws on insights from psychology and sociology. More recently, it has become clear that such concerns are crucial in the development of security-related functionality. A seminal paper (Whitten and Tygar 1999) reported the difficulty that "ordinary" users had in making use of mainstream email encryption software.

The problem is seen clearly in the issue of password management. The requirements placed upon users in choice of passwords and frequency of changes are driven (at least in part) by sound technical analysis, but often take no account of the functioning of human memories, or of the social functions surrounding, say, password sharing in an office environment. Moreover, the burdens placed upon users are driven in part by an economic analysis: it is cheaper to ask users to manage difficult passwords than to implement systems which avoid the need for such passwords. Inter-disciplinary studies have thrown these issues into sharp relief, leading ultimately to radical changes to official password guidance (NCSC 2016; Grassi et al. 2017).

## Example security challenge: attribution

Hackers have access to several technical tools that help them cover their tracks, thereby making it difficult for states to definitively name a perpetrator – something that has become increasingly necessary as hacking has taken on a geopolitical dimension (Newman 2016).[3] To overcome the inherent challenges of attribution, a "constellation of evidence" is required: drawing on a variety of sources and investigative techniques can help to make a more compelling case about an aggressor's identity. Crucially, if a combination of strategic, operational and technical data makes attribution more convincing (Rid and Buchanan, 2015), it follows that a variety of skill sets are required to overcome the problem.

Demonstrating that the Russian government acquired, and subsequently leaked, Democratic National Committee (DNC) documents during the 2016 US presidential election provides a case in point. Technical forensic evidence was naturally a vital component of attribution attempts. For example, the command-and-control server (essentially a digital fingerprint) used on the DNC server was linked to a previous attack on the German parliament that German security agencies has publicly attributed to Russian military intelligence (Rid 2016).

Linguistics analysis also helped to understand the context of the hack. Gucifer 2.0, the online pseudonym that declared responsibility for the hack, claimed to be Romanian. Yet, this was disproven after Guccifer 2.0 was asked to explain the hack in Romanian; a linguistic analysis quickly showed that Guccifer 2.0's sentence constructions were unusual for Romanian natives, with a strange use of diacritics and accented letters (Franceschi-Bicchierai 2016). In addition, there was significant variety in the pseudonym's written English, possibly suggesting that a team of operators were behind the online persona (Rid 2016).

Political and strategic analysis also help to provide context. Rid argued that the DNC hack sits comfortably within the wider framework of Russia's evolving military doctrine which comprises a broader view of what can qualify as a military target or military tactic (Adamsky 2015). This shows that consideration of political factors can be highly informative in providing a contextual backdrop (Healey 2012).

## Reflections on experience

The authors have first-hand knowledge of several relevant initiatives in this area, and in this section, we reflect on our experience of these.[4]

### MSc in Software and Systems Security

Launched in 2008, the Oxford University Master of Science programme in Software and Systems Security grew out of more long-standing provision in a similar MSc in Software Engineering. Both are offered solely on a part-time basis, designed to meet the needs of mid-career professionals in their respective fields. Each one recruits around 50 students per year, and the part-time students typically take four years to complete the degree. The first module in Security Principles was offered on the Software Engineering course in 2001, and has proved to be the most popular module offered. A second module – on People and Security – was added soon afterwards; one of the first anywhere to offer dedicated tuition in human factors in security. From this beginning, the selection of available modules has grown to encompass many topics in both technical and process/governance fields in security (Simpson et al. 2015).

Because of the constituency from which the students are drawn, the selection of students seen appears to represent a fair cross-section of the practitioner community. The close but distinct fields of the two degrees – and the offer of modules from each one to students of the other – presents an opportunity for academics teaching cyber security to reflect on the distinct skills and abilities of the professionals in the two areas. In particular:

- Many working in the security field – even those who will benefit from a Master's degree with quite a technical focus – have little or no experience of software development. Many professional software engineers – even today – have little insight into the security implications of their work, nor how to avoid introducing vulnerabilities.
- The first author was particularly struck by one quiet request from a senior (and well-paid) operations manager who asked for "a quick reminder of how the binary system works": the level of basic technical knowledge present in those holding security-related technical roles can be surprisingly low.
- Moreover, the two constituencies conceive of themselves quite differently. Security professionals, whether taking roles of security specialist, or network administrator; auditor or secure systems designer, are emphatically not software engineers. This disconnect between specialisms is unsurprising to those close to the field – but from a distance might surprise those who expect "the technical people" to fix problems.
- Insight into the human factors covered in the People and Security module does not come at all naturally to those who spend most of their time designing, writing and testing software. People do not behave according to the elegant algebraic patterns of binary arithmetic, and this is a difficult lesson to grasp for those whose whole education has been in STEM.
- Despite decades of teaching of "formal methods" and rigorous development techniques in undergraduate programmes, the great majority of software engineers are largely unaware of development practices which minimise software vulnerabilities, tools to discover and eliminate design flaws, and so on. Many have remarked on the irony of teaching "secure programming" as an advanced topic – as if *insecure programming* were a reasonable entry-level course.

There is a widespread assumption that those who work with software for a living are fully up to speed with issues of creating and maintaining secure systems: nothing could be further from the truth, as is evident from the number of profoundly vulnerable systems reportedly attacked on a daily basis. Conversely, in just a few years, practitioners of cyber security as a technical topic have become quite far removed from the everyday practice of software development.

These distinct specialisations serve to illustrate the depth of the challenge of disciplinary integration described in this chapter. Security challenges are not merely misunderstood by those working in management, policy, or law, but also by the very software engineers who are tasked with building (more) secure systems.

### Cyber Security Oxford

At the University of Oxford, we have developed a network of interest around the topic of cyber security. This began as a relatively small collaboration between academics in the Computer Science department and the Oxford Internet Institute (which largely studies the social science of the Internet). To these have been added links with the Saïd Business School, the Department of Politics and International Relations, and others. It now involves two dozen academic departments and centres, and covers well over 40 academics (with their associated students and researchers).

Deliberately keeping a broad definition of cyber security, it has been evident that very many avenues of research within the university are either strongly connected to cyber security, or at least have a bearing upon it. Indeed, that was our motivation: too many technical talks in this field display a naïve understanding of, say, the politics and culture of a certain country, whereas academics in the university understand this in great depth; too many talks about organisational or national responses miss the point entirely with regard to particular technologies, whereas colleagues in other departments can offer deep understanding of the important issues.

The network is founded on three pillars. To place research at the centre is, of course, natural. As a university, we are also committed, of course, to education – and finding that educational programmes in cyber security and related topics also need to span the disciplines is something else that drives the development of the network. A third pillar is the university's own practice of security: an open dialogue with the University Chief Information Security Officer (CISO) and good relations with the network security team help to drive good practice and to motivate research. A good example of benefit here is in undertaking academic research based on network data derived from the campus network: empirical research on network data is notoriously hard because of the complexities over ownership and disclosure. The university must also, of course, exercise due care with data generated internally, but by building trust between research and operational teams, a great deal is possible with the right safeguards in place.

Two things have particularly helped catalyse this network. A facilitator – tasked with making connections and enabling collaborations – has been invaluable in seeking out such groups and individuals, and connecting them where possible. Second, the Centre for Doctoral Training in Cyber Security at the university has brought into the network a wide range of students eager to pursue research at the boundaries of disciplines, and able, through the university's structures, to seek out collaborators who can help make this possible. The ideas and integration achieved by setting this workforce loose within the university cannot be under-estimated.

Of course, work across the disciplines (whether characterised as cross-, multi- or inter-disciplinary) quickly runs into well-known problems of resourcing and incentives, and of profound differences in academic norms. Our approach – of a largely bottom-up, organic structure, based on individual good will, small and serendipitous collaborations, small-scale projects, and opportunistic publications – has been successful perhaps because it offers little threat to existing structures, but simply adds additional resources to them. We have always been clear that inter-disciplinarity is no excuse for poor scholarship, and by expecting all work in cyber security to retain one or more disciplinary homes, we ensure that appropriate quality control stays in place.

It is appropriate to give special mention of the Cyber Studies Programme led by Lucas Kello in the Department of Politics and International Relations.[5] This initiative arose independently of, and without reference to, the collaboration that was growing elsewhere in the university – but subsequently provided an extra strong dimension to the wide network.

The network led to Oxford being one of the first universities recognised in the UK EPSRC-GCHQ (NCSC) scheme to recognise Academic Centres of Excellence in Cyber Security Research (ACE-CSR). Though this scheme carries little funding, it also has helped to drive integration and provide a shop window for the university's activity. In connection with others in this network, we helped to create through the Oxford University Press an inter-disciplinary journal, *Journal of Cyber Security*.

## Centre for Doctoral Training in Cyber Security

The Centre for Doctoral Training in Cyber Security is a model promoted by the UK Research Councils as one of the main routes of support for doctoral study and research – often in innovative areas, or fields that benefit from cross-disciplinary study. A typical pattern has students receiving intensive instruction as a cohort during the first year of the doctorate, followed by three years of independent research.

The Oxford University Centre for Doctoral Training in Cyber Security (CDT) embraces this model fully. It opened in 2013, and admits around 15 students per year to undertake advanced research in cyber security. The intention of the programme is that 60–70 per cent of the intake, the teaching, and the research should come from computer science, with the remaining contributions coming from a wide range of other disciplines, predominantly in the social sciences. A distinctive feature of this model is that students are admitted to doctoral study without an assigned supervisor or research topic: the structures of the first year of study are designed to allow them to explore possibilities in depth. For students working in the emerging field of cyber security, this is invaluable and often leads to them studying something quite different from the topic they initially imagined they might pursue.

Some of the highlights are:

- Two students studying Internet censorship, privacy, anonymity, and tracking: considering both the motivations and intentions of censorship, for example, and the technical means by which it is being undertaken, and the measures used to evade it.
- A study of malware ecologies – involving a substantial ethnographic study of the behaviour of malware analysis. The student spent months embedded in an analysis lab, learning the skills used by analysts, and reflecting on the extensive connections which span cyberspace and the more physical and business worlds.
- A project jointly supervised between Computer Science and Business, exploring supply chain risks in cloud computing, and the effect of transparency on risk assessment.
- A thesis on software as a weapon – again, jointly supervised, this time between Computer Science and International Relations.

Following their studies, student destinations vary from academic teaching and research posts; through starting up a consultancy based on the insights from the research; and a variety of public service roles.

It is of course difficult to say with certainty how these students' research and careers would have differed without the disciplinary integration they learned in the CDT. However, when interviewed, they very consistently remark on the powerful effect of a diverse cohort whose members they can draw on for insights and constructive criticism, especially on the cyber security contextual issues outside their own (original) expertise. The faculty members teaching and supervising these students are confident that they will not be those who simply imagine that security can be delegated to "the tech guy", nor that policy can be made without reference to the capabilities of the technologies which underlie it.

## The UK NCSC Certified Masters' Programme

The UK's National Cyber Security Centre (NCSC) has taken a lead in promoting professionalism in cyber security in the UK. One of the initiatives within this programme of activity is a certification scheme for degree programmes which cover cyber security. This began with a focus on MSc courses intending to address "general cyber security". In order to gain certification, courses must meet the criteria in covering institutional support, covering the team delivering the courses, the curriculum, and quality control measures. The Oxford MSc described above gained certification in the first round, for a particular learning pathway (choice of modules).

The certification stands in contrast to that undertaken by professional bodies in cognate disciplines. For example, the British Computer Society (BCS) certifies Computer Science degrees mainly on the basis of an assessment of teaching quality and process, with quite a lightweight evaluation of content, and only one compulsory topic. The cyber security Master's certification is in many ways much more prescriptive. The security content of the course must be high, as defined by a mapping to the IISP skills framework,[6] and a high proportion of the framework topics must be covered.

This construction is deliberate: clearly many universities see offering a Master's degree in cyber security as a lucrative proposition. The clear intent is that only those offering substantial specialist content should be able to qualify (in contrast to offering a specially badged MSc which contains just one or two genuine security modules). The assessment is rigorous, and quite a number of applicants have failed to gain certification, but at the time of writing, 25 have succeeded – the programme is gradually being expanded to cover other specialisms (Digital Forensics, as the first example).

Clearly this approach promotes strong, content-filled degrees. But it entails several significant risks. One is that by prescribing the content quite closely, the programme becomes a straitjacket, inhibiting innovation or discouraging diversity. This is potentially very dangerous in a fast-moving area. The other is that it encourages emphasis on a specialism (cyber security) at the potential risk of failing to promote the topic in a wider range of degrees. As we remarked above, for example, there is a surprising gulf between professional software engineering and security engineering, etc. It remains to be seen whether this is bridged by adding "security modules" to a software engineering degree, or whether it can be truly addressed only by a profound change in the way that software engineering is taught. By promoting neither (but probably edging towards the former), there is a risk of further entrenching professional practices which have (arguably) led to the present unhappy situation with vulnerable software. Precisely how general software engineering should (or could) be redesigned to take account of present realities is a much bigger question that has not begun to be addressed.

There is, in addition, some interest from some quarters in certifying undergraduate degrees, with a small number presently holding provisional certification. This runs the same risks as those outlined above – perhaps more strongly. Security is not, generally, an abstract topic, but is about the security *of* something: insufficient depth in the study of the *something* runs a risk of delivering learning which is inherently ephemeral and unable to adapt to changing circumstances.

The role of a Master's degree in professional development varies from field to field. The Master's in Cyber Security programmes helps to develop individuals with the skills of a "cyber security professional". It is far from clear that this helps to equip society with the expertise needed for the inter-disciplinary expertise we have discussed earlier in this chapter.

## Cyber Security Body of Knowledge (CyBOK)

Another initiative of the NCSC, born partly of the scope and definition questions arising in the degree certifications scheme, is a major project to develop a *Guide to the Body of Knowledge in Cyber Security* ( CyBOK).[7] The design of the document draws on the SWEBOK (Bourque et al. 2014), a similar effort in the field of software engineering.

The project began in February 2017, undertaking a nine-month scoping phase before moving into a further 18 months of drafting. Thereafter, the project moved into a maintenance phase – one which will, presumably, continue indefinitely in one form or another. Scoping involved a large range of community engagement activities: structured workshops, a questionnaire, position papers, interviews, as well as desk-based research on extant documentation, textbooks, and conference scopes. At the end of the scoping phase, the initial list of 19 topics (Knowledge Areas) for the document was as shown in Figure 3.1.

The Knowledge Areas possibly identify a slightly narrower scope than that explored in this chapter, but certainly serve to begin to explore the dimensions of the cyber security challenge. As the CyBOK develops and the content is socialised ever more widely, it will be instructive to see the extent to which this breakdown of Knowledge Areas is challenged and developed.

The sponsors and the project team were of course aware of many of the attendant risks of developing such a document. Great care has been taken to have as

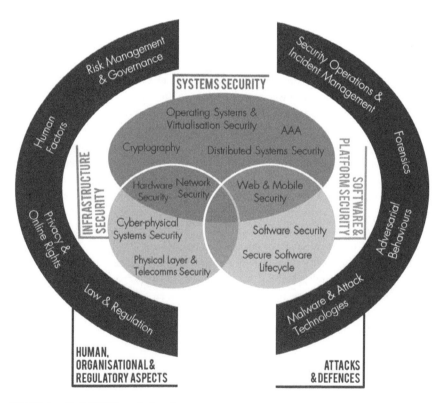

**FIGURE 3.1** CyBOK Knowledge Areas
Source: Figure 1 from CyBOK Version 1.0 © Crown Copyright, The National Cyber Security Centre 2019, licensed under the Open Government Licence: www.nationala rchives.gov.uk/doc/open-government-licence/.

open and transparent process as possible, and to consult as widely as is feasible. There is no single accepted taxonomy of cyber security, and so any such structure will be contentious: certainly, various counter-proposals have been received, even if the overall scope seems to represent a fair emergent consensus. The picture is (figuratively, and literally, at present) quite techno-centric. The topic is of course a moving target: some of the content will be out of date before the project concludes, and ongoing maintenance will be essential if the guide to the body of knowledge is to remain meaningful for even a few years. Finally, many topics contribute to the understanding of cyber security without themselves being part of the field (one cannot understand operating systems security without first understanding operating systems, and probably computer architecture also, for example): and these dependencies are documented.

## Cyber skills shortage: in the academy

Much has been made of a general need of more individuals with cyber security skills across global society. Whether we see that as a need for specialists, or of raising the skill level of other professionals, some level of need is evident. Training and mentoring of individuals can come from many quarters – but clearly the universities have a role to play.

However, it is pertinent to ask whether the universities have the requisite skills to help address the security challenges identified here. Anecdotal evidence says not. Much as the rounded needs of cyber security have surprised the wider community, so too they have caught the universities off guard. There are quite a number of specialists in cryptography, or certain aspects of systems security, and, increasingly, privacy and online rights. But, for reasons already explored, the generalist is harder to find – because academic careers reward specialism.

Yet, because cyber security is so diverse, and the adversary so resourceful (choosing technical means if those lead to the best outcome; psychological or social engineering if this is more fruitful or less expensive, and so on), a group of general, inter-disciplinary thinkers is needed. This much is evident to the second author: many head-hunters are searching for individuals who will lead wide-ranging academic cyber security programmes – in response to demand, and to government encouragement. We hope that the CDT outlined above will help to provide such leaders of the future – but its graduates are of course in high demand.

## Conclusion: the difficulties and promise of an interdisciplinary approach

While an interdisciplinary approach has been advocated throughout this chapter, there are clear difficulties in its implementation. These difficulties should not discourage organisations from adopting such an approach; but it is important to understand these inherent challenges. Three stand out.

First, the various divisions of an organisation often have different cultures. The "hoodie vs suits" caricature might be unfair, but it is certainly true that there are significant differences on a variety of factors, including the expected uniform, working hours, the emphasis between hard and soft skills, and so on. Even differences in language can even cause significant confusion. For example, while *active defence* is conventionally understood within a political context as the use of offensive action to deny a potential aggressor a contested area or position, the technical cyber security community understand the term to mean an active involvement in identifying and countering threat to a network and its systems (Lee 2015). Crucially, with such divergence in culture (and language, and approach), it cannot be assumed that fostering a more cohesive approach will be straightforward.

Second, incentive mechanisms do not routinely promote behaviours which enhance security. While this is seen narrowly in a reluctance to invest in a field which is in essence insurance against future harm, it applies also in a lack of willingness (or reward) to develop a deep understanding – across business and organisational boundaries – of processes and priorities, wherein security challenges may lurk. As we have noted, the same is true for academia. Academics are largely rewarded for publications in prestigious journals and conferences in their specific discipline – publishing genuinely interdisciplinarily often does not help at all with career advancement.

Third, the entrance of new actors and cultures becoming involved in cyber security can be a source of tension. Those who have been working on cyber security for a long time understandably take offence at policy-makers – in business or government – intervening in the issue without them truly engaging with the substance of the underlying issues. Rather than working together and engaging in constructive dialogue, interaction between different cultures and groups often becomes hostile. While this is understandable given the realities of basic human nature, it is not necessarily conducive to future progress on cyber security.

Our judgement is that the current fragmented approach to cyber security is unsustainable; a complete change of mentality is required. Many instances of bad cyber security practice today are completely understandable as a by-product of a fractured approach to the challenges at hand. Of course, the existence of narrowly focused pockets of expertise will remain vital. It should also be recognised that an interdisciplinary approach that crosses silos will not solve the current cyber security challenges. It is also true that developing approaches that cross thought and professional silos comes with both difficulties and risks.

At the same time, there are dangerous tendencies afoot to try to solve human problems with technology, and technical problems with human endeavour. Just as the solution to poorly-designed authentication systems is *not* to ask users to remember ever longer and more complex passwords, so too, a system designed to replace by a machine all decision-making and data processing seldom delivers the robust and secure solution that might be imagined: life is more complicated than that. Conversely, technology continuously improves and develops, and it would be foolhardy to entrench poor organisational solutions to security problems when a better solution is new technology.

The experience we have described suggests that there are indeed movements in the direction of increased interdisciplinary or inter-silo thinking: we hope and trust that this is true outside our own experience also. If one is a solitary example of a new approach, over a period of many years, one begins to wonder whether one's enthusiasm has been misplaced. Overall, an interdisciplinary, cross-silo approach to cyber security is surely essential. Cyberspace may represent a subtle reconfiguration of all the things which have traditionally composed society: an understanding of the medium and its behaviours is necessary but by no means sufficient. One needs, too, an understanding of how people interact at every scale of endeavour – for good and ill. In this regard, current skill shortages in topics such as cyber security go far beyond a deficit of technical skills. While many aspects of an organisation now recognise that cyber security should extend beyond the IT department, it is time for those in other areas to wake up to this fact. This issue area is in urgent need of leadership.

## Notes

1  This analysis of the ecology of WannaCry is due to Andrew Dwyer, a student in the Oxford University Centre for Doctoral Training in Cyber Security, whose doctoral thesis was on Malware Ecologies, in the School of Geography and the Environment.
2  "Bring Your Own Device" (BYOD) refers to an approach that allows employees to use their own personal devices (such as phones, tablets and laptops) for their work.
3  For example, hackers have used techniques such as jump hosts, VPNs, Tor and open relays to obscure their origin for decades. See (Schneier 2017).
4  The first author initiated the first three and participates strongly in the next two; the second author is enrolled as a doctoral researcher in the Centre for Doctoral Training.
5  See www.politics.ox.ac.uk/centre/cyber-studies-programme.html.
6  See www.iisp.org.
7  See www.cybok.org.

## Acknowledgements

The authors are grateful to Lucas Kello for discussions and suggestions which have improved this chapter. Moreover, the insights drawn from experience cover the work of many academics, researchers, and students: there are too many to name here, but we are grateful to count them as colleagues and friends.

## References

Adamsky, D. 2015. Cross-Domain Coercion: The Current Russian Art of Strategy. *Proliferation Papers* 54(November).
Aitel, D. 2017a. UNGGE and Tallinn 2.0 Revisited. *CyberSecPolitics*, 23 August. Available at: https://cybersecpolitics.blogspot.com/2017/08/ungge-and-tallinn-20-revisited.html (accessed 7 January 2020).
Aitel, D. 2017b. Reflections on the GGE "failure". *CyberSecPolitics*, 7 July. Available at: https://cybersecpolitics.blogspot.com/2017/07/reflections-on-gge-failure.html (accessed 7 January 2020).

Bada, M., A. Sasse and J. Nurse. 2015. *Cyber Security Awareness Campaigns: Why Do they Fail to Change Behaviour?* Paper presented at International Conference on Cyber Security for Sustainable Society, pp. 118–131.

Bourque, P., R. Fairley and IEEE Computer Society. 2014. *Guide to the Software Engineering Body of Knowledge (SWEBOK(R)): Version 3.0,* 3rd edn. Washington, DC: IEEE Computer Society Press. doi:10.5555/2616205.

Cavoukian, A. 2009. Privacy by Design: The 7 Foundational Principles. Ontario, Canada: Information and Privacy Commissioner of Ontario. Available at: www.ipc.on.ca/wp-content/uploads/Resources/7foundationalprinciples.pdf (accessed 30 April 2020).

European Union. 2016. Regulation (EU) 2016/679 of the European Parliament and of the Council of 27 April 2016 on the Protection of Natural Persons with Regard to the Processing of Personal Data and on the Free Movement f Such Data. Available at: https://eur-lex.europa.eu/eli/reg/2016/679/oj.

Fischer-Hübner, S. 2001. *IT-Security and Privacy: Design and Use of Privacy-Enhancing Security Mechanisms.* Berlin: Springer-Verlag.

Franceschi-Bicchierai, L. 2016. Why Does DNC Hacker 'Guccifer 2.0' Talk Like This? *Motherboard,* 23 June. Available at: https://motherboard.vice.com/en_us/article/d7ydwy/why-does-dnc-hacker-guccifer-20-talk-like-this (accessed 7 January 2020).

Grassi, P. A., J. L. Fenton, E. M. Newton, R. A. Perlner, A. R. Regenscheid, et al. 2017. *Digital Identity Guidelines.* Gaithersburg, MD: NIST. doi:10.6028/NIST.SP.800-63b.

grugq, t. t. 2016. Cyber Terrorists Can't Cyber. *Medium,* 1 January, Available at: https://medium.com/@thegrugq/cyber-terrorists-can-t-cyber-144406a2d78b(accessed 7 January 2020).

Hancock, A. 2017. Skills Shortage Exposes UK Companies to Cyber Crime. *Financial Times,* 14 March. Available at: www.ft.com/content/4cabd0fe-8940-11e5-90de-f44762bf9896 (accessed 7 January 2020).

Healey, J. 2012. Beyond Attribution: Seeking National Responsibility for Cyber Attacks. Washington, DC: Atlantic Council. Available at: www.atlanticcouncil.org/wp-content/uploads/2012/02/022212_ACUS_NatlResponsibilityCyber.PDF (accessed 7 January 2020).

Henry, A. P. 2017. Mastering the Cyber Security Skills Crisis: Realigning Educational Outcomes to Industry Requirements. Discussion Paper No. 4. ACCS.

Kello, L. 2017. *The Virtual Weapon and International Order.* New Haven, CT: Yale University Press.

Kiss, J. 2010. Google Admits Collecting Wi-Fi Data Through Street View Cars. *The Guardian,* 15 May. Available at: www.theguardian.com/technology/2010/may/15/google-admits-storing-private-data (accessed 7 January 2020).

Lee, R. M. 2015. Threat Intelligence in an Active Cyber Defense (Part 1). *Recorded Future,* 17 February. Available at: www.recordedfuture.com/active-cyber-defense-part-1/ (accessed 7 January 2020).

Megaw, N. 2015. Cyber Security Sector Struggles to Fill Skills Gap. *Financial Times,* 18 November. Available at: www.ft.com/content/4cabd0fe-8940-11e5-90de-f44762bf9896. (accessed 7 January 2020).

Mellor, D. 2017. Cybersecurity Anthropotechnics: Social Immunology, Future Ethics, and the Digital Technosphere. DPhil thesis, University of Oxford Centre for Doctoral Training in Cyber Security.

NCSC. 2016. Password Guidance: Simplifying Your Approach. Available at: www.ncsc.gov.uk/guidance/password-guidance-simplifying-your-approach.

Newman, L. M. 2016. Hacker Lexicon: What Is the Attribution Problem? *Wired,* 23 December. Available at: www.wired.com/2016/12/hacker-lexicon-attribution-problem/ (accessed 7 January 2020).

Nunns, J. 2017. Cyber Security Skills Shortage to Hit 1.8 Million by 2022. *Computer Business Review*, 6 June. Available at: www.cbronline.com/news/cybersecurity/protection/cyber-security-skills-shortage-hit-1-8-million-2022/ (accessed 7 January 2020).

Rid, T. 2016. All Signs Point to Russia Being Behind the DNC Hack. *Motherboard*, 25 July. Available at: www.vice.com/en_us/article/4xa5g9/all-signs-point-to-russia-being-behind-the-dnc-hack (accessed 7 January 2020).

Rid, T. and Buchanan, B. 2015. Attributing Cyber Attacks. *The Journal of Strategic Studies*, 38 (1–2): 4–37. doi:10.1080/01402390.2014.977382.

Rudd, A. 2017. We Don't Want to Ban Encryption, but Our Inability to See What Terrorists Are Plotting Undermines Our Security. *The Telegraph*, 31 July. Available at: www.telegraph.co.uk/news/2017/07/31/dont-want-ban-encryption-inability-see-terrorists-plotting-online/.

Schneier, B. 2017. Attributing the DNC Hacks to Russia. *Schneier on Security*, 9 January. Available at: www.schneier.com/blog/archives/2017/01/attributing_the_1.html (accessed 7 January 2020).

Simpson, A., Martin, A., Cremers, C., Flechais, I., Martinovic, I. and Rasmussen, K. 2015. Experiences in Developing and Delivering a Programme of Part-Time Education in Software and Systems Security. In *Proceedings of the 37th International Conference on Software Engineering (ICSE'15)*, pp. 435–444.

Sukumar, A. M. 2017. The UN GGE Failed: Is International Law in Cyberspace Doomed as Well? *Lawfare*, 4 July. Available at: www.lawfareblog.com/un-gge-failed-international-law-cyberspace-doomed-well (accessed 7 January 2020).

Thomson, I. 2017. Germany, France Lobby Hard for Terror-Busting Encryption Backdoors – Europe Seems to Agree. *The Register*, 28 February. Available at: www.theregister.co.uk/2017/02/28/german_french_ministers_breaking_encryption.

Whitten, A. and Tygar, J. D. 1999. Why Johnny Can't Encrypt: A Usability Evaluation of PGP 5.0. In *SSYM'99: Proceedings of the 8th Conference on USENIX Security Symposium*, p. 14.

# 4

# EDUCATING FUTURE MULTIDISCIPLINARY CYBER SECURITY TEAMS

*Jean R.S. Blair, Andrew O. Hall and Edward Sobiesk*

Cyber security is inherently interdisciplinary at the individual level and multidisciplinary at the team level. The ubiquitous and increasingly complex nature of cyberspace necessarily demands the application of expertise in so many disparate disciplines that a single cyber security curriculum cannot provide sufficient breadth and depth. In this chapter, we present a vision of the cyber security team of the future, along with the disciplines and the multidisciplinary curricular foundations needed to produce such a team. We believe that, although many programs and curricula aspire to a multidisciplinary viewpoint, the current curricular models claiming to support a multidisciplinary perspective primarily integrate notions of other disciplines into an individual and are, therefore, more interdisciplinary in nature.

The cyber security team is driven by the assumption of ever-present, intelligent, adaptive, evolving adversaries—both human and artificial. The threats in cyberspace range from nation states to hacker collectives to industrial spies who target academia, governments, and industry. The risk decisions made to ensure success of the firm or organization cannot address only technical vulnerabilities. They must also holistically address risk as well as the impacts of cyber security policies on people and processes.

Our viewpoint is consistent with the multidisciplinary approach briefly suggested by Conti and Raymond (2017) as well as with the complexity of environments and disciplinary perspectives displayed in the case studies of Shakarian et al. (2013) and Green (2015). Further, because of the critical interdependency between cyber security and success across core business areas, we feel members of the cyber security team will be involved throughout all business processes to determine acceptable risk; ensure business solutions, products, and services are designed, developed, and provided with full consideration of the latest security threats to the customers; and best protect the organization.

## Background

This chapter extends our 2015 and 2017 articles (Sobiesk et al. 2015; Hall and Sobiesk 2017) that describe a holistic multilevel, multidisciplinary approach to cyber education used to achieve the goal of "providing all educated individuals a level of cyber education appropriate for their role in society" (Sobiesk et al. 2015). Our previous works reviewed established best practices and provided a foundation for viewing cyber security from a multidisciplinary perspective. They also provided tangible examples of how this is done both inside and outside the classroom at the U.S. Military Academy.

A highly informative and definitive description of the past, and potentially future, evolution of cyber security education, along with numerous relevant references, can be found in Parrish et al. (2018). This report from the Innovation and Technology in Computer Science Education (ITiCSE) group traces its previous initiatives and other international efforts in the evolution of cyber security education to its current state today as a meta-discipline that is largely centered around computing. The report also covers the integration of cyber security into the various Association for Computing Machinery curricula recommendations, including the disciplines of computer science, information systems, information technology, computer engineering, software engineering, and cyber security itself, and the impact of these curricular recommendations on Accreditation Board for Engineering and Technology (ABET) accreditation criteria. The report advocates for an interdisciplinary perspective toward cyber security and provides a generic competency model that could be used across all disciplines to specify the cyber security competencies needed in the 2030s.

Many distinct, well-established professions have begun to frame how their profession's knowledge, principles, practices, and skills need to progress and evolve given the exponentially growing cyber-enabled threats and opportunities in the world. Some professions have established task forces to address this. For example, see the well-thought-out reports from the computing-focused National Initiative for Cyber Security Education (NICE 2018), the Joint Task Force on Cyber security Education (ACM 2017), the Health Care Industry Cyber security Task Force (2017), and the Attorney General's Cyber Digital Task Force (United States Government 2018a). Leaders in other professions have proactively undertaken steps to frame key issues and make recommendations from their profession's perspective. For examples, see works coming from the communities of international relations (New York Cyber Task Force 2018), political science (United States Government 2018b), and organizational behavior (ENISA 2018). These reports, for the most part, focus on discipline-centric issues and recommendations. As such, the resulting reports deeply address how individuals might apply what is currently considered to be the professions' knowledge, principles, practices, and skills; many describe how cyber threats could cause a disaster if the profession, society, and government do not guard against such attacks.

Business, government, and higher education in general have acknowledged for some time that teams of diverse individuals are likely to do better and accomplish more than teams of people with similar backgrounds. Of particular interest is that cyber security itself is a discipline that crosses traditional disciplinary boundaries. It is the dynamic blending of people and processes from diverse disciplinary backgrounds that clearly realizes what Johansson (2017) describes as *the Medici effect*—breakthrough innovations happen at the boundaries or intersections between different fields and cultures. Despite acknowledging that innovation occurs at the boundaries, current educational curricular guidelines focus on adding broader knowledge and skills within an individual. These efforts are interdisciplinary in that they support a personal approach to problem solving and knowledge development that requires synergy across disciplines within an individual. In the long term, the adding of breadth in an individual cannot scale and necessitates a tradeoff with depth of expertise.

Our work is motivated by the need to develop the skills in each cyber security team member to effectively work with experts who have a background in complementary disciplines so that the team can collectively accomplish more than the sum of their individual contributions. This is what we call multidisciplinary, a process that involves a team of individuals with diverse disciplinary backgrounds and perspectives working together to develop solutions that can be created only by truly integrating aspects of many disciplines in innovative ways at a team level. Only with this approach will we start to build teams that can begin to actually address the inherently complex current and future cyber security issues.

## A vision for multidisciplinary cyber security teams

The cyber security team of the future will be intrinsically multidisciplinary, composed of internal and external expertise (consisting of both people and artificial intelligence) from multiple diverse relevant fields. The people involved will have a proclivity for combining their deep areas of expertise with others on the team who possess complementary deep knowledge, abilities, and experiences. Because of cyber security's interdependencies across core business functions, members of the cyber security team will examine each business process to determine acceptable levels of risk. They will also protect the organization by ensuring that business solutions, products, and services are designed, developed, provided, and maintained with full consideration of the latest security risks to the customers.

Each member of the team will address security tasks within his or her own specialized domain and readily provide essential unique contributions to team efforts to successfully manage risk in the presence of ever-evolving cyber threats and respond to new cyber security opportunities and challenges. Each member individually, and the team as a whole, will adapt, use, and integrate automation and emerging technologies to optimally employ human–machine collaborations. There will be a synergy across the multidisciplinary team that enables its members to collectively combine individual disciplinary contributions to create innovative solutions and perspectives that would not otherwise be possible, including procuring just-in-time expertise as needed. Together, the team will identify, utilize, and develop innovations that facilitate stability and operational success across the organization, society, or nation state.

These diverse cyber security teams will be of variable size and experience levels, with each team's composition as unique as its members. In larger organizations, the team may be mainly in-house cyber security experts across computing, mathematics, statistics, artificial intelligence, electrical engineering, cognitive science, law, organizational management, political science, international relations, marketing, and possibly core business operations. Smaller organizations will most likely have a core team that matrixes support from across the organization, with contracted support to round out capability. In either case, individuals will fulfill their role by applying and lending expertise in their field. The following list of disciplines and roles is not definitive but is rather meant to inspire a realization of the depth of the required multidisciplinary effort. Although a single individual may have knowledge and skills in several of these areas, the diversity and number of disciplines preclude any one individual from having a deep knowledge in all of these areas.

## Computing

There are likely several, or even many, cyber security computing professionals with various areas and levels of expertise and responsibility. Some will have complex technical positions, while others will be more broadly involved in the cyber security team. Computing professionals will include individuals with primary expertise in computing (e.g. computer science, information technology, network engineering, and information systems) complemented with substantive knowledge and abilities on cyber security principles and practices who team with individuals with a broader and deeper cyber security background complemented with sufficient knowledge and abilities in computing fundamentals. All computing professionals will work closely with the rest of the cyber security team to provide software and networking defenses that comply with laws, policies, and regulations; effectively use artificial intelligence and other emerging technologies; capitalize on fundamental principles of communication media of the day; and make it easy for workers in the enterprise to use the systems, adhere to policies regarding their employment, and judiciously assume an acceptable amount of risk.

## Operations research

Operations research includes elements from mathematics, statistics, systems engineering, economics, and computing. These diverse fields will collectively provide professionals with expertise across a vast range of subjects, including cryptography, mathematical foundations of what can and cannot be computed in a timely fashion, game theory, project management, optimization, machine learning, and quantum computing. They will play a significant role in evaluating levels of risk as well as simulating and modeling the impact of cyber security team solutions based on potential technical and human behaviors. They will work with the artificial intelligence experts, computing professionals, cognitive scientists, marketing professionals, lawyers, and political scientists to provide valuable, legal, and intelligent use of data analytics.

## Artificial intelligence and data science

These experts will play a crucial role on the cyber security team, working closely with the computing and operations research professionals to refine and improve their automated tools so that the human–machine defenses and opportunities can be used across all disciplines to combat the ever-increasing automated and intelligent capabilities of adversaries. They will develop, train, update, and evaluate machine learning recommendation systems that provide the kind of advice and guidance that customers currently get from companies such as Amazon or Netflix. These systems will undoubtedly also be used for numerous other tasks such as quality assurance.

## Electrical and computer engineering

Electrical and computer engineers provide expertise on hardware, communications systems, network infrastructure, and photonics. They will develop or ensure the security of everything from chips to hardware components, embedded processes, sensors, drives, controllers, computer architectures, communication systems, and other disciplinary equipment and concepts. In particular, with the increased presence of the Internet-of-Things (including many sensors and devices within humans), this currently underrepresented domain will be critical.

## Cognitive science and psychology

Cyber security cognitive scientists and psychologists will address issues related to human factors, human–machine interfaces and teaming, human behavior, talent assessment, team performance, and team communication. They will also provide explanations for and remove bias from artificial intelligence, develop effective training materials, and understand human limitations in decision-making. They will create models to analyze work flow and estimate cognitive load as well as predict human behavior.

## Law

Cyber security lawyers provide legal and ethical expertise related to issues involving privacy, security, contracting, intelligence, and surveillance at the local, state, national, and international levels. In military domains, they will possess knowledge on the intersection of cyber security with the Law of Armed Conflict, the Geneva

Conventions, and other issues related to sovereignty and international norms. Cyber security lawyers will also provide knowledge and expertise on public–private partnerships and information sharing among various government agencies and the private sector. As in-house counsel, they may, among other things, proactively engage with the team and enterprise about liability, lawsuits, and intellectual property rights to ensure that both the cyber security solutions/practices and the enterprise services are in compliance, including as products are developed. From inside both government agencies and private companies, they may work to influence and change government policies, laws, and international agreements to facilitate stronger cyber security practices for both the public and the private sector.

## Political science and international relations

These policy professionals provide a wide variety of expertise in strategy and policy issues, ranging from defense and deterrence to escalation and influence campaigns. They will bring broad knowledge of current and past events, with a clear understanding of the impact of cyber events on people, and on the private and public sectors, as well as the complex interplay between those impacts. They will actively work at understanding what the cyber security team is considering doing, describing potential unintended consequences and working with the management and marketing professionals to develop internal policies as well as strategies for incentivizing behaviors. The cyber security international relations experts will provide strategy, policy, and cyber threat intelligence expertise at the nation-state level. They will help the team understand how differing values, laws, ethics, and perspectives will impact operations that cross national boundaries. They will be the experts in evaluating and crafting means to influence cultures and their behavior and in understanding how these contribute to cooperation and conflict in cyberspace. They will maintain diplomatic and global security perspectives and help the organization increase trust and cooperation across international boundaries. Together with the political scientists, international relations experts will work with marketing and management to develop information-sharing policies and partnership practices that facilitate mutually maintaining security and bringing a broader perspective on the full range of levers of national power, how nations use them to coerce or compel one another, and how they can either lead to success or unintended consequences.

## Business

The impact of cyber security is felt throughout the organization. Each of the key departments within a modern corporation—i.e., operations, finance, and marketing—leverage modern information technology systems, with success or failure inextricably linked to cyber security. Business specialists will team with computing professionals who may still be learning the business processes of the organization. There is also now a realization that hacking attacks are sometimes a combination of relatively simple security exploits adapted to create public embarrassment or damage. These individuals will lead the efforts to identify such vulnerabilities and prevent such incidents. Depending on the organization, they may be from a mix of professions, such as public affairs and communications, engineers, health professionals, transportation experts, financial wizards, intelligence gatherers, members of the military, or government employees.

## Management

Leadership of the cyber security team of the future is still an open question. As with chief information officers, it is unclear whether a technical, business, or interdisciplinary background will provide the preponderance of leaders. It is also unknown whether leadership of future cyber security teams will evolve from the chief information security officer position and whether it warrants a board-level position. It is clear, however, that leaders of future cyber security teams will have to be masters of putting together and mentoring great teams, perhaps in a manner similar to the abilities of general managers and head coaches of successful professional sports teams. Leadership of the cyber security team will also work with several other interested parties to facilitate and conduct information sharing, both internal and external to the organization.

## Delineating responsibilities in multidisciplinary cyber security teams

Although it may be possible for the cyber security team to be distributed throughout the organization (i.e., each individual being embedded in a section that has people with their expertise, as in the law department, the cyber operations department, the human resources department, and so on) and then provide matrixed support to respond to cyber incidents, the best organizations will work together proactively to reduce cyber risk and create habitual relationships. Few organizations will be able to provide lawyers or marketers who are 100 percent dedicated to a cyber security team. We recommend that, if individuals on the cyber security team have split responsibilities, their contribution to the cyber security team must be clearly delineated. For smaller organizations, some expertise might need to be external or contracted.

## Curricular foundations for the cyber security team

The premise of this chapter is that cyber security is so complex and inherently multidisciplinary that to contribute effectively to a cyber security team, each member must not only be educated in an appropriate cyber-focused discipline but also must be well educated in the skills necessary to be an effective contributor and facilitator on a diverse multidisciplinary team. Today's educational systems generally are designed to give an individual a discipline-centric foundation, often stretching the student to work on teams that include other members from closely related disciplines. Many also gain some level of interdisciplinary skills—which requires synergy across disciplines within an individual. This is in contrast to deliberately developing multidisciplinary skills—an approach that requires working together with individuals with dissimilar disciplinary backgrounds to develop solutions that can be created only by truly integrating aspects of the various disciplines in innovative ways at a team level. These skills are arguably more important for the cyber security professional than having rudimentary awareness of the other disciplinary facets of cyber security. In what follows, we propose desired multidisciplinary-focused outcomes of graduates from any cyber security-related higher-education degree and then briefly discuss how a faculty and curriculum might develop those characteristics in the students. Each discipline's body of knowledge likely includes some requirements for abilities related to the legal and ethical issues as well as communication skills and team skills. The focus here is on the portions of those skills that the cyber security professional needs to work with others across disciplines.

The most essential multidisciplinary-focused knowledge, skills, and abilities for a cyber security team member are consistent with the directions in higher education of the last decade and encompass many of the key components in the Association of American Colleges and Universities VALUE rubrics. These rubrics (Rhodes 2009) include:

- integrative and applied learning
- teamwork
- critical thinking
- creative thinking
- inquiry and analysis
- intercultural knowledge and competence (to a lesser extent).

To be an effective member of a cyber security team, graduates of a higher education cyber security-focused degree program should exhibit skills and behaviors, such as the following. The cyber security graduate:

- *actively seeks input*: has a propensity to garner relevant issues and limitations from each of the other disciplinary experts before and during any work in progress, including efforts to evaluate the level of risk; actively seeks critical feedback on the level of success and areas for improvement after implementing a cyber security solution;
- *listens and pursues full understanding*: carefully listens to other team members, asks questions, and persists until both are confident that the relevant cyber security issues are understood and both agree on acceptable risk and what the next steps ought to be;
- *effectively communicates to others*: effectively communicates to other members of the team critical relevant issues from their own disciplinary perspective;

- *addresses conflict*: directly addresses conflict to help manage and resolve issues, usually helping strengthen both the cyber security solution and the team;
- *facilitates synergy*: is interested in and appreciative of each team member's unique strengths and disciplinary background; engages teammates and constructively builds on their contributions; suggests ways to synthesize contributions;
- *recognizes and exploits innovation*: is forward-thinking; recognizes novel solutions and unique ideas; extends, transforms, and integrates innovative ideas to create new improved solutions;
- *thinks critically*: views a situation from both micro and macro levels and discerns potential impacts; is respectful and constructive while questioning assumptions; formulates recommendations based on logic and informed evaluations;
- *promotes and practices resiliency*: is agile; recovers swiftly and appropriately; is a consequential contributor to effective teamwork during recovery;
- *capitalizes on interrelationships*: is cognizant of the interrelationships among authorities, policies, laws, personal responsibilities, and ethics associated with information-based activities; facilitates integration by fellow cyber security team members.

In total, a cyber security-related curriculum that is designed to develop students into valuable members of cyber security teams should develop both the skills just described and the knowledge, skills, and abilities relevant to the cyber-focused host discipline. Previous works on cyber security education address the curricular foundations relevant to the cyber-focused degree in a host discipline, and Parrish et al. (2018) propose a general model that can help all professions describe cyber security competencies within their given discipline. This chapter calls for integrating into those curricula developmental experiences that prepare graduates for multi-disciplinary interactions.

There are several detailed works that each describe one or more ideas for how to develop and assess some of the skills listed previously (e.g. see Wagner 2012, on developing creative and innovative thinkers). To be most effective at teaching these multidisciplinary skills, the curriculum should include learning experiences that give the students practice working with people with different disciplinary and cultural backgrounds. Ideally, these types of experiences would be strategically placed throughout the curriculum, leading to a large culminating open-ended team project.

The faculty members who deliver the curriculum will need to have had multidisciplinary experiences themselves. How they obtain this is likely to vary widely, but, without having had some set of experiences that helps them understand and appreciate the skills needed to effectively work with people who have very different disciplinary expertise, it is unlikely that they will be able to succeed in developing those skills in their students.

## Examples of multidisciplinary cyber teams

The 60-person Army Cyber Institute (ACI) is a concrete example of the power and value of successful multidisciplinary cyber security teams made up of experts from different fields. Located as part of the U.S. Military Academy at West Point, New York, the ACI has researchers and faculty spanning eight different academic departments: behavioral sciences and leadership; electrical engineering and computer science; English and philosophy; history; law; mathematical sciences; social sciences; and systems engineering. The ACI's unique mix of civilian academics with active-duty military officers promotes a blend of basic and applied research that advances the body of knowledge while also creating internal and external partnerships to conduct applied research that brings pragmatic value and sets future direction.

One ACI example of a research initiative that creates synergies across multiple disciplines and domains is Jack Voltaic—the ACI's research dedicated to protecting critical infrastructure (Army Cyber Institute and AECOM 2018). Jack Voltaic is a series of multiday, multisector, public–private events that explore preparation, prevention, and response during simulated cyberspace-physical attacks on a large city. Exercises have been conducted thus far in New York City and Houston. The 2016 New York City event involved about 20 organizations and 100 participants. The 2018 Houston event involved about 40 organizations and 400 participants. The New York City event was co-led with Citigroup (a financial institution) and the Houston event with AECOM (a national engineering company).

Overall, the critical infrastructure sectors involved included communications, defense industrial base, emergency services, energy, financial services, government facilities, health care, and transportation systems. The design of the event included three components: governance coordination, a facilitated tabletop exercise for mid-level managers, and a virtual environment component in which operators encountered a notional adversary.

Prior to the Jack Voltaic research efforts, a challenge recognized within the U.S. critical infrastructure communities was that too many of their preparations were siloed within their own sector. The true purpose and value of the Jack Voltaic research are that it forces communication and coordination across sectors, including encountering many boundary issues and assumptions. These unique events each simultaneously engage multiple areas of expertise, creating an environment in which leaders from different domains must collaborate with one another to resolve crises. In each of the two past Jack Voltaic events, the domains spanned many disciplines including computing, electrical and computer engineering, operations research, political science and international relations, law, business, cognitive science, public affairs, and management.

A second ACI example of multidisciplinary efforts succeeding is research that explored the vulnerability equities process in which "offensive equities are weighed against potential harms caused by delayed disclosure or nondisclosure of zero-day vulnerabilities" (Pell and Finocchiaro 2017). The power behind this research and publication was the collaboration between a lawyer who is an expert on national policy for cyber ethics, privacy, security, and surveillance and an intelligence officer who had served in operational cyber assignments and possessed a computing and engineering background. This research not only spanned the deep expertise of both these individuals but also covered the intersection and boundaries of their disciplines, which are so often either ignored or misunderstood.

Overall, almost all outreach, partnerships, and research conducted by the ACI are multidisciplinary in nature. These efforts are aided by the fact that several other U.S. Military Academy faculty members from across various departments are actively conducting cyber research and cyber educational initiatives in conjunction with the ACI.

The multidisciplinary paradigm also correlates well with cyber security colleagues from the private sector with whom we have spoken. The market need for multidisciplinary cyber security teams has created an environment in which innovative cyber solution companies have arisen.

GRIMM is a private-sector cyber security company that provides another concrete example of a successful multidisciplinary cyber security team. The roughly 60 internal GRIMM employees come from a mix of technical and social science backgrounds. The company maintains a holistic, multidisciplinary perspective and organizes in a matrixed manner, pulling in expertise based on the needs of the situation. GRIMM founder Bryson Bort (pers. comm. 2018) emphasized that "innovation and compromise happen at the edge."

Recently, GRIMM solved a high-level fraud challenge for one of the world's largest banking institutions by pulling together in-house policy, government, criminal-tracking, technical, and strategic minds. Combining deep in-house expertise in developing technologies with the understanding of policy and strategic implications, GRIMM was able to swiftly identify a single source of fraud risk for the bank. This approach saved the bank more than US$90 million in fraud avoidance (a figure determined after the fraud trend turned toward the now-prepared bank) as well as countless millions of dollars in fines and legal fees. In this example, it was the multidisciplinary skills across the team that enabled its members to quickly solve a complex problem with a combination of technical and nontechnical approaches.

In this chapter, we argued that cyber security is inherently both interdisciplinary at the individual level and multidisciplinary at the team level. We submit that the ubiquitous and ever-increasingly complex nature of cyberspace requires breadth and depth beyond that which can be included in a single cyber security curriculum. We presented a vision for the cyber security team of the future, along with the disciplines and the multidisciplinary curricular foundations needed to produce such a team. We noted that, while many programs and curricula aspire to a multidisciplinary viewpoint, the current curricular models claiming to support a multidisciplinary perspective primarily integrate notions of other disciplines into an individual and are therefore more interdisciplinary in nature. We believe that effective and stable cyber security can be achieved and maintained only by teams of experts from multiple disciplines, focusing their efforts against omnipresent, intelligent, adaptive, and ever-changing human and autonomous adversaries. Because of the critical interdependency between cyber security and success across core business areas, we feel that members of the cyber security team will be involved throughout all business processes to determine acceptable risk; ensure that business solutions, products, and services are designed, developed, and provided with full consideration of the latest security threats to the customers; and best protect the organization.

Future work will involve fully integrating content and experiences into the various cyber security-focused educational systems that develop the much-needed multidisciplinary attributes and culture. Ideally, students will be taught these skills, given constructive feedback after practicing them, and provided with an opportunity to experience a true multidisciplinary cyber security team effort. Another interesting avenue for future work would be to holistically pull together the bodies of knowledge (curricular models) for cyber security-focused degrees in the different disciplines and to use those to help educators in each of the disparate fields better understand how their graduates will interact with other members of the cyber security team. Both of these directions reinforce the concept that cyber security is a meta-discipline spanning many traditional boundaries.

## Acknowledgments

The authors would like to acknowledge and profoundly thank the talented and diverse group of cyber security professionals who generously shared their expertise and perspectives to shape and inform the content of this chapter. These included Robert Barnsby, Nathaniel Bastian, Erica Borghard, Bryson Bort, Judy Esquibel, Jason Healey, Maxim Kovalsky, Paul Maxwell, Clay Moody, Stephanie Pell, Aryn Pyke, Roy Ragsdale, and Robert Thomson. The views expressed in this chapter are those of the authors and do not reflect the official policy or position of the U.S. Military Academy, the Department of the Army, the Department of Defense, or the U.S. Government.

## References

ACM. (Association for Computing Machinery). 2017. Cyber Security Curricula 2017. Available at: www.acm.org/education/curricula-recommendations.

Army Cyber Institute and AECOM. 2018. Jack Voltaic 2.0 Executive Summary. Available at: https://cyber.army.mil/.

Conti, G. and D. Raymond. 2017. *On Cyber: Towards an Operational Art for Cyber Conflict*. New York: Kopidion Press.

ENISA. (European Union Agency for Cyber Security). 2018. Cyber Security Culture in Organizations. Available at: www.enisa.europa.eu/publications/cyber-security-culture-in-organisations.

Green, J. 2015. *Cyber Warfare: A Multidisciplinary Analysis*. New York: Routledge.

Hall, A. and E. Sobiesk. 2017. Integration of the Cyber Domain at the United States Military Academy. In Proceedings of the International Workshops: Realigning Cyber Security Education, Melbourne, Australia, 2017. doi:10.1145/3293881.3295778.

Johansson, F. 2017. *The Medici Effect*. Boston: Harvard Business Review Press.

New York Cyber Task Force. 2018. Building a Defensible Cyberspace. Available at: https://sipa.columbia.edu/ideas-lab/techpolicy/building-defensible-cyberspace.

NICE. (National Initiative for Cyber Security Education). 2018. NICE Cyber Security Workforce Framework.. Available at: https://niccs.us-cert.gov/workforce-development/cyber-security-workforce-framework.

Parrish, A., J. Impagliazzo, R. K. Raj, H. Santos, M. T. Asghar, *et al.*2018. Global Perspectives on Cyber Security Education for 2030: A Case for a Meta-Discipline. In Proceedings of Conference on Innovation and Technology in Computer Science Education. Larnaca, Cyprus. doi:10.1145/3293881.3295778.

Pell, S. and J. Finocchiaro. 2017. The Ethical Imperative for a Vulnerability Equities Process and How the Common Vulnerability Scoring System Can Aid that Process. *Connecticut Law Review* 49(5): 1549–1589.

Rhodes, T. 2009. *Accessing Outcomes and Improving Achievement: Tips and Tools for Using the Rubrics*. Washington, DC: Association of American Colleges and Universities.

Shakarian, P., J. Shakarian, and A. Ruef. 2013. *Introduction to Cyber-Warfare: A Multidisciplinary Approach*. Waltham, MA: Syngress.

Sobiesk, E., J. Blair, G. Conti, M. Lanham, and H. Taylor. 2015. Cyber Education: A Multi-Level, Multi-Discipline Approach. In Proceedings of Conference Information Technology Education. Chicago, pp. 43–47.

United States Government. 2018a. A Report of the Attorney General's Cyber Digital Task Force. Washington, DC: Department of Justice. Available at: www.justice.gov/ag/page/file/1076696/download.

United States Government. 2018b. Supporting the Growth and Sustainment of the Nation's Cyber Security Workforce: Building the Foundation for a More Secure American Future. Washington, DC: Secretary of Commerce and the Secretary of Homeland Security. Available at: www.cisa.gov/publication/supporting-growth-and-sustainment-nations-cyber security-workforce.

Wagner, T. 2012. *Creating Innovators: The Making of Young People Who Will Change the World*. New York: Scribner.

# 5

# WHAT THE PROFESSION OF CYBER SECURITY NEEDS TO KNOW AND DO

*Dan Shoemaker, Anne Kohnke and Ken Sigler*

It has been well documented that we have a problem securing cyberspace (Hatchimonji 2013, Symantec 2014; Trend-Micro 2015; Privacy Rights Clearinghouse 2017; NIAC 2018). However, the price of that failure might not be so clear. Therefore, this chapter uses two global concerns as illustrations – the escalating cost of cyber crime and the threat of attacks on the national infrastructure.

In 2015, cyber crime cost the world $500 billion. By 2018, that amount had escalated six-fold to $3 trillion (Microsoft Security Team 2016). And by 2021, the price is expected to double again to $6 trillion (ibid.). An annual loss that exceeds the combined gross domestic products of Great Britain, Germany, and France is going to impact every business in every industrialised country in the world.

Given what we have said, one would think that every organisation's top priority would be the creation of a complete and comprehensive virtual asset protection scheme. However, the sad truth is that cyber security is a lot like the weather; everybody talks about it, but nobody does anything about it. For example, only 38 per cent of the organisations that were surveyed by the Information Systems Audit and Control Association in its 2015 *Global Cyber Security Status Report* felt that they were doing anything substantive to address the problem of cyber threats (Laberis 2016).

That is understandable, given the fact that the advent of the Internet is perhaps the most significant technical breakthrough since the invention of moveable type. The difference between these two revolutions is that our culture took three centuries to accommodate the profound impact of mass printed information, whereas we have had a mere 20 years to adjust to the even more momentous and exponentially growing impact that immediate access to every virtual thing in the world implies. Accordingly, it is not surprising that society's mechanisms have had a hard time keeping up.

So, the bad guys are ahead of us, which is an especially egregious indictment of the overall profession of cyber security. This is because the only justifiable reason to establish a cyber security operation is to prevent the loss or subversion of virtual assets. Hence, a protection scheme that is unable to guarantee the confidentiality, integrity, and availability of its protection objects has not achieved its basic purpose. It should be noted here that there is no exception to this rule. A loss of virtual value is a loss, no matter how the exploit was carried out. Therefore, it is axiomatic that the cyber security function is obliged to close off every potential avenue of attack for all the virtual assets for which it is held accountable. The problem is that 10 years of loss data make it crystal clear that we are getting worse at that task, not better.

## We must re-evaluate our assumptions

The saying goes, "We fight the last war." That has never been truer than with cyberspace. On the surface, the justification for adopting our current approach seems simple enough. The virtual world is enabled by computers. Computers have an explicit set of rules associated with them. Those rules are dictated by the rigid architecture of the machine. Therefore, it seems obvious that we should base our cyber security protection paradigms on the well-established scientific principles of computer engineering and networking architecture. This has been the case since the beginning of the field, but perhaps we have misunderstood the meaning of the term "cyber security".

Cyber security is a combination of the words cyber, meaning "computer", and "security". We understand the reason for the cyber part as virtual information is kept and transmitted by computers. So, it's just common sense to hand the responsibility for cyber security to the technical part of the organisation. After all, these are the people who are expert in computer system development and use. The problem is that "security" is its own independent concept and it carries a different set of requirements. Security implies the act of safeguarding something.

Cyber security does that in some respects. For instance, it is well documented that the effective percentage of successful electronic exploits has decreased over the past decade. Even so, it is one thing to protect virtual assets from unauthorised electronic access, while it is another thing to ensure that those same assets cannot be lost or harmed due to any credible type of attack.

In this respect, then, the "security" factor expands the mission of the "cyber security" function to include the responsibility to safeguard every virtual object of value. Therefore, the protection obligation goes from simply regulating the coming-and-going of data through a highly restricted point of electronic access, like a firewall, to assuring that the entire virtual asset cannot be harmed by any foreseeable means. The latter is a much more rigorous test, but it is still an inescapable fact that, "A loss of value is a loss no matter what the cause."

Until now it has been acceptable for organisations to concentrate their cyber defences strictly on electronic protection. That head-down focus on a conventional technological attack-surface appears to be perfectly reasonable and it has been relatively successful. This is to be expected. Almost universally, the people who are responsible for the creation of an organisation's cyber defensive scheme work in the information technology function. And those people are experts in addressing threats associated with electronic types of attacks.

However, there are two highly credible types of attack that are inevitably part of the overall attack surface. Those are human and physical exploits. Arguably, ignoring a plausible line of attack pre-programmes failure into the protection mission. Because the evidence is abundantly clear that electronic exploits constitute less than one-third of the attack surface, the rest of the attack surface involves such real-world factors as insider theft and social engineering, or even natural disasters like fire or flood. So, the question remains, who should be responsible for deploying and coordinating a defence against those types of exploits?

In most organisations, human or physical types of threats are simply not part of traditional cyber defence thinking. In fact, most active cyber defence solutions do not consider embodying tightly integrated, well-defined, and uniformly applied behavioural controls into the overall cyber security process (Laberis 2016). As a result, well-executed attacks against the non-electronic attack surface are almost certain to succeed. The question is, "What causes such a clear disconnect in our planning?"

## The adversary changes things

Computers are technological devices so, therefore, the steps to ensure the security of virtual space must be technological. This would be a safe assumption if it were not for two confounding factors. First and foremost, there is the presence of the adversary. Dropping an adversary into the equation imposes a different set of demands on Information Technology's traditional operating assumptions.

The aim of the adversary is to break into the system, not use it. And those adversaries are not constrained by conventional rules of engagement. So, besides the traditional task of ensuring that the system operates as intended, system developers and maintainers are now expected to ensure that its day-to-day functioning is fully safeguarded from any foreseeable kind of malicious exploitation. That task is an entirely dissimilar and much more difficult proposition.

In the case of a determined adversary, the scope of the protection perimeter is not simply limited to the cosy, rational world of science. It is now opened to any means necessary to achieve the ends of a wide range of hackers. Thus, a failure to consider every legitimate avenue of attack will build inevitable failure into every protection scheme. This is because logically the smart hacker will always seek to attack undefended gaps.

This makes perfect sense if you view this from the adversary's standpoint. Consider if the adversary's aim is to subvert or acquire a virtual asset, then the easiest way to accomplish that would be through the path of least resistance. As far back as the 1970s Saltzer and Schroeder codified this as the "Work Factor" principle (Saltzer and Schroeder 1974). The adversary will adopt the approach that is the easiest to execute and the most likely to succeed. Sun Tzu characterised this thinking best when he wrote, "Attack weakness not strength." Or in practical terms, the form of the hack will be dictated by the shape of the soft spots in the cyber defence.

So, if the organisation has constructed a strong electronic defence, a smart adversary will launch anything BUT an electronic attack. The data bear this out. In 2006, the predominant percentage of loss was from exploits that could be classified as "electronic" (Privacy Rights Clearinghouse 2017). Fast forward 10 years and the preponderance of the losses are due to exploits that are classified as "behavioural" (ibid.). This change in tactics illustrates how the adversary has simply shifted their line of attack to sidestep our improved capability in the electronic realm. It is also, most probably, the reason why our loss statistics continue to grow at exponential rates.

From a terminology standpoint, the exploits we have been talking about are called *non-technical hacks*. Both human-centred and physical types of attacks fall into the category of non-technical hacks. And as the term implies, non-technical hacks do not target the technology directly. Rather than electronic types of approaches, non-technical hacks target existing behavioural or physical weaknesses. Thus, in real-world terms, non-technical hacks are aimed at the "human attack surface". That term simply denotes every possible way that intentional behaviour executed in the physical space could compromise an asset or compromise its confidentiality. Microsoft estimates that by 2020, the human attack surface will encompass four to six billion people (Microsoft Security Team 2016).

Because human behaviour is distinctive, creative, and unpredictable, there are an infinite number of ways that a non-technical hack can be executed. The most popular approaches include such well-known exploits as insider and social engineering attacks. But non-technical impacts can also be the result of humble, everyday operational errors like procedural glitches and even simple worker negligence (Tech Target 2018).

It is hard to estimate what non-technical hacks represent in terms of actual harm. This is because the really damaging exploits such as industrial espionage or theft of proprietary trade secrets are rarely reported and simple human negligence or error tends to get missed or covered up. Therefore, it is impossible to accurately describe the impact of such a set of occurrences. Nevertheless, it is believed that the overall extent of the problem is most certainly far greater than what is currently estimated (Laberis 2016). There are two perfectly logical reasons why non-technical hacks go unreported or, for that matter, unnoticed. Both illustrate the challenge organisations face when it comes to building a complete and effective cyber defence.

First, companies and particularly top-level decision-makers simply do not associate human behaviour with virtual losses, and so the threats that malicious insiders and bumbling employees represent tend to fly under their radar (ibid.). Nevertheless, non-technical hacks are now the dominant path of least resistance (Privacy Rights Clearinghouse 2017). And since the adversary is becoming increasingly reliant on their use, we will have to learn how to close off all the alternative paths. In this respect, the ability to identify, classify, and counter non-technical exploits will have to be amalgamated into every organisation's overall understanding and approach to cyber security going forward.

Second, human behaviour is impossible to accurately predict and/or effectually monitor. More importantly, an insider is part of the organisation. Therefore, they are trusted to some extent and have legitimate credentials. Accordingly, it is almost impossible to spot a capable insider who is planning to undertake an attack and because humans are creative, their harmful actions are almost impossible to assure by automated means (Laberis 2016). Nonetheless, most of our present-day cyber defences are still exclusively oriented towards countering electronic types of attack. And this is reflected in the loss statistics.

Presently, 71 per cent of annual losses are due to failures in the physical and human attack domains, while electronic breaches account for roughly 29 per cent (Privacy Rights Clearinghouse 2017). Specifically, the leading cause of record loss (36 per cent) over the past decade is attributable to physical exploits (ibid.). A physical exploit is any hands-on theft, harm, or loss. A stolen laptop containing sensitive information is one example. Human behaviour is the second leading cause of record loss (35 per cent). Human behaviour exploits include such categories as insider theft, social engineering, or human error (ibid.). While the lowest percentage of losses (29 per cent) falls into the area of the classic technology-based attacks, unfortunately these are often the only kind of attacks factored into an organisation's cyber security planning.

## The three-legged stool

Given what we have said so far, it ought to be self-evident that a complete cyber defence rests on a three-legged stool: electronic, human, and physical controls. So it goes without saying that the requisite planning for effective cyber defence needs to involve those three distinctly different operational functions. Nonetheless, the steps to integrate these functions into a single unified approach are often overlooked in the cyber security strategic planning process. Therefore, the practical starting point is to begin to assimilate the other two important areas into the overall strategic planning. The problem is that, in most cases, the three component domains have traditionally operated independently of each other, yet all three are vital components of the cyber security protection mission. So, the question is, how do we start the process?

We start by knocking down the stovepipes, because those stovepipes are the reason why credible threats like insider attacks or social engineering are not called out and addressed in the formal protection planning process. Cyber security suffers from something called the "Six Blind Men and the Elephant" syndrome. In that classic Indian fable, six blind men are asked to describe an elephant based on what they are touching. To one, it's a snake, to another it's a wall, and to another it's a tree, and so on. But, in the end, "Although each was partly in the right, all were entirely wrong."

The people who need to be involved in constructing the cyber security defence are not aware of the aspects of the problem that they do not touch. Thus, they do not feel the need to counter threats that arise in other areas. Again, this is an understandable stance. The job of network security is to secure the network, not conduct a background check and to periodically investigate the network manager, as Human Resources do not consider ways to regulate the firewall or restrict facility access as part of their mandate. And the Director of Physical Security does not think she or he needs to worry about bent insiders or the system configuration. So, the present state of the practice is hamstrung by three, mutual, limited views of the world. This simple fact puts the cyber security function into dysfunctional stovepipes.

Certainly, there are established elements of the field that can competently protect the part of the elephant that they touch. However, none of these conventional elements is an entirely effective solution in-and-of-itself. And, if every practical aspect of the solution is not fully integrated into the response, the path-of-least-resistance gaps are bound to appear in the protection scheme.

## Learning to play better with each other

As we have seen, exploitable gaps are created when the important actors in the cyber defence process do not play well together. In fact, most of the requisite set of actors are probably unaware of the actual necessity to cooperate. For instance, the failure to lock and monitor the computer room, or to thoroughly vet the system manager will always invalidate any elegant firewall solution. That is because direct access to the machine trumps every other form of countermeasure.

These two situations are sources of the types of "exploitable gaps" just discussed. However, the design of substantive steps to limit every form of direct physical access to the computer, such as locks and employee monitoring and supervision, would require explicit participation of the relevant players from the Human Resources and physical security areas, and these experts are rarely involved in the cyber security operation.

Every factor must be considered for a cyber defence to be gap-free. However, because the planning for cyber security is seen as a strictly technological exercise, the organisation is not able to deploy the full set of controls necessary to completely and adequately protect its assets from every conceivable source of harm. Accordingly the challenge is clear, the profession must find ways to ensure that the real-world practice of cyber security involves the creation of a complete, correct, and highly effective set of well-defined and commonly accepted controls; ones that are capable of closing off every feasible type of adversarial action.

## Creating a holistic solution

The term "holistic" was adopted to describe a state of comprehensive cyber security. Holistic simply means that every type of threat has been identified and countered by a formal control mechanism. Holistic implies that the cyber security scheme embodies a complete set of essential activities, which are enough to close off every reasonable avenue of attack. In practical terms, holistic designates an organisational situation where ALL likely threats have been effectively countered by an actual and fully integrated set of electronic, physical and human-centred actions.

Therefore, a holistic cyber defence contains all the critical counter-measures necessary to address every possible avenue of attack. Holistic solutions are enabled by a systematic planning process. Thus, good cyber security practice involves strategic architecture and design. That architectural process must consider all reasonable avenues of exploitation, not just the electronic ones, and it must ensure that all the necessary controls are implemented and deployed as a rational, real-world, day-to-day frame-work of mutually supportive and interacting counter-measures.

The aim of counter-measures is to ensure a complete and correct cyber defence. This is not just a matter of putting together a list of controls. There must be a specific organisational mechanism in place, to rationally integrate every one of these controls into a complete and effective cyber defence.

## The importance of knowing what to do

We will not be able to implement a holistic solution until we are able to bring all the essential players into the main tent. Since this consolidation of protection responsibilities is likely to incorporate a range of skills and interests, we are also going to need universal agreement about the elements that constitute correct practice. To be completely effective, the definition must amalgamate all the essential concepts of cyber defence into a single unifying practice model, one that has real-world currency.

The problem to this point has been that the contents and boundaries of the pro-fession are not well defined. Thus, it is perfectly acceptable to think of cyber security protection as nothing more than a scientific/engineering exercise. This perception is clearly not correct since there is irrefutable evidence that human behaviour is an important contributor to the overall losses. So, in application, good cyber security solutions are a combination of things that are both scientific and practical.

Every profession is built around a common understanding of the correct prac-tices of the field. In this respect, a formal statement of the fundamental underlying knowledge requirements is the necessary point of departure. The statement then serves as the basis for understanding what needs to be done and the basic knowl-edge requirements tell the practitioner what they need to know and do, which helps them understand all of the elements of their field as they relate to a real-world solution. In practical terms, it itemises the basic responsibilities of the cyber security professional.

Nevertheless, there has never been an official, commonly accepted definition of the fundamental elements that constitute legitimate cyber security work. The learned societies are the entities who have traditionally developed and documented the essential concepts of the fields that they are appointed to oversee.

Best practices are a perfectly acceptable way to guide any professional field (e.g. business, law, or engineering). But there must be "expert" entities to study, authorise and validate the common best practices, as well as to sanction the applicability of those practices in professional usage once they have been identified and promulgated. That is the reason why professional societies exist. Professional societies serve as the developers and sanctioners of the fundamental ideas in their respective fields. Thus, it is the professional societies who are responsible for the promulgation and accreditation of a recognised body of knowledge and professional practice. Examples of professional bodies include such well-known groups as: the American Medical Association for doctors, the American Bar Association for lawyers, and the National Society of Professional Engineers for engineers.

Occasionally all the societies come together to develop a single unified set of recommendations for a topic of vital mutual interest. The CSEC2017 document is specifically dedicated to providing an authoritative statement of the elements of the field of cyber security for a broad array of practitioners. It should be noted that the CSEC2017 thought model is authoritative in the sense that the computer societies have made the commitment to make them so. Within that thought model, the knowledge elements that are specified for the discipline can be explicitly tailored to need.

These recommendations represent a single conceptual model for cyber security. The CSEC2017 document is not prescriptive. Instead, the Cyber Security Education Curriculum (CSEC) body of knowledge can be used either completely or in part to develop relevant applications or modify a broad range of existing programmes (Joint Task Force on Cyber Security Education 2017). As defined in the CSEC, there are eight generic knowledge areas. These knowledge areas represent the complete body of knowledge within the field. Taken as a set, these distinctive areas constitute a common definition of the discipline as well as the learning elements that should be involved in the delivery of an acceptable cyber security learning experience. These knowledge areas, according to the CSEC, are:

- data security
- software security
- component security
- connection security
- system security
- human security
- organisational security
- societal security.

### Knowledge area one: data security

The data security knowledge area is the perfect area to lead off with. Data security defines what needs to be known in order to ensure the security of data assets either at rest, during processing, or in transit. This is a well-accepted and commonly understood part of the current discipline and there is no disagreement about its importance in the overall protection of electronic assets. The knowledge elements associated with that protection include the usual set of commonly acknowledged suspects, such as basic cryptography concepts, digital forensics concepts, and methods for secure communications, including data integrity and authentication and information storage security (Joint Task Force on Cyber Security Education 2017).

## Knowledge area two: software security

Software assurance goes back to the very origins of the field and predates any concerns about security. In the 1990s, the methods and techniques in this area focused on creating defect-free code and the general area of practice was called "software quality assurance" (SQA). Since most of the knowledge, skills and abilities associated with SQA transfer to the identification of exploitable flaws, the knowledge elements for this area are well defined and commonly accepted as correct among both academics and business people.

The focus of the CSEC knowledge areas are an assurance of the security properties of the information and systems the software protects (ibid.). Thus, the CSEC2017 recommendations centre on such accepted areas of practice as security requirements, design concepts and practice, software implementation and deployment issues, static and dynamic testing, configuration management, and ethics, especially in development, testing and vulnerability disclosure (ibid.).

## Knowledge area three: component security

The component security knowledge area is somewhat novel in that it is not an element of most of the predecessor bodies of knowledge for cyber security. However, it is not surprising to see it here given the inclusion of Computer Engineering in the CC2005 set of disciplines. Component security's body of knowledge focuses on the design, procurement, testing, analysis and maintenance of the tangible components that are integrated into larger systems (ibid.). Thus, the elements of this area include such well-accepted hardware aspects as identification and elimination of vulnerabilities present in system components, component lifecycle maintenance and configuration management, secure hardware component design principles, security testing and reverse engineering. Finally, there is a healthy dose of supply chain management security knowledge elements due to the industry's commitment to commercial-off-the-shelf integration of components.

## Knowledge area four: connection security

This area is what is colloquially known as "network security". The security of networks is another quality that is both commonly accepted as well as an essential aspect of good cyber security practice. The knowledge in this area focuses on the security of the connections between components, including both physical and logical connections (ibid.). Thus, the recommendations entail assurance practices for networked systems, networking architecture, and standard secure transmission models, physical component interconnections and interfaces, software component interfaces and the common types of connection and transmission attacks.

### Knowledge area five: system security

This knowledge area begins the move away from the technology and into the area of standard organisational processes. Thus, the system security knowledge area focuses primarily on those common embedded organisational practices that ensure the articulated security requirements of systems, which are composed of interconnected components and connections and the networking software that supports those interconnections (ibid.). Consequently, the knowledge elements in this area embody recommendations that spell out the necessity for a holistic approach to systems, the importance of security policy, as well as organised identification and authentication management processes, this area also contains recommendations for system access control and operational system monitoring processes, as well as the standard recovery, system testing and system documentation best practices.

### Knowledge area six: human security

This knowledge area represents the first serious attempt to provide recommendations with respect to the human attack surface. As we have said, this is unknown territory for the traditional study of cyber security and though it might not be as mature as areas 1–5, it represents a pioneering step in the attempt to compile a complete body of knowledge for the field.

The first five knowledge areas comprise what might be considered the "usual suspects" in the cyber security profession. They are essentially hard, technology-focused, elements that encompass generally well-known and commonly accepted axioms regarding the practice of data, software, component and system assurance. The human security area attempts to make benchmark recommendations about the assurance of human behaviour and the study of human behaviour as it relates to the maintenance of a state of cyber security.

This is a new area and one that will probably be susceptible to refinement over a period of time. However, the loss statistics make it clear that the focus on protecting individuals' data and privacy in the context of their role as employees and in their personal lives is an important area of teaching and research (ibid.). The recommended knowledge elements in the human security knowledge area include identity management, social engineering prevention, assurance of workforce and individual awareness and understanding, assurance of broad-scale social behavioural privacy and security, and the elements of personal data privacy and security protection.

### Knowledge area seven: organisational security

Organisational security is historically the best-known and most commonly discussed aspect of all the non-technical areas. The general content and focus of this area are embodied in the recommendations of the National Institute of Standards and Technology's workforce framework (NIST 800–181) as Knowledge Area Seven, "Oversee and Govern" (Newhouse et al. 2017). The organisational security area encompasses all the relevant processes and behaviours for the rational oversight and control of the overall cyber security function. This is understandably a very large element of the CSEC2017 model since these controls embody all the traditional counter-measures that are associated with the general protection of the organisation. This includes the deployment and oversight of controls to ensure proper monitoring and response to intrusions on the technological attack surface, as well as the entire set of standard behaviours associated with the human attack surface.

The purpose of the knowledge that is embodied in the Organisational Security area is to ensure the organisation against all relevant cyber security threats as well as manage the inherent risks that are associated with the successful accomplishment of the organisation's mission (Joint Task Force on Cyber Security Education 2017). Consequently, the elements in this area include a detailed set of recommendations for the risk management process, the setting of governance and policy strategies, long- and short-term planning, as well as legal, regulatory and ethical compliance.

## Knowledge area eight: societal security

The societal security knowledge area is revolutionary, and it reflects the growing awareness of the impact of virtual space on the average person's life. The knowledge items in this category are mostly large societal factors that might, for better or for worse, broadly impact every citizen in our society. These knowledge elements are essentially still in need of refinement, but their inclusion opens the door to their integration into the overall understanding of how virtual space needs to be channelled into institutional actions that are beneficial to the community. This includes thought models for approaching the problems of cyber crime, the legal and ethical dictates associated with good citizenship as well as social policy, personal privacy, and how that relates to the formal mechanisms of conventional cyberspace (ibid.). The specific recommendations promulgated in this area centre on the general behaviours to prevent or alleviate cyber crime, make and enforce laws in cyberspace, and ensure ethical thinking when it comes to functioning in cyberspace, as well as the elements of what constitutes proper cyber policies and privacy regulation.

## References

Hatchimonji, G. 2013. Survey Results Reveal Both IT Pros' Greatest Fears and Apparent Needs. CSO. Online. 18 September. Available at: www.csoonline.com/article/2133933 strategic-planning-erm/survey-results-reveal-both-it-pros–greatest-fears-and-apparen t-needs.html.

Joint Task Force (JTF) on Cyber Security Education. 2017. Cyber Security Curricula 2017, Curriculum Guidelines for Post-Secondary Degree Programs in Cyber Security: A Report in The Computing Curricula Series. ACM/IEEE-CS/AIS SIGSEC/IFIP WG 11.8, Version 1.0, New York.

Laberis, B. 2016. 20 Eye-Opening Cybercrime Statistics. Security Intelligence, IBM. Available at: https://securityintelligence.com/20-eye-opening-cybercrime-statistics/.

Microsoft Security Team. 2016. The Emerging Era of Cyber Defence and Cybercrime. Microsoft Secure. 27 January. Available at: https://cloudblogs.microsoft.com/microsoftse cure/2016/01/27/the-emerging-era-of-cyber-defence-and-cybercrime/.

Newhouse, W., S. Keith, B. Scribner and G. Witte. 2017. *National Initiative for Cyber Security Education (NICE) Cyber Security Workforce Framework*. Gaithersburg, MD: National Institute of Standards and Technology.

NIAC. (National Infrastructure Advisory Council) 2018. *Surviving a Catastrophic Power Outage*. Washington, DC: Department of Homeland Security.

Privacy Rights Clearinghouse. 2017. *A Chronology of Data Breaches*. San Diego, CA: PRC.

Saltzer, J. H. and M. D. Schroeder. 1974. The Protection of Information in Computer Systems. *Communications of the ACM 17*. New York: ACM Digital Library.

Symantec. 2014. *A Manifesto for Cyber Resilience*. Mountain View, CA: Symantec.

TechTarget. 2018. Human Attack Surface. Available at: www.Whatis.com.

Trend Micro. 2015. *Report on Cyber Security and Critical Infrastructure in the Americas*. Washington, DC: Organisation of American States.

# 6

# CREATING SOCIAL CYBER VALUE AS THE BROADER GOAL

*Greg Austin and Glenn Withers*

This chapter argues that social science should be a central foundation for managing the key technologies of cyberspace. We also argue that this approach gives rise to a massive research agenda, in both scope and scale, and that the associated emergence of social cyber science is both necessary and desirable.

The need for new social science approaches to modern cyberspace problems has been confirmed in a recent report by the U.S. National Academies on social science and national intelligence (National Academies 2019). The report includes a key chapter on "social cyber security" and distinguishes it from engineering and computer science approaches that consider social science at the margins only and not as an equal centrepiece of analysis.

To ground this argument, consider the following examples of "Five Cyber I" problems in cyber systems that a social science perspective can help mitigate:

- *Cyber insecurity*: as documented by Greenberg (2018), one random cyber attack caused one company to lose US$340 million. Known losses across all companies from the same attack, NotPetya, reached a total of US$10 billion.
- *Cyber incompetence*: an Australian government agency, AUSTRAC, imposed a fine of US$500 million[1] on the Commonwealth Bank of Australia for its failure to monitor possible money laundering through its Intelligent Deposit Machines (Austrac 2018).
- *Cyber intransigence*: the estimated loss from slow digital transformation and slow uptake of related technologies is estimated for the case of Australia to be A$37 billion[2] over a decade (PWC 2014: 2).
- *Cyber ignorance*: Standard & Poor's stocks fell on Wall Street by US$136.5 billion in 6 minutes in response to a mistaken claim on Twitter that there had been an attack on President Obama in the White House (CNBC 2013).

- *Cyber insensitivity*: Facebook saw its share value drop by 44 per cent in 2018 and 2019 as it struggled to meet reshaped global expectations for privacy and security. By July 2019, Facebook was forced to pay a fine of US$5 billion for its errors and omissions in cyberspace (Brody and McLaughlin 2019).

From these case illustrations we can see, anecdotally, the need for new approaches for each of the following five problem sets made prominent by the cyber era: maximising security in cyberspace, minimising incompetence in digital choices, avoiding technological lock-in, defending against information uncertainty, and creating solid ethical foundations for navigating the information revolution.

It is the contention of this chapter that there may be substantial benefit in an overarching approach that treats the five problem sets as unified, in the sense of them all deriving from an inadequate understanding of the human factors in cyberspace. If this is correct, an approach that adds the social to the technical could optimise financial outcomes in big business, and community outcomes in non-profits, as well as policy outcomes for government. The proposed approach is to manage them all through the concept of the social cyber ecosystem. The key foundation feature of the ecosystem that cuts across the five problem sets is perceiving the human component operating through the lens of human capital and its capacity to generate social cyber value.

Currently, the world faces a severe and worsening shortage in many aspects of workforce development for information technology, to the extent that the US President has declared an arms race in cyberspace human capital dimensions (Austin 2019: 34). In China's case alone, by 2020, this shortage – in the field of cyber security alone – is estimated to reach 1.4 million cyber security posts for which suitably trained applicants are not available (ibid.: 34). In a situation of shortage of appropriately trained people, an increased percentage of people will be promoted to sensitive jobs that are beyond their individual competence levels unless specific steps are taken in anticipation, to compensate for gaps in individual knowledge and skills through building an appropriate human ecosystem of talent. To that can be added an appreciation of also building trust and ethical behaviour within organisational cyber communities to maximise the positive human benefit.

## A mature and comprehensive information ecosystem approach

The concept of information ecosystem was usefully defined in a paper for the Institute of Electrical and Electronic Engineers as follows:

> A digital ecosystem is defined as an open, loosely coupled, demand-driven, domain clustered, agent-based, self-organised environment where species/agents form short- and long-term coalitions for specific purposes or goals, and everyone is proactive and responsive for its own benefit or profit. Interactions among peers

in Digital Ecosystems may involve, besides unbridled competition, new modalities of pre-competitive and collaborative partnerships. Digital ecosystems are characterised by complexity – demanding radically new solutions.

*(Guetl, Ismail and Lexar 2013)*

What is notable in this definition coming from an engineering professional association is how much the 14 separate descriptor terms of a digital ecosystem so specified (such as loosely coupled, unbridled competition, collaborative partnerships, to name just three) already represent highly complex social phenomena, and not just technical ones.

The recent further evolution of this holistic information ecosystem approach can be tracked through key contributions. See Wang et al. (2017) for a literature survey:

- Yurcik and Doss (2002) provide an early recognition of the value of an ecosystem approach (entirely technical rather than socio-technical) for the value of security, but they recognise that "over-reliance on protection solutions for system components at a singular layer" contributes to the fragility of information systems when viewed as a whole. For example, the use of authentication and encryption "may actually add more vulnerabilities to the system as a whole than they eliminate".
- Schwartz (1999; 2002), at the same time, proposes the idea of digital Darwinism for the evolution of such systems with adaptable businesses being the vehicle for advance along with new technology, a conception furthered by Walton (2015). Walton concludes, however, that the "realities of information exchange" are being transformed more quickly than the "conventions of exchange" are able to adapt.
- Floridi (2002) extends the introduction of such a social phenomenon into these ecosystems by also investigating the moral philosophy of these developments in the digital age.
- Arina (2009), building on Iansiti and Levien (2004), identified several species of information actors in contestation, with some exploiting the new environment and others enhancing their society with the balance determining advance or detriment.
- Masys (2015) observed correctly that resilience is as important as security and that "this does not reside purely in cyber security patches and technical solutions but requires a more comprehensive and collaborative approach that embraces the social, organizational, economic, political and technical domains".
- Kovács et al. (2017: 5) suggested that there is a need for "new approaches for exploring technology and society relationships" and that the "pervasive ICT ecosystem shapes interactions and relationships between humans and technology on different levels".
- Richards et al. (2008) developed similar ideas for the technical architecture of space systems, where risk aversion is high because of cost penalties, They propose five design principles as listed in Table 6.1 to correct five major flaws in contemporary approaches, notably including recognising that "architecting for survivability is a poorly understood, socio-technical issue".

**TABLE 6.1** Design principles for space system survivability

| Corrective design principles | To fix contemporary design flaws |
| --- | --- |
| Incorporate survivability as an active trade in the design process | Treatment of survivability as a constraint |
| Capture the dynamics of operational environments over the entire lifecycle of systems | Static threat reports (selected operational scenarios are not likely to truly represent future conflicts); "unanticipated technological developments will affect combat operations"; and "adversaries in real conflicts will adapt to our capabilities in unanticipated ways" (citing Anderson and Williamsen 2007) |
| Capture path dependencies of system susceptibility and vulnerability to disturbances | Assumption of independent disturbance encounters: "Perrow (1999) finds that failures may also arise from unanticipated, dysfunctional interactions among components and then subsequently be exacerbated by the rapid propagation of local failures due to tight coupling in complex systems." |
| Extend the scope of architecture-level survivability assessments | Narrow scope of survivability design and analysis ("tremendous amount of progress has been made to improve the survivability of individual elements in aerospace system architecture) (Nordin and Kong 1999; Paterson 1999). Less progress has been made at the architecture-level where systems tend to evolve in an ad-hoc manner—accommodating constraints from legacy systems and forming temporary coalitions to support emergent missions. More generally, architecting for survivability is a poorly understood, socio-technical issue." |
| Take a value-centric perspective to allow alternative value-delivery mechanisms | Lack of a value-centric perspective. "Success of a system is dependent on how much value it is perceived to deliver to its stakeholders" but stakeholders have to document the value proposition. |

Scholars, therefore, have a clear focus on how complex systems evolve under the influence of technological development and stakeholder actions, but there is equally a clear consensus that these influences should be further defined, refined and elaborated.

## The socio-technical aspects: how visible is social science?

The socio-technical character of cyber security and the importance of associated analysis are now clear. There has been growing recognition of how vast, complex and deceptively (un)manageable the social dimensions have become. What is less clear is what this involves and how it should proceed.

Conceptually, rational knowledge is created through logic and evidence, as opposed to intuition and experience. Such rational knowledge is what formal research pursues and formal education conveys, in both cases, in open, transparent, accessible, systemic documented form. The documentation is the foundation of sharing the knowledge. The social mechanisms of disseminating knowledge have become profoundly disturbed by the information age.

Where the knowledge is focused on the natural and physical world, it is seen as science, technology, engineering and mathematics (STEM) knowledge. Where the knowledge relates to human behaviour and interaction, whether individually or through community and cultural, business, economic or political and governmental collectivity, it is seen as humanities, arts, and social science (HASS) knowledge.

For the cyber world, understanding the imminent social complexities identified above as crucial is made more difficult by the persistent dominance of technical practitioners of cyber security within the policy and research domains. This is understandable as the issues first required physical world insight to be developed and, while social implications still follow inexorably, codified social science knowledge of that aspect has yet to catch up to and inform the technology imperatives.

At the most simple level, in spite of thousands of scholarly research articles over more than two decades, we have arrived at the point where three UK specialists concluded that "industry, policymakers, law enforcement, public and private sector organizations are yet to realize the impact individual cyber behaviour has on security" (Benson, McAlaney and Baranowski 2019: 1264). They called for recognition that "cybersecurity is inherently a complex socio-technical system". With a focus on behavioural psychology, they advocated especially for new work practices that reflect research on the workplace behaviour of individuals (ibid.: 1269). This is perhaps the best recognised social consideration. The individual human is, however, as indicated above, only part of the picture.

There are institutional factors as well. Given the business imperative to capitalise on the new technology, it has been natural to look to the structure and practices of organisations as a starting point for moving beyond individual behaviour, abstracted from social context. As some American scholars found a little earlier in 2017: "Contrary to our theorizing, the use of more IT security is not directly responsible for reducing breaches, but instead, institutional factors create the conditions under which IT security investments can be more effective." They went on to say that the implications of their results "are significant for policy and practice", particularly the "discovery that firms need to consider how adoption is influenced by institutional factors and how this should be balanced with technological solutions" (Angst, Block, D'Arcy and Kelley 2017: 893). Other researchers have travelled the same terrain (Kraemer, Carayon and Clem 2009; Tang and Zhang 2016). On the other hand, ecosystem factors such as legal regulation can have a negative impact on cyber security (Clark-Ginsberg and Slayton 2018).

A series of studies take this further and look at the links between IT governance, risk management and information security (De Smet and Mayer 2016). They concluded that more research would be needed to "define how to well integrate security and risk management in the IT governance framework" and they suggested sector-based approaches in research on IT governance to take better account of the unique context of different organisations.

Beyond organisational factors, there is less research. But an emergent literature is to be found on questions of cyber security as a complex social system (Salasin 1976; Baskerville 1996; Courtney et al. 2009; Rebovich 2010). There is also work on the impact of complex social systems in turn on broader resilience questions for other relevant domains, such as Bellavita (2006) for general homeland defence missions; Lafond and DuCharme (2011) and Dimitrova (2017) for general security policy; Clarke et al. (2015) on environmental security.

The research is embracing further issues of path dependence and complex dependencies and recognising these as new, even more complex problems (Kovács et al. 2017). Here social science moves beyond the individualism or organisation analysis common in behavioural social science and management, through to the aggregations often used in social science areas, such as sociology, economics and political science and to the evaluative questions posed by ethics.

Researchers at Carnegie Mellon University saw "social cyber security" at present as self-limiting to political or cultural manipulation of victims (Carley et al. 2018: 389). They, therefore, proposed moving beyond this by seeing the field as multidisciplinary, carving out a new field that mirrors the term "socio-technical". They see social cyber security as a "computational social science" which, they say, is "noticeably distinct from a pure computer science approach or a pure social science approach". The methods and theories being developed:

> (a) take the socio-political context into account methodologically and empirically; (b) are predicated on issues of influence, persuasion, manipulation, and theories that link human behavior to behavior in the cyber-mediated environment; and (c) are focused on operational utility rather than just improving scores for machine learning algorithms or theory testing.
>
> *(ibid.: 390)*

The focus of this approach is to address negative impacts on security through malign influence or manipulation, and it does not appear to extend to the concept of second- or third-order effects of cyber security practices back inside the broader information ecosystems of organisations, communities or countries from the perspective of IT governance outside security or digital transformation in the broad sense. Even so, within the narrower remit, they observe that "new research is needed in many areas", and they single out "bias estimation and reduction in data; movement of actors and ideas within and between media; semi-automated identification, assessment of impact of, and effectiveness of counter-messaging" (ibid.: 393). In the longer run, the concept can also turn to emphasise methods of analysis for focus on enhanced use of cyber, not only in relation to security but in the positive use of the technology in general for organisational and social advance.

Such new interest in the social dimensions of cyber security can be discerned in the emergence of the term "social cyber physical". But there is a long way to go before this displays mainstream acceptance. The Scopus database records the first entry for that term in 2003, and five for 2018 at the date of the search.[3] Of these, only two distinct articles mention the term "cyber ecosystem". For the search term, "cyber social", as keyword in the Abstract, Scopus records 67 articles, with the first in 2003, and eight for 2018 at the date of search. Of these, only three mention the word ecosystem. The SSRN database returns zero articles showing "social cyber" as in "abstract, title and keywords", and only two that reflect the term "cyber ecosystem".[4] Some 16 articles reflect the search terms "cyber" AND "ecosystem". Of the items identified by the above searches, there were three that touch on aspects relevant to this chapter.

Zeng et al. (2016) observed correctly therefore that studies of cyber physical social systems "are still at their infancy, most recent studies are application-specific and lack systematic design methodology".

Trautman's quite short (2017) paper goes to a foundational problem (a departure point) in developing research on social cyber security. Having observed the complexity of the cyber security problem for many of the social and organisational factors mentioned already, he notes the lack of a common discourse among key stakeholders (business, government and individuals). He suggests that over time, group dynamics have produced disincentives for more rational approaches and even working against candour in discussion of problems between various groups. He suggests that "navigating the cyber ecosystem and structuring effective solutions to the cyber problem will require recognizing and overcoming difficult truths about organizational and human behavior".

It will also need to recognise and overcome difficult truths about research methodology. Scholars are rooted in disciplinary specialisation. This has indeed been a productive engine for insight. It allows deep insight through understood shared and well-defined specialist concepts and methods. But problems of interest to decision-makers and stakeholders beyond the Academy are often searching for integrated or holistic insight.

The current state of play was foreshadowed in a 2013 analysis of the state of cyber security research. In a long list of under-researched areas, the last mentioned was the social aspect. Referring to a paper on "Reducing Systemic Cybersecurity Risk" by Sommer and Brown (2011) prepared for the OECD project on global economic shock, the authors (Craigen, Walsh and White 2013: 14) suggest that research responses should adopt a cross-disciplinary approach that combines "hard computer science" with the need to understand social science dimensions because "information system security are achieved only by a fusion of technology and the ways in which people and organizations actually try to deploy them".

One of the best guides to this nascent but emerging field of social cyber research is a report from the U.S. National Academies (2019) on strengthening the role of social and behavioural sciences in intelligence analysis. Using the term, "social cybersecurity science", and following a somewhat forced and limiting definition of the emerging field, it says that the term serves two primary objectives (cited verbatim):

- to characterize, understand, and forecast cyber-mediated changes in human behavior and in social, cultural, and political outcomes; and
- to build a social cyber infrastructure that will allow the essential character of a society to persist in a cyber-mediated information environment that is characterized by changing conditions, actual or imminent social cyber-threats, and cyber-mediated threats.

*(ibid.)*

The report distinguishes between cyber security dominated by engineering perspectives that can take account of social science considerations and social cyber security, where the researchers are linked by their commitment to doing the following:

- take the sociopolitical context of cyber activity into account both methodologically and empirically;
- integrate theory and research on influence, persuasion, and manipulation with study of human behaviour in the cyber-mediated environment; and
- focus on identifying operationally useful applications of their research.

*(ibid.)*

There is a useful summary assessment of the interactions between social cyber security and other disciplines. Box 6.1 lists the main findings and proposed research directions for this field as defined by the report. The report is valuable for its scoping analysis but is limited by its narrow focus on national security intelligence analysis and its bias towards understanding the impacts of potential human-machine interaction in that field. Wider social science in law, ethics, economics, management, politics and community awaits like examination.

---

**BOX 6.1 MAIN FINDINGS ON SOCIAL CYBER SECURITY IN THE U.S. NATIONAL ACADEMIES REPORT**

Conclusions 6.1 and 6.2 call for:

- a comprehensive multidisciplinary research strategy for the study of social cyber attacks;
- scientific methods for assessing bias in online data;
- new computational social science methods for monitoring social networks and narratives;
- operational computational social science theories of influence and manipulation in cyber-mediated environments.

The chapter has seven specific proposed lines of future research:

1. Continue work on developing better theories and methods for identifying perpetrators of cyber attacks.
2. Conduct interdisciplinary research to develop computational models and theories about information manoeuvres in cyberspace and the respective strategies of influence and manipulation.
3. Conduct research to develop techniques and tools with the capabilities to determine automatically and rapidly the intent of those conducting social cyber security information manoeuvres.
4. Conduct research to develop multimedia diffusion theories and a better understanding of the co-movement of people and ideas through cyberspace.
5. Develop methods for measuring the impact of an information campaign, in both the short and long terms.
6. Better characterise those groups at risk of social cyber attacks, and identify ways to increase awareness of malicious information manoeuvres and strengthen the resistance of at-risk topic groups to such attacks.
7. Support the design of counter-messaging strategies in cyberspace.

Thus, while social considerations are certainly increasingly evident in modern approaches to cyber security, they have rarely been analysed as part of a complex socio-technical system. The preference has been either to see the people problem as distinguishable and separate from the technical challenges; or in the case of some research, to see the human as an extension of the machine. Prevailing approaches include security vetting of personnel or subsequent monitoring of them, and courses in basic cyber hygiene (especially phishing and password control). There has been little exploration of incentive-based approaches to cyber security and cyber competence, or the construction of new cyber ecosystems. The idea of linking IT governance and digital transformation to the security challenge has not been researched widely, and nor has the impact of cyber incompetence as a broader social phenomenon independently of the specific cases referenced in the first pages of this chapter.

What is needed is a more conscious and systematic cyber ecosystem approach as outlined later in this chapter to optimise social cyber value, but drawing on the full range of social science disciplines seen as basic to achieving a full system integration approach:

- individualist theory foundations: behavioural psychology, organisational analysis;
- quantitative data interpretation: statistical and computational analysis including for big data;
- institutional aggregation: political, economic, social and cultural modes of analysis;
- ethical and value interrogation: philosophy.

These are applied to the activities being generated by science, technology, engineering, and mathematics disciplines as they too come together to generate the new cyber universe.

## Interdisciplinarity and integrating social science influence

There is as yet no accepted meta-discipline of interdisciplinarity. The intellectual challenge of defining the standards and methods of excellence for such work is evolving.

In 2015, Australia's Council of Learned Academies (ACOLA) sought to pursue a multidisciplinary analysis of the closely related issues around innovation. This took a wide definition of relevant disciplines across each of the natural and physical sciences, engineering and technology, social sciences and humanities, and sought to use that approach to analyse the impact of technological lock-in on that country's innovation (Williams et al. 2015). This "lock-in" phenomenon might offer some explanation for the lack of progress globally towards more comprehensive and up-to-date policies for cyber security. One need only cite the persistence of the highly insecure Microsoft Windows as an acceptable operating platform. But the challenge is not confined to the technologies. As Gaycken and Austin (2014) observed, that software system represents an inherently insecure technology (tens of millions of lines of code that require regular patching to prevent major security breaches) yet the market dominance of such systems effectively prevents or delays the advent of "highly secure computing".

The bigger challenge still arises from the social foundations of the inertia. Referencing Leo Marx (1999), the Australian study calls these foundations a "socio-technical complex", a system that "consists of manufacturers, developers, businesses, industry and users, and includes cultures of manufacture, regulation, and the networked and interlinked technologies and infrastructure" (Williams et al. 2015). Referring to "sunk costs and vested interests", the report (ibid.: 24) sees these as barriers to change "even when there would be clear benefits" from it.

The summary of how "lock-in" occurs that is offered in the report is highly relevant to understanding the current dominance of the "technological" approach to cyber security. It says:

> Once a market is established, institutions such as technical and professional associations often emerge as gatekeepers between end-users and individual professionals. Voluntary associations such as social automobile clubs, unions, industry associations or media channels such as magazines or electronic social media sites can act as non-market (i.e. social, cultural or governance) forces of "lock-in". Emergent technologies can also create brand new academic disciplines which are then absorbed into research and teaching institutions. Social norms play a part in 'lock-in' when people can become locked into new social practices associated with the uses of technologies.

*(ibid.: 25)*

The report mentions an important set of break-out measures to overcome technological "lock-in":

> Lock-in created by technological inertia and vested interests means that a substantial technical performance improvement is often needed in order to induce a transition from a widely adopted technology to a new technology. Such substantial improvements often come from niche and entrepreneurial entrants to the market. To achieve structural change, policy must support the growth of new technologies and industries. Legislation can help to create niche markets, and if there is variety in the niche markets created, then technical advances are more to likely occur.
>
> *(ibid.: 25)*

The report later addressed the specific case of Australia, calling out a list of 11 factors that were likely to shape Australia's response to advanced technology (ibid.: 31–32). See Box 6.2. At least five of these have sharp resonance for the discussion in this chapter. They will be revisited later in this chapter.

---

## BOX 6.2 ONE SET OF AGENDA ITEMS FOR SOCIAL CYBER RESEARCH

### 1 Attitudes to changing technology and practices

- Model best practice in organisational and workforce change, taking into consideration how new technology will require new roles, work patterns, modes of communication, reward systems, leadership models and workplace training.
- Mitigate against negative attitudes to new technology in general by ensuring that there are effective retraining schemes and social safety nets for affected workers.

### 2 Approach to risk and failure

- Through education, vocational training and lifelong learning, develop a business/industry/national culture that accepts the uncertainty and failure inherent in innovation. Train people to experiment, and how to learn from (and benefit from) failure.
- Recognise there is also risk in maintaining the status quo, and not adopting new technologies.
- Experiment with multiple technological options for a given problem, recognising that it is unlikely there is only one solution.

---

## 3 Skills

- Recognise advanced skills are needed to make use of a new technology effectively, as well as for its invention and creation.
- Influence training and education schemes to encourage flexibility, creativity and the ability to try new things.
- Minimise constraints on worker mobility, e.g. stringent visa rules.
- Ensure training content is sufficiently generic to enable workers to adapt to the evolving job requirements imposed by new technologies, rather than highly specific content that is focused on existing technologies employed in past and present jobs.

## 4 Open data

- Ensure data that is owned by the government, or that the government is a custodian of, is made freely available and shared by default.

## 5 Privacy and security

- Impediments to adopting wireless and cloud technologies in many businesses include security and privacy concerns. This is particularly important in industries such as healthcare where high security standards need to be achieved to ensure patient confidentiality.

The proposition that the cyber security scene globally is dominated by some sort of technological lock-in would seem to be confounded by the vast creativity and invention we see in the sector. But it is possible to see even the creativity as bounded by a preference for technological solutions to security in cyberspace. There is little evidence globally of the necessary adjustment of policy at national, enterprise or community level that gives due weight to the reality that cyber security is a socio-technical phenomenon. This is evidenced by the sharp imbalance between investments in technology as against social science at almost every level where prosperity and security are affected by cyberspace.

The potential scope of social cyber research was flagged quite comprehensively if indirectly in the report by the Australian Council of Learned Academies just mentioned (William et al. 2015: 31–32), and as reproduced in Box 6.2. That is a fairly traditional set of social science topics. An agenda laid out in the National Academies (2019) report, and referred to in Box 6.1, is more ambitious because it takes account of both the revolutionary changes in social cyber ecosystems under the influence of technology and, at the same time, the new and unrealised potential of the same technologies to better study (and document) the novel social interactions catalysed by them.

## Social cyber value: a new concept

This chapter proposes that such social science inputs can be achieved by focusing on optimised information ecosystem value derived from a more comprehensive accounting of the interaction between technical, social, political and ethical realities inside and outside the corporate entities (in business, government or the community). We call this "social cyber value".

The departure point for this concept was cyber security. But the stream of research in recent times just outlined leads us to see the problem as lying well beyond the traditional positioning of cyber security as a separate domain of largely defensive activity led by a class of technically qualified "cyber guardians".

Rather, we conclude, as some in business and government already have, that a preferred approach is a broader one. In the same way that national security depends on deeper social and economic realities of a country, so too security in cyberspace, either for a large corporatised entity or a country, depends on the harmonisation of the social, ethical and economic aspects of cyberspace with the technical. The arrival point therefore is one of optimising full social cyber system value.

The concept of social cyber value that results is represented graphically in Figure 6.1. It proposes an integration of management of four pillars of business activity: cyber security, digital infrastructure management, strategies for digital transformation (business processes), and human resources (social information vectors) (a function which has to

**FIGURE 6.1** Information ecosystem optimised for social cyber value

become human resources for digital life as well as digital competency). Underpinning the proposed new interaction between all of these four pillars is the consideration of ethics underpinning the social and political values of the enterprise.

## Enterprise-level adoption of cyber social value

An ecosystem approach to cyber instinctively connotes big picture complexity. It is important, however, to recognise that the social cyber issues can be canvassed at each of the micro, meso and macro levels; and that the units of analysis, as indicated, can stretch across a spectrum from individual focus to individual nations and the globe. Components of the ecosystem can be examined through "deep dive" research as well as in wider context. But the core unit for intermediating all the forces at play is the organisation. It is therefore affirmed that rich analysis of organisations is necessarily central, if not sufficient, for the success of the ecosystem perspective.

The premier information age utilities companies, such as Google, Facebook and Microsoft, are the principal organisations currently under scrutiny. They have all now set themselves high aspirational benchmarks through integrated, ethics-based approaches to their entire enterprise and its information ecosystem. None have quite cracked the challenge, as evidenced by repeat stumbles of one kind or another, especially on the ethics front. Nevertheless, the aspiration of these corporations to set new standards also saw them create novel forms of management to address the challenges. What we can take from the leadership example of these corporations, if only at an anecdotal level, is this. If your corporate structure operates more or less as it did a decade ago, and if the lines of authority between the pillars of your information ecosystem represented in Figure 6.1 (information security, digital transformation, resilience of legacy systems, and human capital) remain largely in silos, then it may be reasonable to assume that your enterprise is at a higher risk of digital disaster than ones that have made fairly fundamental and integrative changes. That said, change by itself, without continuing validation of the success of the change, can often be more destructive than no change at all.

If the basic proposition in this chapter is valid, and it certainly remains under-researched and untested, one might imagine that large corporations and government agencies might realign their organisational structures around an ecosystem approach that would see the creation of new posts, perhaps with the title such as Vice President for social cyber ecosystems. Perhaps governments will even create new ministerial appointments for social cyber systems, instead of drawing ad hoc on separate portfolios for cyber security, digital transformation, education, industry and employment.

As just one illustration of the potential for change, Figure 6.2 shows how a new post, Senior VP for Cyber Ecosystems might be genetically inserted into the current cyber DNA of an organisation. The concept reorganises the reporting lines and diffuses the functionality of four existing separate functions: the VP for Human Resources (digital human capital),[5] the CIO (functionality of current IT), the

CISO (security of current IT), and the VP Strategy (seizing profit gains from future IT transformation). They would all report to a Senior VP for information ecosystem management. The concept, like the diagram, is indicative only.

Figure 6.2 illustrates this concept using the image of a triple helix where three broad strands (technical, socio-technical, and social) constitute the DNA of any information ecosystem. A central assumption of this idea of optimised social cyber value is that solutions will be unique to each organisation and that each organisation needs to invest in longitudinal social science research by in-house teams to devise optimal outcomes. The field of activity is simply too complex to leave to the imagined leadership judgement of senior executives uninformed of detailed consequences, for the reasons discussed in this chapter.

While the preceding paragraph illustrates the concept with an intra-firm approach, the concept is as relevant to large communities, countries and even transborder relationships. We can and should imagine single political entities as a

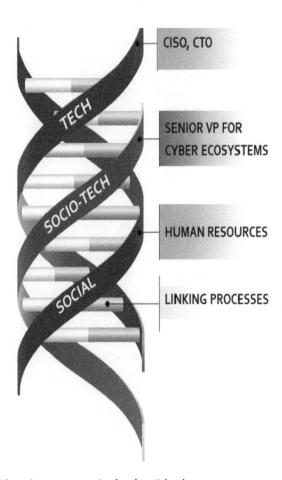

FIGURE 6.2 Managing an enterprise-level social cyber ecosystem

cyber ecosystem, comprising many component cyber ecosystems. Cyber sovereignty does exist. But the national authority of the sovereign is now seriously diluted, whatever the intent, by disruptive influences of trans-national cyber ecosystems or business ecosystems that cut across politically bounded ones. These disruptive influences can be structured or chaotic. But they are all too real, so this calls for a new wider vison of the international (cross-border) character of cyberspace through cyber ecosystem analysis.

## Conclusion

Few businesses and few governments around the world have well-developed policies to respond to the fundamental social behaviour and ethical transformations under way as result of the information revolution. Policy and management have been oriented largely towards both the technologies and the business preferences of the technologists. Where broader interests have come into play, these have been confined largely to workplace regimes (efficiency from automation) or to exploiting consumer responses to technology products. We have not seen social and ethical questions arise much in new types of "information training" for government and business. Leading moral philosophers of the information age, such as Floridi, signal ways in which we should expect society to respond to the new moral qualities of the information age, but we don't see it.

In this chapter, we suggest an ecosystem approach that sees leaders and executives construct a vision of the specific cyber ecosystem in which their enterprise activity takes place and in which they can create new forms of social cyber value. The chapter takes as its departure point and end point the dualistic Floridi proposition that diffusion of power (democratisation) is a central organising principle of the information age, and that what will matter most is how that power is re-aggregated. Business and government have to adapt, profoundly, in ways that respond to the new sentiments of direct democracy and millennial "rights sensitivity". The main direction of that change needs to be in the high-level ranks of organisations who need to yield authority both to lower levels and to social scientists. In the same way that the technology of the information revolution transformed workplaces several decades ago with new work roles, including Vice President for Information Technology and large-scale lay-offs because of efficiencies from automation, then the emergent sociology of the information revolution – including the human rights aspects—will bring forth new work roles and work structures. In addition to specialised roles that have emerged more recently, such as the Chief Information Security Officer, will we now look to appoint Chief Information Sociology Officers? They will have not only a narrowly commercial function but will be the main champions of human rights promotion inside business ecosystems because in the information age, there will be higher costs to those corporations and government agencies which ignore human rights.

Drawing on Floridi (2002; 2012), the chapter assumes that the norm of freedom of information objectively shapes concrete outcomes in the business world, both within a single enterprise and between the enterprise and the outside world. The chapter ties that proposition to an evolving concept of "social cyber" management which identifies important gains and penalties for corporations or large government agencies which fail to take into account the centrality of non-technical aspects in the outcomes produced by their technology-based information objects. The non-technical aspects include the ethics of the workforce, the corporation, and international society writ large. But the non-technical aspects also include considerations of how to manage business outcomes for digital transformation at the same time as managing for cyber security and for cyber competence.

The chapter argues that by addressing these limitations and bringing social science to bear on the cyber ecosystems, all actors could simultaneously unleash the untapped positive potential for digital transformation that has hitherto been constrained by the focus on the technical domain (tools and inventions, such as autonomous vehicles and robots). The new spirit might be based on the conviction that a social retooling at a system level is not only feasible but is also a moral duty.

An additional important outcome of the social science study of specific cyber ecosystems will be enhanced protection from information threats, such as malicious campaigns to destroy national confidence, undermine shareholder value, or direct attack on key actors in the workforce. An overarching benefit of addressing social ecosystem development and issues in this comprehensive fashion (insecurity, incompetence, digital transformation and information threats) is that it creates the conditions for the appropriate reflection on important ethical questions (especially privacy but also worker values) that are unique to the information age.

This chapter imagines how a process of radical adjustment to the social and systemic influences of security in cyber space might be undertaken to begin to deliver more viable social ecosystems that can match the escalating threats while exploiting more effectively the untapped potential of the information revolution, still in its early stages. The keys are to adopt a wide perspective, make it socially aware and embrace all levels of insight while being ecosystem-focused, multidisciplinary and with firm micro-foundations. This is a big agenda for analysts but with huge potential pay-off, intellectually and in the cyber worlds of government, business and individuals.

## Notes

1  Exchange rate as of the date of the announcement.
2  Exchange rate as of 30 June 2014.
3  As of 2 December 2018.
4  As of 2 December 2018.
5  There is a basic assumption that the digital aspect of human resources management and development is today and into the future, one that over-rides all others. The central idea is an ecosystem approach. Social influences and interactions involved in managing an information ecosystem are "path-dependent"; the basic assumption is that the boundaries, character and destiny of a cyber ecosystem, however fluid, are defined by the people in it.

## References

Anderson, T. and J. Williamsen. 2007.*Force Protection Evaluation for Combat Aircraft Crews*. Paper presented at the 48th AIAA Structures, Structural Dynamics, and Materials Conference, Honolulu, HI.

Angst, C. M., E. S. Block, J. D'Arcy and K. Kelley. 2017. When Do IT Security Investments Matter? Accounting for the Influence of Institutional Factors in the Context of Healthcare Data Breaches. *MIS Quarterly* 41(3).

Arina, T. 2009. *Digital Ecosystems*. Paper presented at Finnish Digibusiness seminar. 13 January 2009. Available at: www.slideshare.net/infe/digital-ecosystems-presentation-913157.

Austin, G. 2019. Digital China: Has Australia Been Spooked? *Asia Society*. Available at: https://asiasociety.org/australia/digital-china-has-australia-been-spooked.

AUSTRAC. 2018. AUSTRAC and CBA Agree $700m Penalty. Press release. 7 June 2018. Available at: www.austrac.gov.au/media/media-releases/austrac-and-cba-agree-700m-penalty.

Baskerville, R. 1996. The Second-Order Security Dilemma. In *Information Technology and Changes in Organizational Work*. Berlin: Springer, pp. 239–249.

Bellavita, C. 2006. *Changing Homeland Security: Shape, Patterns, Not Programs*. Monterey, CA: Center for Homeland Defense and Security, Naval Postgraduate School.

Benson, V., J. McAlaney and L. A. Frumkin. 2019. Emerging Threats for the Human Element and Countermeasures in Current Cyber Security Landscape. In V. Benson, J. McAlaney and L.A. Frumkin (eds), *Cyber Law, Privacy, and Security: Concepts, Methodologies, Tools, and Applications*. Hershey, PA: IGI Global, pp. 1264–1269.

Brody, B. and D. McLaughlin. 2019. Facebook Agrees to Pay Record $5 B, *Time*. 24 July Available at: https://time.com/5633513/facebook-ftc-settlement/.

Carley, K. M., G. Cervone, N. Agarwal and H. Liu. 2018.. Social Cyber-Security. In *Proceedings of International Conference on Social Computing, Behavioral-Cultural Modeling and Prediction and Behavior Representation in Modeling and Simulation*, pp. 389–394.

Clarke, J. , J. Coaffee, R. Rowlands, J. Finger, S. Hasenstein and U. Siebold. 2015. Resilience Evaluation and SOTA Summary Report. European Union. Horizon 2020 Program. Available at: http://resilens.eu/wp-content/uploads/2016/08/D1.1-Resilience-Evaluation-and-SOTA-Summary-Report.pdf.

Clark-Ginsberg, A. and R. Slayton. 2018. Regulating Risks Within Complex Sociotechnical Systems: Evidence from Critical Infrastructure Cybersecurity Standards. *Science and Public Policy*. Available at: https://academic.oup.com/spp/advance-article-abstract/doi/10.1093/scipol/scy061/5184558?redirectedFrom=fulltext.

CNBC. 2013. False Rumor of Explosion at White House Causes Stocks to Briefly Plunge; AP Confirms Its Twitter Feed Was Hacked. 23 April 2013. Available at: www.cnbc.com/id/100646197.

Courtney, T., S. Gaonkar, K. Keefe, E. W. Rozier and W. H. Sanders. 2009. Möbius 2.3: An Extensible Tool for Dependability, Security, and Performance Evaluation of Large and Complex System Models. In *Proceedings of 2009 IEEE/IFIP International Conference on Dependable Systems & Networks* pp. 353–358.

Craigen, D., D. A. Walsh and D. Whyte. 2013. Securing Canada's Information-Technology Infrastructure: Context, Principles, and Focus Areas of Cybersecurity Research. *Technology Innovation Management Review* 3(7): 12–18.

De Smet, D. and N. Mayer. 2016Integration of IT Governance and Security Risk Management: A Systematic Literature Review. In *Proceedings of IEEE 2016 International Conference on Information Society (i-Society)*, pp. 143–148.

Dimitrova, S. 2017. Challenges of the Security Environment Before the Correlation "Resources-Capabilities-Effects". In *Proceedings of International Conference Knowledge-Based Organization* 23(1): 89–93.

Floridi, L. 2002. Information Ethics: An Environmental Approach to the Digital Divide. *Philosophy in the Contemporary World* 9(1): 39–45.

Floridi, L. 2012. Hyperhistory and the Philosophy of Information Policies. *Philosophy & Technology* 25(2): 129–131.

Gaycken, S. and G. Austin. 2014. Resetting the System: Why Highly Secure Computing Should Be the Priority of Cybersecurity Policies. East West Institute. Available at: www. issuu.com/ewipublications/docs/resetting_the_system.

Greenberg, A. 2018. The Untold Story of NotPetya, the Most Devastating Cyberattack in History. *Wired* 22 August 2018. Available at: www.wired.com/story/notpetya-cyberatta ck-ukraine-russia-code-crashed-the-world/.

Guetl, C., L. Ismail and C. Lexar. 2013. Track A: Foundations of Digital Ecosystems and Complex Environment Engineering. In *Proceedings of 2013 7th IEEE International Conference on Digital Ecosystems and Technologies (DEST)*, pp. 1–10.

Iansiti, M. and R. Levien. 2004. *The Keystone Advantage: What the New Dynamics of Business Ecosystems Mean for Strategy, Innovation and Sustainability*. Boston: Harvard Business School Press.

Kovács, L., A. Nemeslaki, Á. Orbók and A. Szabó. 2017. Structuration Theory and Strategic Alignment in Information Security Management: Introduction of a Comprehensive Research Approach and Program. *AARMS* 16(1): 5–16.

Kraemer, S., P. Carayon and J. Clem. 2009. Human and Organizational Factors in Computer and Information Security: Pathways to Vulnerabilities. *Computers & Security* 28(7): 509–520.

Lafond, D. and M. B. DuCharme. 2011. Complex Decision Making Experimental Platform (CODEM): A Counter-Insurgency Scenario. In *Proceedings of 2011 IEEE Symposium on Computational Intelligence for Security and Defense Applications (CISDA)*, pp. 72–79.

Marx, L. 1997. Technology: The Emergence of a Hazardous Concept. *Social Research* 64(4): 965–988.

Masys, A. J. 2015. The Cyber-Ecosystem Enabling Resilience Through the Comprehensive Approach. In A. J. Masys, *Disaster Management: Enabling Resilience*. New York: Springer, pp. 143–154.

National Academies. 2019. A Decadal Survey of the Social and Behavioral Sciences: A Research Agenda for Advancing Intelligence Analysis. Available at: www.nap.edu/down load/25335.

Nordin, P. and M. Kong. 1999. Hardness and Survivability Requirements, in J. R. Wertz and W. J. Larson (eds), *Space Mission Analysis and Design*. El Segundo, CA: Microcosm Press.

Paterson, J. 1999. Overview of Low Observable Technology and Its Effects on Combat Aircraft Survivability. *Journal of Aircraft* 36(2): 380–388.

Perrow, C. 1999. *Normal Accidents: Living with High-Risk Technologies*. Princeton, NJ: Princeton University Press.

PWC. 2014. Expanding Australia's Economy: How Digital Can Drive the Change. Available at: www.pwc.com.au/consulting/assets/publications/expanding-australias-economy-apr14.pdf.

Rebovich, G. 2010. Systems Thinking for the Enterprise: A Thought Piece. In G. Rebovich, *Unifying Themes in Complex Systems*. Berlin: Springer, pp. 556–563.

Richards, M., D. Hastings, D. H. Rhodes and A. L. Weigel. 2008. Systems Architecting for Survivability: Limitations of Existing Methods for Aerospace Systems. Available at: http:// seari.mit.edu/documents/preprints/RICHARDS_CSER08.pdf.

Salasin, J. 1976. A Control Systems Model of Privacy. In *Proceedings of the June 7–10 1976 National Computer Conference and Exposition*, pp. 45–51.

Schwartz, E. 1999. *Digital Darwinism: 7 Breakthrough Business Strategies for Surviving in the Cutthroat Web Economy.* New York: Broadway Books.

Schwartz, E. 2002. *Digital Darwinism: 7 Breakthrough Business Strategies for Surviving in the Cutthroat Web Economy.* 2nd edn. New York: Broadway Books.

Sommer, P. and I. Brown. 2011. Reducing Systemic Cybersecurity Risk. Organisation for Economic Cooperation and Development, Working Paper No. IFP/WKP/FGS (2011)3.

Tang, M. and T. Zhang. 2016. The Impacts of Organizational Culture on Information Security Culture: A Case Study. *Information Technology and Management* 17(2) :179–186.

Trautman, L. J. 2017. Governing Risk and the Information Silo Problem: Engineering a Systemic Cultural and Communications Solution for Cyber. *SSRN*, 6 March.

Walton, P. 2015. Digital Information and Value. *Information* 6(4): 733–749.

Wang, X., Y. Guo, M. Yang, Y. Chen and W. Zhang. 2017. Information Ecology Research: Past, Present, and Future. *Information Technology and Management* 18(1): 27–39.

Williams, R. C., M. Raghnaill, K. Douglas and D. Sanchez 2015. Technology and Australia's Future. New Technologies and Their Role in Australia's Security, Cultural, Democratic, Social and Economic Systems. Australian Council of Learned Academies. Securing Australia's Future. Final Report 05. Available at: https://acola.org.au/wp/PDF/SAF05/SAF05_Report_web_17Sept.pdf.

Yurcik, W. and D. Doss 2002 . *A Survivability-Over-Security (SOS) Approach to Holistic Cyber-Ecosystem Assurance.* Paper presented at IEEE Workshop on Information Assurance, June.

Zeng, J., L.T. Yang, M. Lin, H. Ning and J. Ma 2016. A Survey: Cyber-Physical-Social Systems and Their System-Level Design Methodology. *Future Generation Computer Systems* 105: 1028–1042.

# 7

# EDUCATION FOR CYBER DISASTER RESPONSE AND RESILIENCE

*Adam P. Henry*

The accelerating development within the digital world creates a dynamic new age. Organisations and governments alike have sought to catch the digital wave, transforming their processes, procedures and product offerings to match the ever-increasing appetite of consumer citizens globally. Although the digital age has generated many new technological benefits, it has also generated new threats. The world has experienced an explosion of access to the Internet, with another three billion Internet users expected in the next decade or so (Morgan 2019). There are already more Internet-of-Things (IoT) devices than humans and this is expected to jump to over 150 billion in the not-so-distant future (Afshar 2017). The increasing interconnectivity of the digital ecosystem has created gaps in peoples' understanding of the threats. As new technology continues to be implemented, the risks increase.

This acceleration of technological advance is unprecedented, and no one truly knows what lies ahead. The increase in reliance on technology and the threats and risks associated, have transformed the field of cyber security beyond recognition and into one that might as well be completely new. It has no close peer in spite of efforts at analogy and metaphor, such as comparisons with public health management.

Cyber security is multifaceted, and touches all aspects of our lives, including political, social, legal, technical and personal. Yet as a field of knowledge it is very much in its infancy. This is especially the case for education research and preparation for major cyber incidents.

The cyber security skills crisis is growing as both the use and reliance on technology and the threats and risks expand. The cyber security employment forecasts have been unable to keep pace with the dramatic rise in cyber crime, which has doubled and is expected to cost up to $6 trillion by 2021 (*Cybercrime Magazine* 2018).

The current cyberspace climate is complicated. Multiple factors work against each other in developing an effective cyber workforce. A dire skills shortage threatens to see all nations fall behind in the digital economy. It is not just technical skills that are required. Multifaceted and multidisciplinary skill sets associated with cyber security and digital literacy are also essential. Expertise in key areas such as policy development, regulation, privacy and law are becoming a primary focus for organisations, boards and governments alike.

Governments and organisations are scrambling to ensure the next generation of workers meet not only the technical requirements necessary to address the challenges, but also related and essential skill sets. This attempt will fall short unless there is a radical change. There is a strong requirement for soft skills and digital literacy to convey the key messages throughout areas of policy, regulation development and international relations (Warner 2018).

This chapter argues that there needs to be a sharper focus on knowledge, skills and abilities to handle cyber incidents, from single vector attacks all the way up to major incidents at the national level. The argument is buttressed by increasing global attention to the concept of "national cyber emergencies" and systemic risk. The former subject was the focus of an international conference held in February 2019, for which this chapter was initially prepared, and which led to a selection of the papers published (Austin 2020a). Those with an education policy focus were reserved for this volume.

As for systemic risk, cyber security challenges have become one of the defining issues of our time. The World Economic Forum Global Risks Report (WEF 2019) listed cyber attacks in the top six global risks in terms of likelihood, three years straight from 2017–2019. Damage from cyber attacks will have a significant impact on sovereign national security, the national and global economy, and the livelihood and safety of individuals throughout the world (Clark and Hakim 2016). Only when an appropriate level of understanding within the general population about national-level emergencies, and even global cyber risks, has been developed can we start to move towards a more cyber-resilient society.

Cyber incident response brings the human element into play (response under pressure) more than everyday system security management. While we need technologies and organisational plans to help build resilience, they will not successful if there is little investment in the corresponding requirements for human and social capital (Siegel 2018). Worldwide, regulators are introducing reporting and compliance requirements associated with cyber events, such as data breaches (European Commission 2019). This has increased the requirement for appropriate cyber professionals, further depleting the staff available to undertake key frontline tasks. Cyber security is first of all a people and process issue, then a technological one. There is a requirement to move from a compliance (tick box) response to a risk-based response as there is no such thing as being 100 per cent secure. Threats and vulnerabilities can be mitigated, but success depends ultimately on how people respond in a crisis.

The human element of cyber crisis management is a primary vector of policy once we move outside the technical realm (where an attack occurs) to the impacts on society and everyday life. We have seen this aspect of the evolving cyber environment, where global, national and city-based events have crippled government and organisational functions with direct impact on the function of communities and countries. The risks are continuing to grow in both prevalence and disruptive potential (British High Commission 2018). The WEF Global Risks Report ranks data fraud or theft and cyber attacks as numbers 4 and 5 in the top 10 risks in terms of likelihood in 2019 (WEF 2019). Cyber attacks throughout the world are now targeting the core functions of economies such as critical infrastructure and healthcare. These attacks, which disrupt services and induce catastrophic damage, are becoming more difficult to defend against (Johnson 2015).

These social impacts of cyber attacks have become one of the defining issues globally. Damage to critical infrastructure through cyber-based attacks will have a significant impact on national security, the economy, and the livelihood and safety of governments and individual citizens throughout the world (Clark and Hakim 2016). Simple ransomware attacks have crippled cities' government functions for months on end. These attacks are growing in frequency, though unfortunately, many go unreported. This creates a false sense of security about the threats and the repercussion on lives and property. This false sense of security further affects the resilience of individuals, organisations (small through to multinationals) and governments alike.

Several reports support the need for enhanced education for cyber disaster preparedness. A 2017 report for the US Government found that offerings in the country's universities were not adequately addressing even the technical aspects of resilience preparedness (McDermott 2017). It found that "Students in Computer Science and Electrical and Computer Engineering are not being sufficiently exposed to these concepts of security in CPS [cyber physical systems] enough to fulfil the competencies" needed for resilience (ibid.: 25). A 2014 report for the Department of Homeland Security reported that "Experts fear that existing techniques to understand technical and societal consequences of a cyber-disaster are insufficient, and we lack approaches to examine the interconnections" (S&TFC and DHS 2014). There is also awareness of the need in particular sectors, such as health (Rajamäki, Nevmerzhitskaya and Virág 2018).

Some universities and other educational institutions have responded but the examples suggest a fairly unimpressive level of recognition. For example, in a search of curriculum materials one can see that the University of Akron offers a whole certificate level program in Cyber Disaster Management, approved in 2018. It includes the following six courses:

- Introduction to Digital Forensics
- Cyber Warfare
- Principles of Emergency Management and Homeland Security
- Introduction to Terrorism
- Intelligence: Cyber and Homeland Security
- Cyber Issues in Emergency Management and Homeland Security.[1]

The University of Alaska Fairbanks offers a bachelor's degree in emergency management, in which one of five possible specialisations is cyber.[2] A professional cyber academy in Mumbai offers a certification in Cyber Disaster Management and

Cyber Incident Response.[3] There is not a large number of peer programmes, though individual course of high relevance can be found. For example, the Emergency Management Institute of the Federal Emergency Management Agency (FEMA) has a three-hour course in "Exercising Continuity Plans for Cyber Incidents".[4] A search of the National Initiative for Cybersecurity Careers and Studies (NICCS) database reveals 92 training programmes in forces in disaster recovery that have some cyber elements.[5] Of these, 50 are classroom-based, and less than 10 are delivered by universities. One of the most relevant appears to be the Certified Disaster Recovery Engineer course offered by Mile-2.[6] This course has nine generic modules for disaster recovery or business continuity, and two are more specific: Cyber Attack and Pandemic. Another relevant course is "Cyber Crisis Management Planning Professional (C2MP2) Certification Boot Camp", offered by a private consulting and training firm in Arizona.[7] Gujurat Technical University in India offers a course in Cyber Disaster Management and Recovery in a two-year Master's programme in Electrical Engineering for cyber security.[8]

## Cyber disaster risk: taxonomy before education

Cyberspace is the primary domain for communications and commerce globally, and as a result, the challenge to protect digital assets will grow quickly and continually. Researchers at the International Institute for Strategic Studies (IISS) in London have highlighted the scale of the stakes by referencing the volume (the value) of daily trades that depend on a secure and well-functioning cyberspace: US$8 trillion per day in foreign currency exchange instruments alone (Austin 2020b). Discussion of "national security" and cyberspace often gravitates towards government, military and intelligence actors. Excluded from the discussion are government, industry and academia stakeholders who create economic wealth and social well-being. These key players are often left both vulnerable to cyber threats and unable to contribute their capabilities to the effort (Scully 2014).

Many governments have only recently focused on the major cyber threat and vulnerabilities that their nations and the global economy face. In 2018, former Australian Prime Minister Malcom Turnbull stated, "We must not and will not wait for a catastrophic cyber incident before we act to prevent future attacks" (Australian Cyber Security Centre 2018a). Yet even governments which have moved to recognise the threat of national cyber incidents have not yet moved as comprehensively as they should have, to develop an agreed taxonomy for such threats (see Austin 2020a). Before we can think about education strategies for cyberspace professionals to address cyber crises, we need to know the framework in which these events will be managed. It will be critical to focus on the proven (non-cyber) disaster recovery mechanisms in place in each local, regional or national setting and adapt them for the digital age.

The taxonomy of a cyber crisis will be threat-determined. Threats in cyberspace originate from a diverse range of actors with varying motives. These include financial and economic gain, personal advantage and revenge, political/military/social advantage or change and corporate or nation state-sponsored espionage. Actors may include interested individuals (hackers), employees, contractors or business partners, cyber criminals, hacktivists, cyber criminals, nation states and nation state-backed advanced persistent threats (APT). These attacks constitute a significant, diverse and rapidly escalating risk element in the global environment. These susceptibilities have a significant potential to inflict widespread harm on targeted countries and possibly globally (Rudner 2013).

To mitigate such events, it is critical to review all potentially affected areas and use risk and emergency management strategies to develop appropriate frameworks. Key areas to focus on will include:

- probability
- consequences
- impact
- human factors
- safety
- mitigation
- cost
- complexity
- exposure
- capacity
- acceptability
- liability.

One critical factor is to shift the focus from events to recovery objectives. It is then possible to consider and plan for anticipated risks as well as build capabilities to handle unanticipated events (Siegel 2018). These aspects should be addressed at all levels of government and organisations within an appropriate framework. As a situation arises, these factors must be considered in ensuring an appropriate response to the event (Manson 2018).

## Strengthening governance and management

It is critical during and after cyber disasters that appropriate governance and management practices are followed. It is essential that clear methodologies from risk and emergency management are established and are used to prepare and respond to cyber disasters. They are characterised by national-level, multi-agency and private sector involvement, evolving priorities, and the exertion of time pressure on responsible cyber emergency management personnel tasked with making risk decisions in the absence of complete, accurate and unequivocal information (Albanese and Paturas 2018). See Table 7.1.

During cyber disaster events it is critical that the right information gets to the right people to ensure appropriate decisions are made. The information required to make sound decisions always includes the following: location, time, cause and

**TABLE 7.1** The four Rs of cyber resilience

| | |
|---|---|
| Reduction | Identify and analyse risk to critical infrastructure, systems and other priority factors such as risk to human life, etc. Take steps to eliminate risk to reduce magnitude of impact or likelihood of occurrence. |
| Readiness | Develop appropriate operational systems and capabilities, including self-help, responses for the public and develop specific programmes for all emergency services, utilities and relevant public/private organisations |
| Response | Action taken by all relevant parties to react and respond to cyber disaster |
| Recovery | Coordinated efforts and processes for immediate, medium- and long-term holistic regeneration |

severity of the incident, weather conditions, resource and personnel availability and how well response agencies work together to share information and resources, i.e. collaborate. The ability to discriminate between what is important and what is irrelevant information is vital for making decisions and implementing optimal response actions (ibid.).

Cyber disaster risk reduction requires an all-of-society engagement and partnership. Addressing underlying disaster risk factors through informed public and private investments is more cost effective than primary reliance on post-disaster response and recovery and contributes to sustainable development. Disaster risk reduction practices need to be inclusive and accessible in order to be efficient and effective (United Nations Office for Disaster Risk Reduction 2015). It is essential to have clear roles and responsibilities when responding to an event. This increases the chances of withstanding the adverse impacts. Coordinated approaches are required. People should know exactly what to do to help manage the situation and support the overall decision-making process.

Proper communications protocols and clear escalation and reporting paths are also necessary so response teams can focus on resolving the situation without various stakeholders interrupting them with demands for situation updates. It is also critical to have appropriate levels of triage, similar to the medical field, to prioritise key areas of response. Each level of priority will have different actors involved to respond appropriately and effectively to each individual situation. These levels will be on an organisational, sector/industry, local through to national scale, each with their own escalation processes (Drachal 2017).

## Investment in cyber disaster reduction for resilience

With the rapid development within the technological world, new essential life skills have formed: cyber foundations and digital literacy. It is imperative that a generational change is implemented. This includes these new skills being taught in schools and tertiary education institutions to develop the new cyber workforce.

A radical rethink of the current processes of educating our school students, tertiary education students and the general public is needed. We need to understand the current cohort of students will be our future digital workforce. It is critical that current leaders focus strategically on developing solutions for the medium to long term and not on immediate solutions. It is essential to educate the public on what they can do to protect themselves generally and the steps that should be taken in the event of a cyber disaster (ibid.).

Digital literacy is just as important as having a grasp on cyber foundations, as they go hand in hand in developing a holistic knowledge base for the digital age. Only when we develop an appropriate level of understanding within the general population can we move towards a more cyber-resilient society and ultimately the new cyber workforce.

As observed in a study on the cyber security skills crisis (Henry 2017), key messages reiterated from current research define the importance of the purpose of the cyber security education and the importance of frameworks (models) for enhancing education and awareness (AustCyber 2018). Typically, this research offers a critical view of the current curricula and the input/output method of education for cyber security which is universally seen as inadequate (Conklin, Cline and Roosa 2014). There is a clear requirement for investment in cyber security education by all governments. It is essential we educate, train and develop cyber security professionals (and all individuals) with the required multidisciplinary skill sets that can protect against cyber threats and vulnerabilities.

For courses to remain relevant, teaching and learning methods should continuously be updated and content must be consistent with industry's new direction. Academics have suggested the relationship between industry and universities needs to be improved, particularly with respect to the development of industry-integrated curricula (Koppi et al. 2008).

This requires an understanding not only of the purpose of the course for the university, but also of the purpose and relevance to the students undertaking the course (Armstrong, Dodge and Armstrong 2013). High quality cyber security programmes need to differentiate between the multidisciplinary aspects of courses and the unique requirements for each course. There is a need for a whole variety of academic degree programmes in cyber security from technical aspects through to courses based on psychology, criminal justice, business, humanities and social sciences (i.e. policy and economics) and more.

The scope of cyber security education must also include programmes for computing professionals and operations staff as well as for the good of the public and the needs of society (McGettrick 2014). A strong technical-based curriculum requires hands-on activities including the use of cyber ranges, simulations and war games. Wide-ranging technical courses are necessary to produce high-quality graduates who can develop into cyber security experts.

To address these problems, the academic community needs to restructure their curricula. Many have a grim view whereby universities only provide cyber security education from the university perspective (Lehto 2016). This is true for many universities, but there are some institutions moving towards industry partnerships to enhance the effectiveness of their programmes as a differential for potential students. This type of cooperation and collaboration is vital for the effectiveness of cyber security educational programmes in general.

There are issues to be addressed to ensure education pathways do not focus solely on organisational cyber security. Austin (2018) proposed setting up a cyber war college because universities cannot deliver this by themselves, and certainly government or the private sector cannot (Austin 2016). This is something to consider. There is a current need for national training facilities that provide high-level simulation capabilities, available at an unclassified level to institutions in the civil sector, police and other public and private institutions. The aim of all the initiatives is to train, equip and provide highly skilled forces responsive to the needs of the nation.

There needs to be further education pathways for cyber disaster response and emergency management. This is a clear area of need in which all cyber security professionals should have an understanding, but it is most critical for policy-makers and governments to ensure effective and informed decision-making. New education pathways are required to develop the necessary workforce to effectively respond to a cyber disaster. This type of national institution would specialise in key areas of importance in cyber security, such as disaster response and recovery and other key requirements such as military cyber education development. This is a completely new form of civil defence, and it may need a new form of organisation to carry it forward. Another potential solution could be a new, dedicated arm of an existing agency, such as emergency services organisations.

## Enhancing cyber disaster preparedness for effective response and recovery

There are many good initiatives that have been established to look at how to respond to major cyber events. These include local through to national strategies and international exercises to test processes and procedures. Reviewing and learning from these exercises help develop effective resilience and areas for improvement. Key to an effective strategy is having a blueprint or a cyber playbook to review current posture, detailing how to effectively address the issues found, and develop an understanding of existing capabilities and functions in terms of people, processes and technologies (Clay 2015).

A cyber disaster blueprint needs to focus on these areas:

- The critical aspects of dealing with a cyber disaster, including ensuring adequate education and awareness between all stakeholders and the general public.
- Assessing cyber resilience for a cyber incident is not a one-size-fits-all exercise. Different levels of government have unique circumstances (strategies, budgets, maturity levels and appetite) that must be scrutinised and rationalised as a first step.
- A comprehensive stocktaking of existing information and communication technology (ICT) and cyber security infrastructure and capabilities to identify strengths and weaknesses.

- Testing the assumption that all existing government institutions, policy-making apparatus and operational agencies are "fit for purpose" when dealing with the cyber threat.
- Importantly, the blueprint would assess the ideological, political, economic, social and cultural factors that would influence subsequent decision-making (Scully 2014).

Ultimately the blueprint would be executed as follows.

- Development of a consistent approach in the application and overarching cyber disaster management framework, encompassing organisational, sector/industry, for all levels of government.
- Development and implementation of key measures and activities that support the framework, including appropriate oversight and coordination in the public sector, industry and academia.
- Development of information-sharing mechanisms, including industry-based, government and organisational information-sharing between all bodies.
- Development of a programme to continue to develop the cyber foundations and digital education of the population.
- Further investigation and development of specific cyber disaster management education.
- International participation and cooperation in the area of cyber security (Galinec, Možnik and Guberina 2017).

It is essential all levels of government work together to address the issue. Beyond this, it is imperative to undertake simulations, exercises and develop appropriate policy and legislation, where required, to ensure organisations are taking appropriate steps.

## What can be done?

In Australia, there have been major movements to address these critical areas. The State, Territory and Federal Governments have been working closely together to address these items. This work is in the early stages, but many successes have been achieved in developing and implementing principles at the government level. Linking the different levels of governments' digital and cyber strategies is an adequate step in addressing their requirements of the blueprint and outcomes.

At a national level, the Council of Australian Governments (COAG) in 2018 released the Cyber Incident Management Arrangements (CIMA). The aim of the CIMA for Australian governments is to reduce the scope, impact and severity of national cyber incidents. The CIMA seeks to provide Australian governments with guidance on how they will collaborate in response to, and reduce the harm associated with, national cyber incidents. This is in line with the blueprint of cross-jurisdictional collaboration.

The CIMA document states that the benefits of strong strategic inter-jurisdictional coordination include:

- improved situational awareness across jurisdictions, which increases the effectiveness and timeliness of response activities
- potential to prevent a national cyber incident from escalating to a national crisis
- more efficient use of jurisdictional response resources, and
- consistent public information from Australian governments to business and the community, to promote confidence and contain the potential spread of a cyber incident (Australian Cyber Security Centre 2018b).

At the state level, the New South Wales (NSW) Government released a cyber policy which states the requirement that all NSW State Government entities must submit a report that outlines each entity's assessment against the Australian Cyber Security Centre's Essential 8, outline cyber security risks with ratings and must identify an entity's "crown jewels". This document is to be submitted by the entity's head. Entities are also required to have a "current cyber security response plan" that is tested at least every year and integrates with the government-wide cyber incident response plan (NSW Government 2018).

The key areas outlined are:

- empower – assist frontline organisations to respond rapidly
- one voice – one key point of contact ensuring consistency, accuracy and reliability
- timely – promote critical information to reduce impending or emerging activity
- understand – how does it rate against identified risk?
- coordinate – clear identification of lead entities
- support – information and specialist skills sharing
- continuous – reassessment during incidents
- share – situational awareness and experiences.

Another example is the U.S. Government's Cyber Storm exercise. The focus outlined by the U.S. Government states the main objectives of the Cyber Storm are:

- exercising coordination mechanisms, information sharing efforts, development of shared situational awareness, and decision-making procedures of the cyber incident response community
- evaluate relevant policy, statutory, and fiscal issues that govern cyber incident response authorities and resource prioritisation
- provide a forum for exercise participants to exercise, evaluate, and improve the processes, procedures, interactions, and information sharing mechanisms within their organisation or community of interest
- assess the role, functions, and capabilities of Department of Homeland Security and other government entities in a cyber event (US Department of Homeland Security 2016).

Some of the lessons learnt from such exercises demonstrate the need for a cyber disaster blueprint. Some findings in Cyber Storm V are the importance of a national-level plan with widespread buy-in, adoption and integration and that information sharing challenges still impact disasters with liability and the speed of the information sharing (ibid.).

These initiatives are being established and provide valuable starting points, but there are still areas that must be addressed to move forward. These include the formalisation of arrangements for collaboration with identified non-governmental partners – particularly the business sector, but also researchers and large non-profit entities and international partners. In this context, critical infrastructure providers, such as electricity companies, should be among the first businesses targeted for collaboration due to the scale of potential fallout if they came under attack. This will be up to governments and relevant critical infrastructure providers to develop and negotiate. This is no easy task as these processes may be subject to competing budget priorities, political appetite, divergent levels of cyber maturity, and, most importantly, staffing requirements (Austin and Henry 2018).

## Conclusion

It is critical that nations start focusing on cyber disaster blueprints and frameworks. Developing an effective cyber response and resilience is a task that requires attention from organisations, academia and all levels of government. This is a major undertaking but using the existing literature and best practice in risk and emergency management principles enables a structured response.

The current cyberspace climate is complicated by multiple factors that work against developing an effective cyber workforce that can effectively react to a major cyber event. A dire skills shortage threatens to see all nations fall behind in the digital economy. It is not just technical skills that are required. The multi-faceted and multidisciplinary skill sets associated with cyber security and digital literacy become more essential. Expertise in areas such as policy development, regulation, privacy and law are becoming a primary focus for organisations boards and governments alike.

Governments need to ensure there is open exchange of information and active engagement at all levels. Government, industry and academia need to work together to develop appropriate frameworks, policies and initiatives. This needs to be complemented and tested through active exercises and simulations. This ensures there are opportunities for collaboration and the holistic integration of cyber disaster risk management practices. These steps, while time-consuming and costly, will ultimately enable nations to effectively participate in the digital economy.

Education in cyber disaster management needs to be a component of any nation's blueprint and strategic focus. A focus on the education and awareness requirements on the above points will ultimately lead to a cyber-resilient economy.

## Notes

1 See https://bulletin.uakron.edu/undergraduate/colleges-programs/applied-science-technol ogy/disaster-science-emergency-services/cyber-disaster-management-certificate/.
2 See www.bestmedicaldegrees.com/best-value-online-bachelors-of-emergency-managem ent-degrees/.
3 See http://130.211.254.80/cyberjureacademy.com/?page_id=3138.
4 See https://training.fema.gov/is/courseoverview.aspx?code=IS-523.
5 See https://niccs.us-cert.gov/training/search?keyword=disaster&distance%5Borigin%5D=& distance%5Bdistance%5D=&items_per_page=20.
6 See https://niccs.us-cert.gov/training/search/mile2/mile2-certified-disaster-recovery-engineer-cdre.
7 "As a certified Cyber Crisis Management Planning Professional (C²MP²), you will have the knowledge to help organizations prepare for a major cyber crisis by leading the development of an integrated plan that serves not only IT, but also functional business and operational groups required to maintain resilience."
8 See www.gtu.ac.in/school_Eng_Tec.aspx.

## References

Afshar, V. 2017. Cisco: Enterprises Are Leading the Internet of Things Innovation. *Huffpost*. Available at: www.huffpost.com/entry/cisco-enterprises-are-leading-the-internet-of-things_b_59a41fcee4b0a62d0987b0c6.

Albanese, J. and J. Paturas. 2018. The Importance of Critical Thinking Skills in Disaster Management. *Journal of Business Continuity & Emergency Planning* 11(4): 326–334.

Armstrong, H., R. Dodge and C. Armstrong. 2013. Reaching Today's Information Security Students. *Information Assurance and Security Education and Training*. Available at: http://link.springer.com/chapter/10.1007%2F978-3-642-39377-8_25.

AustCyber. 2018. Cyber Security Training. Australian Cyber Security Growth Network. Available at: www.austcyber.com/training.

Austin, G. 2016. Australia Rearmed! Future Needs for Cyber-Enabled Warfare. Australian Centre for Cyber Security, UNSW Canberra. ACCS Discussion Paper #1. Available at: www.unsw.adfa.edu.au/unsw-canberra-cyber/sites/accs/files/uploads/DISCUSSION%20PAPER%20AUSTRALIA%20REARMED.pdf.

Austin, G. 2018. *From Cyber Skills to Resilient Cyberspace Talent: Advance Australia!* Paper presented at ACSC 2018, 12 April 2018. Available at: www.unsw.adfa.edu.au/unsw-canberra-cyber/sites/accs/files/uploads/ACSC%20Presentation%202018.pdf.

Austin, G. (ed.). 2020a. *National Cyber Emergencies: The Return to Civil Defence*. London: Routledge.

Austin, G. 2020b. The Geopolitics of Business in Cyberspace: Is Decoupling Possible?Seminar presentation, International Institute for Strategic Studies, London, 22 January 2020.

Austin, G. and A. Henry. 2018. New Guidelines for Responding to Cyber Attacks Don't Go Far Enough. *The Conversation*. 18 December. Available at: https://theconversation.com/new-guidelines-for-responding-to-cyber-attacks-dont-go-far-enough-108908.

Australian Cyber Security Centre. 2018a. A New Approach to Support Cyber Security. Available at: www.cyber.gov.au/news/new-ism-2018.

Australian Cyber Security Centre. 2018b. Cyber Incident Management Arrangements for Australian Governments. Available at: www.cyber.gov.au/sites/default/files/2019-03/cima_2018_A4.pdf.

British High Commission. 2018. Australia-United Kingdom Cyber Statement. Available at: www.gov.uk/government/news/australia-united-kingdom-cyber-statement.

Clark, R.M. and S. Hakim (eds). 2016. *Cyber-Physical Security: Protecting Critical Infrastructure at the State and Local Level*. New York: Springer [e-book].

Clay, P. 2015. A Modern Threat Response Framework. *Network Security* 4: 5–10. Available at: www.sciencedirect.com/science/article/abs/pii/S135348581530026X.

Conklin, W., R. Cline and T. Roosa. 2014. *Re-engineering Cybersecurity Education in the US: An Analysis of the Critical Factors*. Paper presented at 47th Hawaii International Conference on System Sciences. Available at: http://ieeexplore.ieee.org/stamp/stamp.jsp?reload=true&arnumber=6758852.

*Cybercrime Magazine*2018. Cybercrime Damages $6 Trillion by 2021. Available at: https://cybersecurityventures.com/hackerpocalypse-cybercrime-report-2016/.

Drachal, M. 2017. Coordinating Management Disciplines to Build Operational Resilience in Response to a Major Crisis Situation. *Journal of Business Continuity & Emergency Planning* 11(4): 174–183.

European Commission. 2019. Rules for the Protection of Personal Data Inside and Outside the EU: Data Protection. Available at: https://ec.europa.eu/info/law/law-topic/data-protection_en.

Galinec, D., D. Možnik and B. Guberina. 2017. Cybersecurity and Cyber Defence: National Level Strategic Approach. *Automatika*, 58(3): 273–286.

Henry, A. 2017. Mastering the Cyber Security Skills Crisis: Realigning Educational Outcomes to Industry Requirements. ACCS Discussion Paper #4, Australian Centre for Cyber Security, UNSW Canberra. Available at: www.unsw.adfa.edu.au/unsw-canberra-cyber/sites/accs/files/uploads/ACCS-Discussion-Paper-4-Web.pdf.

Johnson, T. (ed.). 2015. *Cybersecurity: Protecting Critical Infrastructures from Cyber Attack and Cyber Warfare*. New York: Routledge.

Koppi, A., F. Naghdy, J. Chicharo, J. Sheard, S. Edwards and D. Wilson. 2008. *The Crisis in ICT Education: An Academic Perspective*. Paper presented at Annual Conference of the Australasian Society for Computers in Learning in Tertiary Education. Available at: http://ro.uow.edu.au/infopapers/901.

Lehto, M. 2016. Cyber Security Education and Research in Finland's Universities and Universities of Applied Sciences. *International Journal of Cyber Warfare and Terrorism (IJCWT)* 6(2):15–31. doi:10.4018/IJCWT.2016040102.

Manson, B. 2018. Understanding Risk in an Emergency Management Context. *Journal of Business Continuity & Emergency Planning* 12(1): 27–39.

McDermott, T. 2017. Human Capital Development – Resilient Cyber Physical Systems. Technical Report. SERC-2017-TR-113. Systems Engineering Research Center, Stevens Institute of Technology. 29 September. Available at: https://apps.dtic.mil/dtic/tr/full text/u2/1040186.pdf.

McGettrick, A.et al. 2014. Toward Curricular Guidelines for Cybersecurity. In *Proceedings of the 45th ACM Technical Symposium on Computer Science Education*, pp. 81–82.

Morgan, S. 2019. Humans on the Internet Will Triple from 2015 to 2022 and Hit 6 Billion. *Cybercrime Magazine*. Available at: https://cybersecurityventures.com/how-many-internet-users-will-the-world-have-in-2022-and-in-2030/.

NSW Government. 2018. Mandatory Requirements. Available at: www.digital.nsw.gov.au/policy/cyber-security-policy/mandatory-requirements.

NSW Government. 2019. NSW Cyber Security Policy. Available at: www.digital.nsw.gov.au/sites/default/files/NSW%20Government%20Cyber%20Security%20Policy.pdf.

Rajamäki, J., J. Nevmerzhitskaya and C. Virág. 2018. *Cybersecurity Education and Training in Hospitals: Proactive Resilience Educational Framework (Prosilience EF)*. Paper presented at 2018 IEEE Global Engineering Education Conference (EDUCON), Tenerife. Available at: https://ieeexplore.ieee.org/abstract/document/8363488.

Rudner, M. 2013. Cyber-Threats to Critical National Infrastructure: An Intelligence Challenge. *International Journal of Intelligence and CounterIntelligence* 26(3): 453–481.

S&TFC and DHS. 2014. US-UK Collaboration on Resilience and Security. Summary Report from November 17–18, 2014. Working Meeting, Science and Technology Facilities Council (UK) and Department of Homeland Security. Available at: www.dhs.gov/sites/default/files/publications/ColoRS_Working_Meeting_Report.pdf.

Scully, T. 2014. A Cyber-Resilience Blueprint for ASEAN. East Asia Forum. 20 December. Available at: www.eastasiaforum.org/2014/12/20/a-cyber-resilience-blueprint-for-asean/.

Siegel, M. 2018. Building Resilient Organisations: Proactive Risk Management in Organisations and Their Supply Chains. *Journal of Business Continuity and Emergency Planning* 11(4): 373–384.

United Nations Office for Disaster Risk Reduction. 2015. Sendai Framework for Disaster Risk Reduction. Available at: www.undrr.org/publication/sendai-framework-disaster-risk-reduction-2015-2030.

US Department of Homeland Security. 2016. Cyber Storm V: National Cyber Exercise. Available at: www.cisa.gov/cyber-storm-v-national-cyber-exercise.

Warner, M. 2018. Cybersecurity: Unis and TAFEs Can Fill the Gap. *The Australian*, 27 February. Available at: https://amp.theaustralian.com.au/business/technology/cybersecurity-unis-and-tafes-can-fill-the-gap/new-story/27551e3844d8a5269ed32d6eb7e7f4b0.

WEF. (World Economic Forum). 2019. *The Global Risks Report 2019*. Available at: www3.weforum.org/docs/WEF_Global_Risks_Report_2019.pdf.

# 8

# NEW KINDS OF LEADERSHIP SKILLS FOR WINNING PEACE IN THE FOURTH INDUSTRIAL REVOLUTION

*Daria Daniels Skodnik*

The world has seen decades of civil wars fuelled by geopolitical competition between major powers. Russia's 2014 split with the West over Ukraine and hybrid warfare against its former Western partner countries is ending Russia's "centuries-long quest to join the West and preparing for 100 years (200? 300?) of geopolitical solitude," as expressed by President Putin's long-time advisor Vladislav Surkov (RFE/RL 2018). China is steadily rising to become a global leader in terms of national strength and international influence. Revived populism and nationalism in Europe are further stranding international relations and multilateral arrangements. Emerging and advanced technologies increase the complexity of our strategic environment, adding unprecedented challenges to the existing security threat landscape.

In the midst of such a highly complex strategic environment, the Fourth Industrial Revolution[1] is marking not only accelerating technological and scientific progress with an overwhelmingly positive impact on society, but also borderless security shocks created by the ingrained "malware" threatening with immeasurable consequences and disruptive effects on a global scale. Specifically, new technologies hold an ominous promise to accelerate further existing enmities by foreign aggression and coercion using modern tools in new warfighting domains. The pace of change and disruption is accelerating across all five warfighting domains: land, air, sea, cyberspace and outer space. Particularly in the cyberspace, in which everything and everybody is intrinsically joined and instantaneously susceptible to multiple "butterfly effects".[2] A combination of geopolitics within the great powers' competition and the manifestation of the unprecedented capacity of new technologies will be the driving force of future wars.

The current security landscape, distinct from the past, is marked by sustained cyberwarfare launched in a "grey zone" of cyberspace, a zone between war and peace, where aggression and coercion persist just below the level that risks military confrontation. This on-going warfare can be labelled in multiple ways, e.g., Hybrid Warfare, Asymmetric Warfare, Digital Cold War with underlined East-West divide, Cyberwar, Codewar, or even "flash war" when AI capabilities apply to the strategic environment (Price, Walker and Wiley 2018). However labelled, we can agree that is not quite a war and no death casualties have been reported to date. Until now, cyber attacks perpetrated either by states or by criminal groups and individuals have never risen to the level of acts of war, despite disruptive waves across cyberspace. Nevertheless, the cyber attacks recorded so far hold the promise of a dire future. Therefore, they need to be perceived as a wake-up call for institutional adaptation to secure and defend against such unprecedented threats with a possible magnitude generating multiple "cyber storms". The remaining missing element for a perfect storm to be imagined we find in artificial intelligence (AI). Its militarised use increases the probability of "hyperwar", a term coined by General John R. Allen,[3] US Marine Corps (Ret.), alluding to the fact that unparalleled speed enabled by automated decision-making and instantaneous deployment of autonomous weapons systems will fundamentally change the character of warfare and war itself.

## The changing geopolitical context

The revived competition between the great powers to dominate in multiple domains of technological advances and to project power across spheres of interest, defines a new geopolitical momentum. More than ever, great powers' politics will drive events, and international rivalries will be decided by the relative capacity of their militaries, their capabilities and, above all, their human capital (Kotkin 2018).

In relation to great powers' politics and under escalating economic, political and military competition, security concerns have risen to an unprecedented level. The great powers' technological advances and related strength elevated by wide-ranging modernisation of their military forces further enable their global impact. Furthermore, the threat landscape is most likely to expand and accelerate, depending on technological innovation. The use of new technologies will challenge nations to alter their defence posture and heighten their military forces' competitiveness. In addition, the great powers have made the cyber domain a highly contested space and a medium that reflects the hostile relationships between them.

The 2017 United States National Security Strategy maintains that, in addition to the threats posed to the United States by rogue regimes and violent extremist organisations that have been a central focus of national security policy since the end of the Cold War, great power rivalry and competition have once again become a central feature of the security landscape (McInnis 2017; White House 2017). Relative to the threats posed by China and Russia, the 2018 United States National Defense Strategy maintains that "inter-state strategic competition, not terrorism, is now the primary concern in U.S. national security" (DoD 2018). French President Macron called for a European Army to protect the continent from China and Russia, and the United States, and wants to build a self-sustainable defence apart from NATO (Meixler 2018). German Foreign Minister, Heiko Maas, called for deeper European defence integration and has pushed for a broad European approach towards Russia (Maas 2018). The US President's policy of "America First", Russia's violations of international law and China's expansionist policies, are shaking the pillars of international liberal order.

The great powers' competition is forcefully unfolding in cyberspace, a domain of the global interconnected technologies. Cyber powers, i.e., the United States, China, Russia, Israel and the United Kingdom, and notable players like Iran and North Korea, all play a part. While China and Russia have very clearly powerful cyber capabilities, North Korea and Iran and some non-state actors are penetrating deep into cyberspace and are contesting it as well.

Undeniably, Russia is one of the two major nuclear weapon states, has a permanent seat on the UN Security Council, and is willing and able to use its military force and engage cyber capabilities in support of its policies (Haas 2018). Russian cyber warfare against Estonia in 2007 set a precedent, making cyberspace a warfighting domain. Russia's employment of cyber attacks, psychological warfare and influencing campaigns, in support of its kinetic power during the war with Georgia in 2008 and in an on-going war with Ukraine since 2014, is seen as "a laboratory to perfecting new forms of warfare" (Greenberg 2017).

One of the central elements of Russian foreign policy for decades has been a category of activities known as "active measures". Active measures campaigns encompass a range of activities that include the media, the use of forgeries, political influence campaigns, the funding of extremist and opposition groups, and directed cyber attacks. Russia has proven to have powerful cyber capabilities that are used aggressively by the Military Intelligence Directorate (GRU) and its collaborators against the West[4] and its spheres of interest. As an example, GRU can effortlessly spread disinformation to particular audiences, quickly test the effectiveness of the messages, and use social "bots" and other modes of automation to multiply their reach dramatically (Galeotti 2017).

It is worth mentioning the "NotPetya" 2017 cyber attacks, a significant indicator of Russia's capabilities. As a new piece of malware hit Ukrainian companies, it has since been dubbed NotPetya, in part because it originally bore an intentional resemblance to encrypting ransomware called Petya. The malware was introduced by Russia into the Ukrainian Internet as part of the Kremlin's on-going attempt to further destabilise Ukraine through enormous sabotage to the state's systems. The virus hit the Ukrainian energy companies and it quickly spread internationally, hitting a Danish power company and moved around the globe. Although Ukraine appeared to be the initial target of the attack, generating suspicions that Russia was to blame, the attack spread worldwide, causing billions of dollars in damage across Europe, Asia, and the Americas. The Russian experiment in Ukraine was successful, blindsiding the machine learning algorithms that otherwise recognise abnormalities (Tucker 2018). There is a widespread belief that NotPetya was a Russian dress rehearsal for an attack on the United States and the West.

Extensive Russian cyber capabilities employed against the United States and Western democracies have become an intrinsic part of warfare. There can be little doubt that Russia actively seeks to undermine the legitimacy of the American government, its capacity to act and its unity of purpose (Galeotti 2017). A roughly 200-page 2018 report, "Putin's Asymmetric Assault on Democracy in Russia and Europe: Implications for U.S. National Security", released by the Senate Foreign Relations Committee, describes in detail a Russian campaign against democratic governments in Europe and beyond (Senate Foreign Relations Committee 2018). It gives a global look at Russia's aims and methods, identifying "military invasions, cyber attacks, disinformation, support for fringe political groups and the weaponisation of energy resources, organized crime and corruption", as the tools employed by Moscow in its influence campaign. Both Russia and China have demonstrated that hybrid warfare, if not pushed too far, can achieve lasting results (*The* Economist 2018). "The strategic alignment between the two geopolitical rivals against the American threat would be the most dangerous scenario," warned Zbigniew Brzezinski. A nuclear superpower alongside an economic superpower is a matter of great concern that will have an impact on the military, economic and diplomatic power balance in the future (Allison 2018).

China's capacity to operate disruptive offensive capabilities is unrivalled in great power competition, and spans the entire spectrum of activities in the cyber domain as well as in space. Some fear China might target US drone operators sitting in their bunkers in the desert, or threaten the homeland with a mass cyber attack on the electric grid, water system, banking or medicine in order to deter the United States from intervening in a fight China may choose to engage. China's cyber corporate espionage runs in all directions, from the East China and South China Sea to the Indian Ocean to Central Asia and even to Africa and Latin America (Kotkin 2018). President Xi has emphasised the importance of accelerating China as a cyber superpower making rules in cyberspace (Kania 2018). To control the narrative, China uses the integrated employment of public opinion warfare, legal warfare, and psychological warfare (Erickson 2007), the force multipliers to material capabilities, reinforcing China's policies and its readiness for future wars (Kania 2018).

In 2018, the U.S. National Defense Strategy Commission analysed the U.S. Defense Strategy in the global geopolitical context (USNI 2018). The assessment was the starkest in the last two decades, exposing the limits of American military power due to diverging multiple security threats. Authoritarian competitors, especially China and Russia, are seeking regional hegemony and the means to project power globally. All adversarial powers, including Iran and North Korea, have developed more advanced cyber capabilities and innovatively employed asymmetric tactics. In multiple regions, intimidation and coercion, in the grey zone, have become the tool of choice for many. The Commission offered a possible scenario as US and NATO forces prepare to respond, Russia declares that a strike against Russian forces is taken as an attack on Russia itself, and a nuclear response is considered. The consequences, said the report, would be severe:

Major cities are paralyzed; use of the Internet and smartphones is disrupted. Financial markets plummet as commerce seizes up and online financial transactions slow to a crawl. The banking system is thrown into chaos. America's ability to defend its allies, its partners, and its own vital interests is increasingly in doubt.

The Commission calls on the nation to act promptly to remedy these circumstances, as the consequences will be grave and lasting (see also Brewster 2018).

As discussed above, the malware inserted in the state system nearly paralysed Ukraine as well as causing significant disruptions across the globe. These are recent and very relevant examples of the possible cyber destruction that can be meted out to a vulnerable society. Cyber attacks are becoming more widely employed by a number of potential adversaries and will accelerate further when enabled by new technologies. Expressed in Clausewitzian terms, "the continuation of political interaction with the addition of other means" is powerfully played out in the new warfighting domain of cyberspace (Singer and Emerson 2018).

## The Fourth Industrial Revolution and future wars

Exponential technological advances and the complexity and the velocity of new dynamic interconnected networks wired across cyberspace and spanning across the globe mark the Fourth Industrial Revolution. The general use of new technologies and techniques will be advantageous. However, multiple state and non-state actors use new technologies for political interference and economic gain, threatening national and international security.

The world's most powerful adversarial nations, Russia and China, have disclosed plans to accelerate the development of new technologies, focusing on AI, until 2035. China has vowed to equal the United States in AI within two years, overtake it by 2025 and become the dominant world force by 2030 (Zwetsloot, Toner and Ding 2018). China, taking an increasingly assertive attitude in public, is reinforcing years of its "peaceful rise" by building one of the most capable and well-funded militaries in the world to become a world-class military by 2049 (Manson 2018). President Xi Jinping called for China to embrace a "new era" and move "closer to center stage" while also calling on military commanders to prepare to fight a war (Friend and Thayer 2018). By focusing its best and brightest on new technologies, Russia has become the global leader in information and telecommunication systems, AI, robotic complexes, supercomputers, technical vision and pattern recognition, information security, nanotechnology, energy tech and the technology life support cycle, as well as bioengineering, biosynthetic, and biosensor technologies. In many respects, Russia is now the strongest country in the world, experts claim (Finch 2018). They also caution that Putin's message about AI dominance expressed as, "'whoever leads in AI will rule the world'", does not occur in a vacuum. The message to the world comes after "intense deliberations and intense experimentation" (Underwood 2018). An ambitious ten-point plan, released by officials in 2018, outlines key public-private partnerships calling for scientific research and development steps. Among its key projects is creating breakthrough technologies such as robotics, autonomous systems, AI prototypes in image recognition, imitating the human thought process, complex data analysis, AI training and education, and many others. The very fact such plans have been revealed deserves attention (Bendett 2018).

China's and Russia's revised strategies reflect plans to effectively integrate new technologies into state systems to gain advantage in the global balance of power. The convergence of hypercompetitive assertiveness and technological innovations in the field of, e.g. artificial intelligence, robotics, machine learning, quantum computing, nanotechnology, biology and bioengineering, will have unpredictable effects on security. Of all the technological advances, AI's impact on cyberspace capabilities, altering human systems, the autonomy of weapon systems, and the military use of outer space, are at the core of the security concerns of liberal democracies. Outer space is becoming more critical as nearly all aspects of national security depend on its stability. Although the Pentagon and other agencies sound alarms about threats to governments, militaries, space agencies, companies, they are reluctant to share any details about cyber attacks on satellites (Erwin 2018). Systems used by militaries, e.g., intelligence, surveillance, reconnaissance, communications systems, precision timing and navigation, attack warning and targeting systems against potential threats, are also exposed to possible attacks as well as civilian systems in space, e.g. global positioning systems, communications, and other services vital to a national economy, are vulnerable.

To consider how AI's transformative ways will affect the character, or conceivably the very nature of war, General John R. Allen, together with Amir Husain, introduced the concept of hyperwar (Allen and Husain 2018). They see hyperwar presenting itself when leading-edge technologies, especially autonomous weapons systems, will be used in strategic attacks leveraged by AI and machine cognition, at unparalleled speeds triggered by automated decision-making. The degree to which the concurrency of action can be achieved by using machine-based instantaneous decision-making will fuel hyperwar, outpacing the human factor. Additionally, a hypothesis persists about the challenge of technological singularity in which artificial super intelligence triggers runaway technological growth, causing limitless changes to human civilisation and eclipses the speed of human decision-making (Husain 2016), marking the point of singularity. It is for future leaders to pick up the argument and plan accordingly. As General Allen rightly argues, "We are only beginning to learn the extent of what conflict looks like in cyberspace" (2018).

The convergence of AI and AI systems will also fundamentally change the way we wage war. In his book entitled *Life 3.0*, Max Tegmark (2017) portrays what a human-machine war in a machine-controlled world would look like. In reality, if AI systems ever become "corrupt" and thus out of control, militaries will be first responders. For militaries, building the right system that is secured and controlled by humans will be vital. "Defense and military sectors need to be part of the most important conversation of our time", appealed Professor Stephen Hawking, "to ask the questions like, what can we do now to improve the chances of reaping the benefits of future AI and avoiding the risks?" To that extent, and in order to best prepare leaders for the demands of their time, professional military education (PME) is vital as the means to inform strategic discussion on AI's military use and its consequences.

There is another aspect to on-going warfare and the future of war, known also as hybrid warfare. The Russian Federation has redefined the meaning of full spectrum warfare, and its very essence is well captured by Valery Gerasimov, the Russian Chief of the General Staff in 2013:

> Wars are not declared but simply begin, so that a completely stable country could be transformed into an arena of the most intense armed conflict in a matter of months or even days. Military means are more effective when combined with non-military means, including political, economic, information, humanitarian and other measures. New information technologies play an important role. Social media is used to spread false messages and create misleading impressions to weaken opponents.
>
> *(Gerasimov 2013)*

The new and emerging security environment will demand different military structures and different leadership skills. Future wars will require the continuous integration of forces across multiple domains and converging capabilities. If considering the Army, the Air Force and the Navy acting together in the critical domains of cyberspace, it is obvious that a major shift in the mindset and military culture must take place to achieve complementarity in action. Thus, a combined comprehensive education process of PME is highly relevant (Townsend 2018).

In 2017, the U.S. Army created an experimental combat unit, a multi-domain task force for all domains of military operations, capable of space, cyber, maritime, air, and ground warfare. Such self-sufficient units offer a potential model for future forces. Furthermore, only combined multiple arms of state power can respond effectively to the challenges of the modern security environment. The multi-domain battlefield demands joint multi-domain military structures, including civilian assets. To achieve dominance across all warfighting domains will be a modern leadership challenge to ensure the alignment and employment of the nation's forces. Thus, the joint system of PME must be challenged to create and to reinforce the intellectual transformation of strategic leadership, taking into account highly complex, technologically advanced, multi-domain warfare.

Although we perceive warfare as a military matter, a balanced joint civilian and military response is needed. An answer to any crisis rests with an approach by the whole of government, even the whole of society. Unity of effort and purpose, through broad-based collaboration, will better secure connected systems in cyberspace. Thus, a successful collaboration calls for a coordinated process among defence, law enforcement, government agencies, the private sector, and academia, with priorities well set and based on the particular capabilities of each entity. A common threat perception and common awareness of possible threats will be the defining condition of this broader spectrum of collaboration. This presents itself as an important foundation for strategic political and military leadership to expand the use of national capabilities in a concerted effort.

That being said, military superiority will greatly rely not only on new technologies but also on human capital, and especially on the leaders' capacity to deal with emerging threats. Therefore, PME must support the reality on the ground by competently following the trends of the military profession. It is for PME to create the common intellectual platform for contemporary leadership and build up the necessary character of core leadership able and fit to take the lead in the most improbable circumstances.

## Professional military education to supply strategic leadership

In a complex and technologically advanced strategic environment, only an agile and adaptive leadership will serve effectively to safeguard the nation and consequently the international community. An organisation's integrity will depend on well-educated, open-minded and innovative leaders. PME plays a significant role in this regard. Given today's strategic environment and demand for specific skills and competencies necessary to be an effective leader, some changes to certain aspects of officers' education must be anticipated.

In a world that is lacking strategic leadership, integrity and character are the two attributes to be promoted in a future conscientious and self-assured leader. PME is best placed to promote education as a continuous life-long learning endeavour at all officers' ranks. Developing strategic thinking based on a comprehensive understanding of the strategic environment and fostering the ability to deal with surprise and unconventional warfare are necessary competencies. The capacity to build a narrative of a mission or situation and curate the real-time media coverage is gaining in importance with social media's overwhelming presence.

Developing military and civilian intellectual leadership skills to successfully deal with emerging challenges, within alliances or coalitions, remains the primary purpose and responsibility of PME. Leaders who can out-think adversaries, reconcile context, manage uncertainty, and surprise, and embrace change, will be the agents of much-needed decisive edge (Lamb and Porro 2015). In order to support such leadership development, it takes determination and the agility of PME leaders to remain highly responsive to new strategic environments, identify the leadership competencies required to confront them, and implement the change to PME accordingly.

The future operational environment will demand autonomous decision-making at every level. AI will shift the culture of future strategic leadership and improve the decision-making process by integrating information, data analytics, and providing insights. The main leadership challenge will be to optimise the response to multiple concurrent crises almost instantaneously (Aitoro 2018). As Amir Husain (2017) explains in his book *The Sentient Machine*, the enormity of the implications of AI lies in the challenge to our societal norms and deficient understanding of what role the artificial machine intelligence should play in the future. In the dawn of a new form of intellectual diversity, more than ever an intellectual edge is fundamental to establish a relationship between AI and *Homo sapiens*, argues Husain. One of the existential questions in the age of AI is about the intrinsic value of humans in an age where machines outwork and outthink humans. Developing a culture of independent strategic thinking will be of critical importance, and questions are rightly being asked about whether the existing system of PME, centred on the military and staff colleges, is suitable for the task.

The evolving technological advances in military affairs need strategic, creative and innovative thinking to analyse the problem and judge the action vs. training to perform specific tasks. Use of accelerated learning, extended reality (augmented reality, virtual reality, mixed reality), robotics and autonomous systems, machine learning, and other enabling technologies, techniques, and requirements, will drive what, why, and how we respond in contested environments and how we prepare for them through training and education. PME traditional military skills are rightly valued but cognitive skills, often called critical thinking, will be the most important attributes necessary to enhance the intellectual agility supportive of effective strategic decision-making.

Joint education should leave the student capable of dissecting security challenges and threats with an anatomical accuracy. Exercises and case studies with multiple crisis scenarios designed to face the new realities of today and the future remain essential for strategic problem-solving, encouraging adaptability and flexibility and readiness to act in uncertainty. Critical thinking with due respect for diversity and difference of opinion argued in a safe environment of PME further promotes strategic thinking and the communication skills necessary to efficiently communicate policy and explain strategy. The collective mindset is not to be underestimated but cultivated towards achieving a common purpose (Danielson 2018).

## Conclusion

In a world in which the exponential technological advances define our time, surprises are the new normal and no security strategy can account for every eventuality that may threaten a society. In response, defence and military sectors have to be at the forefront of major technological innovation and therefore inevitably subjected to transformational change. To lead and advance such a transformation, a highly capable, strategic leadership is critical. Only intellectually agile and adaptable leaders will be ready to lead the nation and especially its military forces when dealing with unprecedented and reoccurring attacks spread across multiple warfighting domains simultaneously.

Empowered and decentralised leadership is a new prerequisite in the decision-making scheme (Lopez 2017). PME's role is to foster the right mindset that will enable military leaders to act effectively in such a sensitive environment. The new era demands that all military ranks are pulled out of their tactical level trenches and are well informed up to the strategic level of war, including an adequate geopolitical context (Palazzo 2017).

Further integration of military forces will profoundly affect the military culture and demand a different strategic leadership. Accordingly, a modernisation of PME approach reflective of the need to achieve synergy across all warfighting domains needs to be examined. The ability to learn concurrently with the change, enhance and adapt structures, and to enable human interoperability, will be crucial in defining the future of nations.

At the pinnacle of recommendations, and an important requirement for PME to be unfailingly perceptive and thus effective, is the competent and comprehensively incorporated development of leaders' intellectual capacity based on scientific research of, e.g. human behaviour, perception, attention, cognition, especially of increasing decision-making accuracy, structuring educational curricula to enhance learning. Nowadays, the need to foster personal qualities, such as the innate drive to learn, adaptability, flexibility and focus, out-of-the-box thinking, and, above all, character, i.e. mental and moral qualities, informed by integrity and social skills, is decisive. Promoting the spirit of innovation and further the cultural shift necessary to fully embrace the future prospects of technological advances will be the driving force of change. Visionary PME curricula will support the development of those who must lead in these difficult and complex environments. To this end, PME curricula have to be constantly assessed for relevance and supervised by the finest academic and other institutions that are at the forefront of development in the above-mentioned areas of expertise. PME must possess human resources and state-of-the-art IT, creating an adequate infrastructure. The personnel systems must diligently select the finest, operationally capable officers and send them on these PME courses. In such an endeavour, one cannot emphasise enough the importance of the human factor (Cherry 2018).

"Each war is unique, a kind of synergy, rather than specific weapons alone, will deliver victories," argued General James Mattis, former U.S. Secretary of Defense (Manson 2018). "Such a shift needs a new military thinking to be tested, turning over vast amounts of data at speeds to reach life-and-death decisions," said Mattis. For the foreseeable future, humans will remain in control over AI. However, leaders will define the future by decisions made today. As stressed by Major General Kathryn Toohey, Head of the Australian Army's Land Capability: "Despite all of our technical advances, the profession of arms remains an inherently human one. Human domain has significant potential to address shortcomings in other domains" (Kimmons 2018).

The responsibilities of leadership will be widespread and will go deeper into the structures than ever before due to the speed of warfare and the mass disruptions caused by adversaries. Decision-making will be entrusted to leaders at all levels. Leaders, including junior ranks, in future warfare will be required to understand the overall context and the purpose of their deployment, and have the competence and confidence to take action to accomplish the mission purpose. The senior leadership will be required to convey the detailed mission data, including the purpose and the wider context, to inform such decision-making. Communication between leaders at all levels will reinforce understanding and further build trust, cohesiveness, and a culture of cooperation, adding to the resilience of strategic leadership and the nation they defend (Ostlund 2018).

These considerations bring us to the final questions that should be reflected in any national security and defence strategy: "What might the future hold for our species?" and "What will the future look like?" As in the book entitled *Homo Deus*, translated as "Human God", Yuval Noah Harari (2017) asks us to consider the next stage of human evolution that may not be human at all. Science may enable life to break out into the inorganic realm. Relevant to the defence sector is our ability to design not only the world around us, but also ourselves, argues Harari and he further questions: "Where is this leading us, and what do we want to become? And how will we protect this fragile world from our own destructive powers?"

The final thought, paraphrasing Professor Leon Megginson's adaption (1963: 4) of Charles Darwin, is: the issue for systems (like species) is always the same: it is not the strongest of the systems that survives, nor the most intelligent, but the one most adaptable to change.

## Notes

1  According to Schwab (2016): "The First Industrial Revolution used water and steam power to mechanize production. The Second used electric power to create mass production. The Third used electronics and information technology to automate production. Now a Fourth Industrial Revolution is building on the Third, the digital revolution that has been occurring since the middle of the last century. It is characterized by a fusion of technologies that is blurring the lines between the physical, digital, and biological spheres."
2  Based on Edward Lorenz's Chaos theory, a seemingly stable system can be exposed to very small influences resulting in nonlinear impacts on a complex system. "The things that change the world, according to Chaos theory, are the tiny things. A butterfly flaps its wings in the Amazonian jungle, and subsequently a storm ravages half of Europe." It is a classic example of how everything in the world is connected. In other words: "Does an extreme event affect societies across the globe?" (Farnham Street 2017).
3  General (Ret.) John R. Allen is current President of the Brookings Institution and former Commander of the NATO International Security Assistance Force and U.S. Forces – Afghanistan, 2011–2013, and the former Special Presidential Envoy for the Global Coalition to Counter Islamic State of Iraq and the Levant, 2014–2015, appointed by President Obama.
4  "West" meaning the liberal democracies of Europe, the United States, Canada and others, under attack by authoritarian powers, e.g., Russia, China, Iran and North Korea.

## References

Aitoro, J. 2018. The Chief of Naval Research on AI: 'If We Don't All Dogpile on This Thing We're Going to Find Ourselves Behind'. *C4ISRnet*. 6 November. Available at: www.c4isrnet.com/it-networks/2018/11/06/the-chief-of-naval-research-on-ai-if-we-dont-all-dogpile-on-this-thing-were-going-to-find-ourselves-behind/.

Allen, J. 2018. *Hyperwar*. Paper presented at SparkCognition. 22 January 2018, Available at: https://learn.sparkcognition.com/videos/tm17-hyperwar-gen-john-allen?utm_medium= orgsearch&utm_source=google.

Allen, R. J. and A. Husain. 2017. On Hyperwar. *US Naval Institute, Proceedings Magazine*, 143/7/1.373, July. Available at: www.usni.org/magazines/proceedings/2017-07/hyperwar.

Allison, G. 2018. China and Russia: A Strategic Alliance in the Making. *The National Interest*, 14 December. Available at: https://nationalinterest.org/print/feature/china-and-russia-stra tegic-alliance-making-38727.

Bendett, S. 2018. Here's How the Russian Military Is Organizing to Develop AI,.*Defense One*, 20 July. Available at: www.defenseone.com/ideas/2018/07/russian-militarys-a i-development-roadmap/149900/print/.

Brewster, M. 2018. Why the U.S. Could Lose the Next Big War and What That Means for Canada. *Canadian Broadcasting Commission*. 18 November. Available at: www.cbc.ca/ news/politics/defence-policy-trump-china-russia-1.4910038.

Cherry, K. 2018. The Basics of Human Factors Psychology: Maximizing Human Capabilities. *VerywellMind*, 4 November. Available at: www.verywellmind.com/what-is-human-fa ctors-psychology-2794905.

Danielsen T. 2018. A Small State's Special Operators, Up Close. *War on the Rocks*, 25 October. Available at: https://warontherocks.com/2018/10/a-small-states-special-opera tors-up-close/.

DoD. 2018. Summary of the 2018 National Defense Strategy of the United States of America; Sharpening the American Military's Competitive Edge. Available at: https://dod.defense. gov/Portals/1/Documents/pubs/2018-National-Defense-Strategy-Summary.pdf.

Erickson, A. S. 2007. An Accessible Window into Chinese Military Thought: The Science of Military Strategy. *Naval War College Review* 60(3). Available at: https://digital-comm ons.usnwc.edu/nwc-review/vol60/iss3/11.

Erwin, S. 2018. Sorry Sci-Fi Fans, Real Wars in Space Not the Stuff of Hollywood. *Space-news*2 January. Available at: https://spacenews.com/sorry-sci-fi-fans-real-wars-in-space-n ot-the-stuff-of-hollywood/?sthash.EAGThJrD.mjjo.

Farnham Street. 2017. Does an Extreme Event Affect Societies Across the Globe? Available at: https://fs.blog/2017/08/the-butterfly-effect/.

Finch, R. 2018. The Tenth Man: Russia's Era Military Innovation Technopark. Mad Scientist Laboratory, (blog). 20 August. Available at: http://madsciblog.tradoc.army.mil/77-the-tenth-man-russias-era-military-innovation-technopark/.

Friend, J. M. and B. A. Thayer. 2018. *How China Sees The World: Han-Centrism and the Balance of Power in International Politics*. New York: Potomac Books.

Galeotti, M. 2017. The 'Trump Dossier', Or How Russia Helped America Break Itself. *Tablet*, 13 June. Available at: www.tabletmag.com/jewish-news-and-politics/237266/ trump-dossier-russia-putin.

Gerasimov, V. 2013. Tsennost' nauki v predvidenii [The Value of Science in Prediction]. *Voenno-promyshlennyi kurier* [in Russian]. Trans. Mark Galeotti. 7 February. Available at: https://vpk-news.ru/sites/default/files/pdf/VPK_08_476.pdf.

Greenberg, A. 2017. How an Entire Nation Became Russia's Test Lab for Cyberwar. *Wired*20 June. Available at: www.wired.com/story/russian-hackers-attack-ukraine/.

Haas, R.N. 2018. *Cold War* II. Council on Foreign Relations. 23 February. Available at: www.cfr.org/article/cold-war-ii.

Harari, Y. N. 2017. *Homo Deus: A Brief History of Tomorrow*. New York: Harper.

Husain, A. 2016. AI on the Battlefield: A Framework for Ethical Autonomy. Forbes Tech-nology Council. 28 November. Available at: www.forbes.com/sites/forbestechcouncil/ 2016/11/28/ai-on-the-battlefield-a-framework-for-ethical-autonomy/#65c1f65c5cf2.

Husain, A. 2017. *The Sentient Machine: The Coming Age of Artificial Intelligence*. New York: Simon & Schuster.

Kania, E. B. 2018. The Right to Speak: Discourse and Chinese Power. Center for Advanced China Research. 27 November. Available at: www.ccpwatch.org/single-post/2018/11/ 27/The-Right-to-Speak-Discourse-and-Chinese-Power.

Kimmons, S. 2018. Second Phase of Multi-domain Task Force Pilot Headed to Europe. *AeroTech News*. Available at: www.aerotechnews.com/blog/2018/10/15/second-pha se-of-multi-domain-task-force-pilot-headed-to-europe/.

Kotkin, S. 2018. Realist World: The Players Change, but the Game Remains. *Foreign Affairs*. 14 June. Available at: www.foreignaffairs.com/articles/world/2018-06-14/realist-world.

Lamb, J. C. and B. Porro. 2015. Next Steps for Transforming Education at National Defense University. *JFQ* 76. Available at: https://apps.dtic.mil/dtic/tr/fulltext/u2/a618534.pdf.

Lopez, T. 2017. Future Warfare Requires 'Disciplined Disobedience', Army Chief Says. *U.S. Army*, 5 May. Available at: www.army.mil/article/187293/future_warfare_requires_discip lined_disobedience_army_chief_says.

Maas, H. 2018. Courage to Stand Up for Europe: #EuropeUnited. Speech by Foreign Minister Heiko Maas. German Federal Foreign Office. Berlin. 13 June. Available at: www.auswaertiges-amt.de/en/newsroom/news/maas-europeunited/2106528.

Manson, K. 2018. Robot-Soldiers, Stealth Jets and Drone Armies: The Future of War. *Financial Times*, 16 November. Available at: www.ft.com/content/442de9aa-e7a 0-11e8-8a85-04b8afea6ea3.

McInnis, J. K. 2017. The 2017 National Security Strategy: Issues for Congress. *CRS INSIGHT*. 19 December. Available at: https://fas.org/sgp/crs/natsec/IN10842.pdf.

Megginson, L. 1963. Lessons from Europe for American Business. *The Southwestern Social Science Quarterly* 44(1): 3–13.

Meixler, E. 2018. French President Emmanuel Macron Calls for a 'European Army' to Defend Against China, Russia and the U.S. *Time*, 7 November. Available at: http://time. com/5446975/emmanuel-macron-european-army-russia-us/.

Ostlund, W. 2018. On Trust and Leadership. Article Based on Interview with Army Chief of Staff Gen. Mark Milley. Modern War Institute at West Point. 9 December. Available at: https://mwi.usma.edu/on-trust-and-leadership/.

Palazzo, A. 2017. Multi-Domain Battle: Getting the Name Right. *Small Wars Journal* (website). Available at: https://smallwarsjournal.com/jrnl/art/multi-domain-battle-getting-name-right.

Price, M., S. Walker and W. Wiley. 2018. The Machine Beneath: Implications of Artificial Intelligence in Strategic Decisionmaking. *PRISM* 7(4): 93–105. Available at: https://cco. ndu.edu/News/Article/1681986/the-machine-beneath-implications-of-artificial-intelli gence-in-strategic-decisi/.

RFE/RL. 2018. Russia Faces 100 Years of Solitude (Or More), Putin Aide Says. 10 April. Available at: www.rferl.org/a/putin-adviser-surkov-says-russia-abandoning-hopes-integra ting-with-west-loneliness-isolation-/29155700.html.

Schwab, K. 2016. The Fourth Industrial Revolution: What It Means, How to Respond. World Economic Forum. 14 January. Available at: www.weforum.org/agenda/2016/01/ the-fourth-industrial-revolution-what-it-means-and-how-to-respond/.

Senate Foreign Relations Committee. 2018. Putin's Asymmetric Assault on Democracy in Russia and Europe: Implications for US National Security. A Minority Report. 10 Jan- uary. Available at: www.foreign.senate.gov/imo/media/doc/FinalRR.pdf.

Singer, P. W. and T. Emerson. 2018. What Clausewitz Can Teach Us about War on Social Media: Military Tactics in the Age of Facebook. *Foreign Affairs*, 4 October. Available at: www.foreignaffairs.com/print/1123057.

SparkCognition. 2019. SparkCognition Releases 'Hyperwar: Conflict and Competition in the AI Century'. 6 November. Available at: www.prnewswire.com/news-releases/spa rkcognition-releases-hyperwar-conflict-and-competition-in-the-ai-century-at-time-ma chine-2018-300744381.html.

Tegmark, M. 2017. *Life 3.0: Being Human in the Age of Artificial Intelligence*. New York: Knopf Publishing Group.

*The Economist.* 2018. Neither War Nor Peace: The Uses of Constructive Ambiguity. *The Economist.* Special Report. 25 January. Available at: www.economist.com/special-report/2018/01/25/neither-war-nor-peace.

Townsend, S. 2018. Accelerating Multi-Domain Operations: Evolution of an Idea. Modern War Institute. 23 July. Available at: https://mwi.usma.edu/accelerating-multi-domain-operations-evolution-idea/.

Tucker, P. 2018. White House Threatens Consequences for 2017 Russian Cyber Attack, *Defense One.* 15 February. Available at: www.defenseone.com/technology/2018/02/white-house-threatens-consequences-2017-notpetya-russian-cyber-attack/146046/.

Underwood, K. 2018. Russia Strengthening Focus on AI Technologies. *Signal.* 10 April. Available at: www.afcea.org/content/russia-strengthening-focus-ai-technologies.

USNI. 2018. Providing for the Common Defense: The Assessment and Recommendations of the National Defense Strategy Commission. *USNI News,* 14 November. Available at: https://news.usni.org/2018/11/14/document-the-assessment-and-recommendations-of-the-national-defense-strategy-commission.

Walsch, K. 2018. Artificial Intelligence Is Not a Technology. *Forbes.* 1 November. Available at: www.forbes.com/sites/cognitiveworld/2018/11/01/artificial-intelligence-is-not-a-technology/#3672d9cf5dcb.

White House. 2017. National Security Strategy of the United States of America 2017. 18 December. Available at: www.whitehouse.gov/wp-content/uploads/2017/12/NSS-Final-12-18-2017-0905.pdf.

Zwetsloot, R., H. Toner and J. Ding. 2018. Beyond the AI Arms Race: America, China, and the Dangers of Zero-Sum Thinking. *Foreign Affairs.* 16 November. Available at: www.foreignaffairs.com/reviews/review-essay/2018-11-16/beyond-ai-arms-race.

# 9

# TACKLING THE CYBER SKILLS GAP

## A survey of UK initiatives

*Monica Kaminska and Jantje Silomon*

Cyberspace has become a core building block of modern society, with the latest trend introducing an ever-increasing number of Internet-of-Things (IoT) devices into an underlying infrastructure already rife with vulnerabilities. While the focus has traditionally been on the physical and digital elements, the human aspects of education and training have often been an afterthought. Combined with the rapid growth of the domain and the increasingly complexity of cyber-physical systems, this has led to a skills gap that many countries are now seeking to address. This chapter will evaluate the initiatives taken in the UK over the last three years to address the skills gap and to develop a cyber-capable workforce, with an emphasis on educational institutions and programmes. These are grouped into three themes: (1) university teaching and research; (2) government strategies; and (3) cyber competitions and wargaming.

The first theme addresses the different approaches taken in academia. At postgraduate level, this includes three different, but not exclusive, aspects: (1) Academic Centres of Excellence in Cyber Security Research (ACE-CSRs); (2) National Cyber Security Centre (NCSC) Certified Degree Providers; and (3) Centres for Doctoral Training in Cyber Security (CDTs) (HMG 2018). This section will discuss the University of Oxford as a case study, focusing particularly on the Centre for Doctoral Training in Cyber Security. The CDT doctorate is a four-year programme in which the first year is taught, and the following three are research-based. The Oxford CDT had its first intake in 2013 and has an average intake of 16 students per year, with largely varying academic backgrounds and experiences. This section will analyse the benefits of a multidisciplinary approach to cyber security, as well as looking at the challenges of integrating such research agendas into traditional university structures.

The second theme, government strategies, examines the approach the UK has taken to fulfilling its commitment in the National Cyber Security Strategy to closing the cyber skills gap. This section will first present the plans the UK government presented in the latest National Cyber Strategy before moving on to discussing the provision of skills for cyber emergencies. This sub-section will focus specifically on the new NCSC, the "one-stop shop for technical advice and support in times of cyber crisis" (UK Parliament 2018a: 45). In closing, the section will look at other government initiatives, such as the CyberFirst programme for school pupils and university students and the NCSC Cyber Accelerator.

The third theme focuses on cyber competitions and wargames, with an emphasis on government competitions, wide-ranging student-led initiatives, such as Capture the Flag (CTF) competitions, and cyber crisis training exercises. Specifically, the section will discuss the Cyber Discovery government initiative, the Cyber Security Challenge and Cyber 9/12. It is argued that these competitions provide a valuable means of encouraging individuals to take an interest in cyber security, though catering to both technical and non-technical/policy interests in the same competition tends to be a challenge.

## Educational initiatives

There are a number of educational initiatives in the UK focused on cyber security research, including Academic Centres of Excellence in Cyber Security Research (ACE-CSRs), Centres for Doctoral Training (CDTs) and NCSC Certified Degree Providers (NCSC 2018: 42).

The ACE project is run by the NCSC and aims to recognise UK universities which are leaders in cyber security research. In 2018, 17 universities were classed as an ACE-CSR, which recognised their research as being at the global forefront, building their profile and showcasing the UK's research capabilities. The NCSC also supports four Research Institutes, such as the one in Secure Hardware and Embedded Systems at Queen's University, Belfast. The quality of Master's and Bachelor's degrees in cyber security (and related areas) can be assured by choosing providers that are NCSC certified. These currently include 14 fully and 11 provisionally certified Master's courses, three provisionally certified Integrated Master's courses, as well as three Bachelor's courses, of which one is fully certified.[1] Two of the universities recognised by the NCSC as ACE-CSRs, the University of Oxford and Royal Holloway University of London, also run Centres for Doctoral Training in Cyber Security and these are financially supported by the Engineering and Physical Sciences Research Council (EPSRC). The next section provides a case study of two cyber security research programmes at the University of Oxford: the Centre for Doctoral Training in Cyber Security and the Centre for Technology and Global Affairs.

### University of Oxford: CDT in Cyber Security

The UK has currently 117 Centres for Doctoral Training in operation, however, only two are focused on Cyber Security, with this case study presenting the one based at the University of Oxford.

The CDT had its first intake in 2013 and since then has been accepting 16 students annually with backgrounds as varied as business, social or political science, law, mathematics and computer science (CDT 2018). The first year of the programme is taught, followed by two mini-projects lasting nine weeks that mark the progression to the three-year research component. Students are given the opportunity to work with prospective supervisors before deciding on a DPhil project. They can also work with industry partners, using the strong ties the CDT has to companies and organisations outside the university. This encourages students to explore projects that hold real-world relevance, gain new skills and experience working in different fields.[2]

The courses in the first year are designed around a core of technical subjects, such as security principles, system architectures and high-integrity systems engineering, while also being supplemented by research methods and ethical principles. These elements are placed in the context of, for example, business, governance and international relations, providing a rounded, multidisciplinary foundation to cyber security. Students are also invited to take part in a number of industry "deep dives", which allow them to see first-hand the working of government and private sector organisations in cyber security and build relationships for collaborative research.

While the varied student backgrounds contribute greatly to the learning experience, these also entail two core challenges. First, the core topics need to be tailored in a manner that is accessible to all, yet also interesting to those who have studied related areas, and, second, given the time restraints, topics cannot be covered in as great a detail as very specialised courses. Lastly, the year of taught courses impacts the overall research time, as many other PhD programmes tend to take three to four years and therefore allow more time to conduct the initial research and decide on a topic. To mitigate elements of this, the programme has been designed with cyber security as the central topic, and the other subjects or topics are tailored around it, instead of vice versa. Furthermore, the structure was adjusted after the first two cohorts by introducing elective modules into the second half of the year, giving the students an option to either focus on different topics or to delve deeper into their interest areas. A major benefit of the CDT structure is that a large part of the learning process happens outside of the lectures during discussions or when students work together on projects and assignments. CDT students also collaborate on a wide variety of initiatives, including educational and charity projects, cyber crisis simulations and in co-authoring academic papers (CDT 2018). The rich diversity of disciplinary backgrounds also provide students with direct points of contact and support in specialised areas, greatly reducing the barrier for those wishing to cross disciplinary boundaries in their doctoral research: something which may otherwise be intimidating. This is particularly important as the problem of cyber security requires multidisciplinary approaches.

Another challenge is presented by the traditional university structure, both for the students as well as the broader research agenda. Currently, students at the Oxford CDT are registered by default in Computer Science, the programme's host department. After the first year, students decide if they wish to remain in Computer Science or move to a different department, depending on whether they intend to pursue research leaning more heavily towards a different discipline, such as business, law or international relations. There is no structure in place for examining cyber security as a single, multidisciplinary course. Instead, the students join their respective departments and, in order to complete their DPhils, are asked to fulfil the new host department's requirements. This can include additional courses or assessments that are compulsory, but it is most obvious at the point of thesis submission and examination. While this structure brings the students closer to their supervisors and embeds them in their departments, it also can also interfere with CDT cohort cohesion. The Oxford CDT has introduced weekly CDT events such as seminars, lunches and coffee afternoons to mitigate this and bring students from different cohorts together, encouraging them to share their research.

## Government strategies

The second theme, government strategies, examines the approach the UK has taken to fulfilling its promise in the National Cyber Security Strategy to closing the skills gap by supporting quality cyber graduate and postgraduate education.

### The National Cyber Security Strategy

In the National Cyber Security Strategy, the UK government puts forward three primary objectives: "defend our cyberspace, deter our adversaries, and develop our capabilities" (HMG 2016: 29). It is this third objective to which we now turn.

The UK government recognises that there is a growing disparity between demand and supply for cyber security roles due to

> [the] lack of young people entering the profession, the shortage of current cyber security specialists, insufficient exposure to cyber and information security concepts in computing courses, a shortage of suitably qualified teachers, and the absence of established career and training pathways into the profession.
>
> *(HMG 2016: 55)*

To remedy this, the government envisages that all education programmes relating to computer science, technology or digital skills will include a cyber security component. In addition, it aims to address the under-representation of women in cyber-related professions and increase diversity among the workforce (ibid.: 56). The Strategy also promises to establish a "skills advisory group" comprised of "government, employers, professional bodies, skills bodies, education providers and academia" (ibid.: 56). Additional initiatives outlined include:

establishing a schools program to create a step change in specialist cyber security education and training for talented 14–19 year olds (involving classroom-based activities, after-school sessions with expert mentors, challenging projects and summer schools); creating higher and degree-level apprenticeships within the energy, finance and transport sectors to address skills gaps in essential areas; establishing a fund to retain candidates already in the workforce who show a high potential for the cyber security profession; identifying and supporting quality cyber graduate and post graduate education, and identifying and filling any specialist skills gap; supporting the accreditation of teacher professional development in cyber security; developing the cyber security profession, including through achieving Royal Chartered status by 2020, reinforcing the recognised body of cyber security excellence within the industry and providing a focal point which can advise, shape and inform national policy; developing a Defence Cyber Academy as a centre of excellence for cyber training and exercise across the Ministry of Defence and wider Government, addressing specialist skills and wider education; developing opportunities for collaboration in training and education between government, the Armed Forces, industry, and academia; working with industry to expand the CyberFirst program, the government's cyber security education and skills program; and embedding cyber security and digital skills as an integral part of relevant courses within the education system, from primary to postgraduate levels.

*(HMG 2016: 56–57)*

The Strategy also explores the government's role in stimulating the development of the cyber security sector and helping companies prosper. More specifically, the government aims to do, among other things,

commercialise innovation in academia by providing training and mentoring to academics; establish two innovation centres to drive the development of cyber products and cyber security companies, including start-ups; allocate a proportion of the £164 million Defence and Cyber Innovation fund to support innovative procurement in defence and security; provide testing facilities for companies to develop their products; and promote agreed international standards that support access to the UK market.

*(ibid.: 58)*

The government has also promised to continue to provide funding and support for the Academic Centres of Excellence, Research Institutes and Centres for Doctoral Training discussed in the first section (ibid.: 59). The government sponsors a number of UK national PhD students at the Academic Centres of Excellence, an initiative aimed to increase the number of UK citizens with cyber skills (ibid.: 60). Finally, the Strategy discusses funding a "grand challenge" to "identify and provide innovative solutions to some of the most pressing problems in cyber security". It gives the example of CyberInvest, a new industry and government partnership which will aim to support "cutting-edge cyber security research" and "protect the UK in cyberspace". This will have the additional benefit of helping build partnerships between academia, government and industry (ibid.: 60).

## Skills provision for cyber emergencies

The NCSC is a new organisation that was opened in February 2017 to "help protect the UK's critical services from cyber attacks, manage major incidents and improve the underlying security of the UK Internet".[3] The organisation is part of GCHQ, the UK signals intelligence agency, and brings together and replaces the Computer Emergency Response Team UK (CERT UK), CESG (the information security arm of GCHQ), the Centre for Cyber Assessment (CCA) and the cyber-related responsibilities of the Centre for the Protection of National Infrastructure (CPNI). The NCSC has 740 staff and a budget of £285 million for the 2016–2021 period (UK Parliament 2018b: 45). One of its main responsibilities is working to support the UK's critical national infrastructure, particularly during large emergencies. The organisation recently developed a new cyber attack categorisation system to enhance the UK's response to incidents. According to the scale, a category one attack is a national cyber emergency which causes "sustained disruption of UK essential services or affects UK national security" and is coordinated by the NCSC with strategic leadership from Ministers and the Cabinet Office and in collaboration with law enforcement.[4]

Worryingly, according to evidence received by the Joint Committee on the National Security Strategy, expectations from CNI operators and regulators already exceed the NCSC's capacity. The WannaCry attack which hit the UK's National Health Service in May 2017 was an example of a cyber emergency: 47 NHS trusts and Foundation Trusts were affected, ambulances were diverted from some hospitals, and a number of operations were cancelled (NCSC 2017b: 13). In its response to the incident, the NCSC worked with NHS England's emergency response teams, the Department of Health, NHS Digital (the national information and technology partner to the UK health and social care system) and NHS Improvement to coordinate actions. Within 24 hours of the incident, the UK Home Secretary ran the first ever cyber crisis response committee and the NCSC provided the communications lead for the meeting (ibid.: 14). However, according to Rob Shaw, the Deputy Chief Executive of NHS Digital, it became apparent after the WannaCry attack that the NCSC does not have enough people with sector-specific knowledge who are able to do things on the ground (UK Parliament 2018a: 45). This is a problem that will arise in the case of any cyber emergency and stems from the difficulty of recruiting deep technical expertise in the diverse areas that the NCSC has to deal with, examples include healthcare, 5G mobile Internet and aviation. This is something the NCSC recognises as a challenge for example, there are only three or four employees at the NCSC with significant expertise in the latter. The organisation does supplement its workforce with secondees from the private sector as part of the "Industry 100" initiative, but, according to the Joint Committee on the National Security Strategy, further development of the NCSC workforce is needed in order to ensure that the organisation is a "one-stop shop" for technical advice and support in times of crisis.

In December 2018, the UK government published a highly anticipated document entitled "The Initial National Cyber Security Skills Strategy". Here, the government outlined how it has been developing the public sector workforce to address the cyber emergencies. The Transforming Government Security Programme (TGSP) was set up in 2017 with the aim of establishing a government-wide Security Profession (GSP) that would ensure that government employees have "the appropriate skills and training to provide world class security services for government" (HMG 2018: 47). In order to recruit talent into the workforce immediately, the GSP set up a recruitment scheme for apprentices for central government. The scheme is targeted at 18–19-year-old students, but it also accommodates individuals in their thirties and forties seeking a career change. The scheme is designed to be the main point of entry into government for cyber security roles and its long-term aim is to address the gap of professionals at High Executive Officer (HEO) and Senior Executive Office (SEO) levels who often leave after training to work for the private sector.

During a 2017 Parliamentary Inquiry into cyber security skills and the UK's critical national infrastructure (CNI), the Joint Committee on the National Security Strategy heard that despite various government programmes intended to address the shortfall in cyber security skills, there were still a number of challenges (UK Parliament 2018b: 7). A major issue that the inquiry identified was the pace of technological change, which presents a challenge to education policy. The long lag time between an individual joining primary school and entering the workforce means the education system is not able to anticipate and deliver the range of specialist skills and knowledge that will be most sought after upon a student's departure from full-time education (ibid.: 16). The Committee went so far as to state that the disparity between the demand and supply of skills in the top two tiers of specialism, highly specialist skills and moderately specialist skills, is now verging on a crisis (ibid.: 9). This was underscored by the CEO of the UK's National Cyber Security Centre (NCSC), Ciaran Martin, who noted that the organisation finds it difficult to recruit deep technical expertise (ibid.: 9). The recruitment issues faced by the public sector are partly due to the fact that individuals rarely hold both information technology *and* operational technology skills, which are especially important for CNI operators as bespoke and legacy industrial control systems increasingly become connected to the Internet (ibid.: 9). The other reasons are higher compensation packages offered by the private sector and the lack of gender diversity, which is affecting the size of the talent pool: women still only comprise about 10 per cent of the cyber security workforce and the problem is expected to worsen after the UK leaves the EU (ibid.: 10).

The Ministry of Defence (MOD) is particularly concerned with preventing and responding to cyber emergencies and has therefore invested in cyber security innovation to "increase national resilience to cyber attacks through both defensive and offensive measures" (HMG 2018: 49). Within its own workforce, the MOD identifies talent through the Defence Cyber Aptitude Test (DCAT). This tests an individual's ability across a range of cognitive challenges but does not measure prior technical knowledge. The MOD is also opening a new Defence Cyber School in Shrivenham next to the existing Defence Academy which works closely with Cranfield University (ibid.: 49).

## Other initiatives

Analyses of the domestic skills gap, particularly in the CNI sector, are difficult due to the lack of a clear definition of what is considered a cyber security job or skill. The report from the Joint Committee on the National Security Strategy presents a solution to this: the creation of a framework which categorises and describes cyber security work, similar to the framework created by the United States' National Initiative for Cybersecurity Education (NICE) (UK Parliament 2018b: 12). The NICE framework establishes a taxonomy and common lexicon that describes cyber security work and workers "regardless of where or for whom the work is performed". It is made up of the following aspects: high-level categories (groupings of common cyber security functions), specialty areas (distinct areas of cyber security work), and work roles (the most detailed groupings of cyber security work, comprised of specific knowledge, skills and abilities required to perform tasks in a work role) (NIST 2017).

Subject area specialists have also suggested that instead of treating cyber security as a technical subject, it might be beneficial to integrate it into relevant subjects across the curriculum, such as business studies or law. This might have the advantage of making a non-technical, specialist career in cyber security more accessible and develop the aptitudes required for functional cyber security skills, as opposed to just technical roles (UK Parliament 2018b: 19). This would necessarily require teachers to develop a greater knowledge of cyber security.

Another government programme that has already been implemented is Cyber-First. This includes a number of initiatives: undergraduate student bursaries; degree apprenticeships; the Cyber Discovery challenge, and CyberFirst opportunities for 14–18-year-olds, such as development days for girls, residential courses for school pupils and an all-girls competition. As of September 2018, the UK government has awarded over 500 CyberFirst bursaries to undergraduate students who will attend paid summer training or work placements across industry and government. The government aims to have awarded 1,000 bursaries by 2020 (Lidington 2018). The NCSC is also piloting two new Cyber Schools Hubs at schools in Gloucestershire, where GCHQ is based. The aim of this initiative is for the schools to use cyber security as a way to encourage a wide range of students to take up computer science.[5] This is in addition to the all-female CyberFirst Defenders course that the organisation has just announced. The initiative will provide 600 girls with the opportunity to undertake four-day courses on cryptography, cyber security, logic and coding and networking (Coughlan 2019).

In August 2018, the UK and the US collaborated on the first US/UK Future Cybersecurity Leaders Exchange programme for 16- and 17-year-olds. The exchange allowed eight British and eight US students to experience a hands-on introduction to a range of cyber security challenges in the US. The UK will be hosting the next exchange in July/August 2019 (ibid.).

Finally, the NCSC also hosts a Cyber Accelerator. The programme lasts nine months and recently enabled nine companies to develop different ideas, including: a service to solve the problem of age verification and parental consent for young people in online transactions and a service that connects Internet-of-Things devices with end-to-end authenticated, encrypted security. The first two accelerator cohorts raised over £20 million in funding and won 15 trials and contracts worth over £3 million (NCSC 2018: 43).

## Cyber competitions and wargames

Gamified teaching programmes have become increasingly popular in the UK, particularly in the context of cyber security. These include specific events aimed at teenagers, such as UK's Cyber Discovery, or a large number of simulations, challenges, cyber tabletops (CTT) and wargames. These can either be very technically focused, including capture-the-flag (CTF) events, or policy-oriented. The former are usually divided into two types: attack-defence competitions consisting of two (or more) attacking teams versus one team defending a network or server, and task-based ones, where individuals or teams pick challenges from various categories to earn points but do not attack each other. The latter, on the other hand, often revolve around a fictional cyber incident that is escalating, with participants having to manage various stakeholders and give policy recommendations. Other types include CTTs, which are often aimed at exploring effects of cyber incidents, as well as operations, and are used in businesses as well as by armed forces (Le Compte, Elizondo and Watson 2015: 203–16; DoD 2018; Amorim et al. 2013: 12).

All these types of exercises provide an interactive learning experience, with participants improving and gaining new skills, preparing them not only for day-to-day activities but also crisis situations. This section will provide a brief overview of the gamified approached promoted in the UK, introducing the Cyber Discovery programme and the Cyber Security Challenge UK. A CTF for UK service personnel is presented next, followed by an example of a student-led initiative. Finally, the policy-oriented Cyber 9/12 Strategy Challenge is introduced, with an emphasis on its UK variant.

### Government-funded initiatives: Cyber Discovery and CyberFirst Girls Competition

In 2017, the UK Department for Digital, Culture, Media and Sport (DCMS) set up a flagship £20 million Cyber Discovery programme for 14–18-year-olds as part of CyberFirst to develop the next generation of cyber security technical leaders.

Participants are guided through a extensive cyber security curriculum which uses gamified learning and covers topics such as digital forensics, defending against web attacks, cryptography, Linux, programming and ethics.[6] The content is delivered over four stages (Assess, Game, Essentials, Elite) through a role-playing game and participants can chat and collaborate all the while receiving guidance from a mentor or club leader. Having qualified through successfully completing the first digital phase, the students take on the role of a security agent, gathering information, cracking codes, finding security flaws and dissecting a cyber criminal's digital trail using in-toll resources and research techniques (HMG 2018: 34). The programme is delivered for the government by the SANS Institute. Over 23,000 students have registered for Cyber Discovery since it launched and 170 of these students have won a place at an industry-led bootcamp and a live CTF event to further develop their skills. Female pupils are also being directly encouraged through an initiative called CyberFirst girls and the past two years saw 12,500 female pupils aged 13–15 participate in teams in schools across the UK (Scotland 2018). The competition consists of two distinct phases: the first phase is an online qualifying round to identify the top ten teams; the second phase is the Grand Final where the top ten teams compete at a high-profile location in London. The competition aims to encourage the next generation of young women to consider a career in cyber security (NCSC 2017a).

## Cyber Security Challenge UK

Cyber Security Challenge UK is aimed at adults with an interest in the technical side of cyber security.[7] This initiative is delivered as a series of national competitions, learning programmes, and networking initiatives in order to develop more cyber security professionals. The competitions are created by a community of sponsors from industry and aim to test cyber security skills. The challenges are accessed through a "play on demand" system, with those performing best then invited to face-to-face competitions. These culminate in the "masterclass final", which is held annually in November, with contestants having to demonstrate not only technical abilities but also interpersonal and decision-making skills. For complete beginners, a novice toolkit is also provided, giving some guidance on the fundamentals of various topics, such as coding languages, malware analysis, web applications and infrastructure security.[8]

Teenagers are encouraged to take part in a separate team challenge called CyberCenturion, which is mirrored on the US CyberPatriot competition. Toolkits are also provided, both for competitors and adult team leaders.[9] It is important to note, however, that while these competitions provide a great introduction to the technical aspects of cyber security and remain a challenge for advanced levels, the bigger picture, such as national or international governance and policy ramifications of cyber crisis are not addressed as part of the competition.

## Other competitions

Another technically focused initiative is the UK's Ministry of Defence CTF-style competition, Inter-Services Cyber Network Defence Challenge, but this is aimed solely at services personnel. In 2017, the Challenge was organised by the Joint Forces Command and saw four teams compete from the Army, the Royal Navy, the Royal Air Force and the Civil Service. The event is designed to test and teach participants to counter cyber attacks and teams are supported by cyber instructors from industry (HMG 2018: 49).

There are also a number of societies or student-led groups and events that centre on cyber security, such as the Competitive Computer Security (CCS) at the University of Oxford,[10] which introduces beginners to CTFs and helps experienced competitors to develop their skills. The University of Cambridge runs an annual Inter-ACE workshop supported by the NCSC focusing on binary exploitation, with winners qualifying for Cambridge2Cambridge, a three-day transatlantic cyber challenge, later in the year.[11]

European exchange and collaboration in cyber security training are also sought, with an example being the European Cyber Security Challenge that the UK hosted in October 2018. This annual competition is promoted by the European Commission and included teams of under-25s from across 18 European countries participating in a CTF-style event (HMG 2018: 52).

On the policy side, the UK has adopted the Cyber 9/12 Strategy Challenge, which is an annual competition created by the Atlantic Council for students across the globe. It is now held in the US, France, the UK, Switzerland and in Australia, and centres around an escalating fictional cyber incident that has to be managed, with competitors taking the role of government advisors. The aim is for participants to develop valuable skills in analysis and presentation, while at the same time contemplating on, and dealing with, national and international ramifications.[12] The UK competition evolves across two days, with three preliminary rounds that are judged by policy experts. Teams compete in groups of four, comprised of university students enrolled in a variety of disciplines. The challenge in 2020 took place at the BT Tower in London in February, partnered with the Royal United Services Institute (RUSI), senior government and industry stakeholders.[13] While the event is highly engaging and greatly improves the understanding of cyber threats and actions, the technical component is very minimal, and it may thus limit the interest of those who are very technically minded.

## Conclusion

This chapter aimed to provide a survey of UK initiatives aimed at developing the cyber security workforce. The first theme focused on academia, explaining the existence of Academic Centres of Excellence in Cyber Security Research, Centres for Doctoral Training in Cyber Security and NCSC Certified Master's and Bachelor's degrees. The section also discussed in detail the benefits and challenges of offering multidisciplinary study of cyber security, focusing on the case study of the Oxford CDT.

The second theme surveyed the UK government's approach to tackling the cyber skills gap, looking particularly at the government's plans outlined in the National Cyber Security Strategy. This section also addressed the UK's approach to skills provision for cyber emergencies. Here, the recent creation of the National Centre for Cyber Security is most pertinent. The chapter discussed how the UK is seriously addressing the problem of cyber skills shortage in the public sector, but there still exists a gap between the expertise that is available, and the needs of organisations embroiled in a cyber incident. The section ended on a brief overview of a number of other government projects like the CyberFirst programme and the NCSC cyber accelerator.

The third theme provided an overview of existing cyber competitions and games. These include the government-funded Cyber Discovery programme and CyberFirst Girls Competition, the more technical Cyber Security Challenge and other competitions including CTFs, the European Cyber Security Challenge and Cyber 9/12. Such games and competitions are highly valuable in encouraging interest in cyber security but tend to be divided into technical competitions and policy-focused competitions. Future initiatives would do well to try and integrate both, thus generating a dialogue between individuals of different strengths and mindsets and supporting the generation of a diversified cyber security workforce.

## Notes

1  For more on the National Cyber Security Centre, see www.nsc.gov.uk/about-us.
2  Centre for Doctoral Training, Oxford University – Cyber Security Oxford. See www.cybersecurity.ox.ac.uk/education/cdt.
3  See www.ncsc.gov.uk/about-us.
4  "New Cyber Attack Categorisation System to Improve UK Response to Incidents", see www.ncsc.gov.uk/news/new-cyber-attack-categorisation-system-improve-uk-response-incidents.
5  Cyber Schools Hubs, see www.ncsc.gov.uk/information/cyber-schools-hubs.
6  "New UK Government Cyber Schools Programme "Cyber Discovery" Launches to Find Next Generation of Cyber Security Talent", see www.cybersecuritychallenge.org.uk/news-events/new-uk-government-cyber-schools-programme-cyber-discovery-launches-find-next-generation-cyber-security-talent.
7  Cyber Security Challenge UK, see www.cybersecuritychallenge.org.uk/.
8  Novice Toolkit, see www.cybersecuritychallenge.org.uk/novice-toolkit.
9  CyberCenturion, see www.cybersecuritychallenge.org.uk/competitions/cybercenturion.
10  Home, see https://ox002147.gitlab.io/.
11  Inter-ACE, see https://inter-ace.org/.
12  Cyber 9/12 Project, see.www.atlanticcouncil.org/programs/brent-scowcroft-center/cyber-statecraft/cyber-9-12.
13  Home, see https://www.cyber912uk.org/en/.

## References

Amorim, J. A., M. Hendrix, S. F. Andler and P. M. Gustavsson. 2013. *Gamified Training for Cyber Defence: Methods and Automated Tools for Situation and Threat Assessment*. Paper presented at NATO Modelling and Simulation Group (MSG) 2013.

CDT. (Centre for Doctoral Training in Cyber Security). 2018. *2018 Yearbook*. Oxford: University of Oxford.

Coughlan, S. 2019. GCHQ Sets up All-Female Training Classes. *BBC News*, 17 January.

DoD. (Department of Defense). 2018. Department of Defense Cyber Table Top Guidebook.. 2 July. Available at: www.acq.osd.mil/dte-trmc/docs/The%20DoD%20Cyber%20Table%20Top%20Guidebook%20v1.pdf.

HMG. 2016. National Cyber Security Strategy 2016–2021. Available at: https://assets.publishing.service.gov.uk/government/uploads/system/uploads/attachment_data/file/567242/national_cyber_security_strategy_2016.pdf.

HMG. 2018. Initial Cyber Security Skills Strategy. 21 December. Available at: https://assets.publishing.service.gov.uk/government/uploads/system/uploads/attachment_data/file/767515/Cyber_security_skills_strategy_211218.pdf.

Le Compte, A., D. Elizondo and T. Watson. 2015. *A Renewed Approach to Serious Games for Cyber Security*. Paper presented at 2015 7th International Conference on Cyber Conflict: Architectures in Cyberspace, 203–216. doi:10.1109/CYCON.2015.7158478.

Lidington, D. 2018. Correspondence from David Lidington to the Chair 12 July 2018. UK Parliament, July 2018. Available at: www.parliament.uk/documents/joint-committees/national-security-strategy/Correspondence/david-lidington-chair-120618.pdf.

NCSC. (National Cyber Security Centre). 2017a. Announcing the CyberFirst Girls Competition. Blog post, 18 January 2017. Available at: www.ncsc.gov.uk/blog-post/announcing-cyberfirst-girls-competition.

NCSC. (National Cyber Security Centre). 2017b. 2017 Annual Review. Available at: www.ncsc.gov.uk/content/files/NCSC-2017-Annual-Review.pdf.

NCSC. (National Cyber Security Centre). 2018. 2018 Annual Review. Available at: www.ncsc.gov.uk/news/annual-review-2018.

NIST (National Institute for Standards and Technology). 2017. NICE Cybersecurity Workforce Framework. 10 January. Available at: www.nist.gov/itl/applied- cybersecurity/nice/resources/nice-cybersecurity-workforce-framework.

UK Parliament. 2018a. Cyber Security of the UK's Critical National Infrastructure Third Report of Session 2017–2019. House of Lords and House of Commons. Joint Committee on the National Security Strategy, 12 November. Available at: https://publications.parliament.uk/pa/jt201719/jtselect/jtnatsec/1708/1708.pdf.

UK Parliament. 2018b. Cyber Security Skills and the UK's Critical National Infrastructure Second Report of Session, 2017–19. House of Lords and House of Commons, 16 July 2018. Available at: https://publications.parliament.uk/pa/jt201719/jtselect/jtnatsec/706/706.pdf.

# 10

# HOLISTIC CYBER EDUCATION

*Jean R.S. Blair, Andrew O. Hall and Edward Sobiesk*

Cyber has permeated all aspects of our lives and society. Consequently, it is a moral imperative that cyber be integrated into all levels of education. This chapter provides a multi-level, multidisciplinary approach to holistically integrating cyber into a student's academic experience. Our approach suggests formally integrating cyber throughout an institution's curriculum, including within the required general education program, in electives from a variety of disciplines, as multi-course threads, as minors, and in numerous cyber-related majors. Our holistic approach complements in-class curricula with both a pervasive cyber-aware environment and experiential, outside-the-classroom activities that apply concepts and skills in real-world environments. The aim of our approach is to provide all educated individuals a level of cyber education appropriate to their role in society. Throughout the description of our approach, we include examples of its implementation at the United States Military Academy (USMA) at West Point.

Throughout this chapter we use the term cyber, but we acknowledge the ambiguity and open-endedness of the term. One current, popular definition of cyber security is:

> A computing-based discipline involving technology, people, information, and processes to enable assured operations in the context of adversaries. It involves the creation, operation, analysis, and testing of secure computer systems. It is an interdisciplinary course of study, including aspects of law, policy, human factors, ethics, and risk management.
>
> *(ACM 2017)*

While this definition describes much of what we mean by the term, we would broaden the concept to include the full multidisciplinary technical and non-technical aspects of cyber.

The next section describes the most relevant related work. This is followed by sections that respectively address the recommended curricular and extracurricular elements of our approach. The final section describes the importance of a pervasive cyber-aware environment.

## Related work

This section briefly highlights the primary related work for teaching cyber, which we organize into the following categories:

- computer security in traditional computing curricula
- NSA/DHS designations
- ABET accreditation criteria
- standalone cybersecurity curriculum and accreditation criteria
- cyber in general education and electives
- extracurricular cyber opportunities

### *Computer security in traditional computing curricula*

Professional societies for computing, including the Association for Computing Machinery (ACM), the IEEE Computer Society (IEEE-CS), and the Association for Information Systems (AIS), have created curricular guidelines for Computer Science (2013), Information Systems (2010), Information Technology (2017), Computer Engineering (2016), and Software Engineering (2014). These model curricula provide frameworks that influence hundreds to thousands of computing programs across the United States and internationally. Each of these model curricula contains recommended computer security content for the associated discipline, under labels such as Information Assurance and Security, Cyber Security, and Information Security. These computer security curricular recommendations are usually meant to be taught across the program's entire curriculum rather than just in a single course. As example, the Computer Science model curriculum recommends nine lesson hours of "concepts where the depth is unique to Information Assurance and Security" and an additional 63.5 lesson hours of Information Assurance and Security content that is "integrated into other Knowledge Areas that reflect naturally implied or specified topics with a strong role in security concepts and topics" (ACM 2013). The content for these curricular recommendations is mostly technical material that applies to the part of the curriculum being covered. Thus, an agreed-upon best practice at the program level for computing disciplines is to teach cyber security across the entire breadth of the curriculum rather than only bolted-on to the curriculum in a single course.

### *NSA/DHS designations*

Additional computing program-level initiatives include the National Security Agency and the Department of Homeland Security jointly sponsoring the National

Centers of Academic Excellence in Cyber Defence (CAE-CD) program that offers CAE-CD designations for Associate, Bachelor, Master's and Doctoral Programs (2020). The CAE-CD program's goal is to "reduce vulnerability in our national information infrastructure by promoting higher education and research in cyber defense and producing professionals with cyber defense expertise" (NSA 2020). Complementing this, the National Security Agency additionally sponsors the National Centers of Academic Excellence (CAE) in Cyber Operations Program (2020) that supports the National Initiative for Cybersecurity Education (NICE) Framework (2019). The CAE-Cyber Operation's aim is to facilitate curricula that meet the goal of being a "deeply technical, inter-disciplinary, higher education program firmly grounded in the computer science, computer engineering, and/or electrical engineering disciplines, with extensive opportunities for hands-on applications via labs and exercises" (ibid.). Currently, there are over 300 institutions with the CAE in Cyber Defence designation and 21 institutions with the CAE in Cyber Operations designation (ibid.).

## ABET accreditation criteria

For program-level computing accreditation, ABET accredits hundreds of traditional computing programs across the United States and internationally. ABET has recently changed their computing accreditation criteria, and starting in the 2018–2020 time period, all computing programs seeking accreditation or reaccreditation will have to demonstrate that they have curriculum content that sufficiently covers "principles and practices for secure computing" appropriate to their discipline (ABET 2020).

## Standalone cybersecurity curriculum and accreditation criteria.

From the viewpoint of cybersecurity as a distinct discipline, and not simply an aspect of a computing discipline, a Joint Task Force on Cybersecurity Education, comprised of four professional societies (the Association for Computing Machinery, the IEEE Computer Society, the Association for Information Systems Special Interest Group on Security, and the International Federation for Information Processing Technical Committee on Information Security Education), has published *Cybersecurity Curricula 2017* (CSEC2017; Joint Task Force on Cyber Security Education 2017). Its vision is, "The CSEC2017 curricular volume will be the leading resource of comprehensive cybersecurity curricular content for global academic institutions seeking to develop a broad range of cybersecurity offerings at the post-secondary level" (ACM 2017). The guidelines frame cyber security through three dimensions: cross-cutting concepts, knowledge areas, and disciplinary lenses. The six cross-cutting concepts are Confidentiality, Integrity, Availability, Risk, Adversarial Thinking, and Systems Thinking. The eight knowledge areas include Data Security, Software Security, Component Security, Connection Security, System Security, Human Security, Organisational Security, and Societal Security (see Chapter 4). The disciplinary lenses represent "the underlying computing discipline from which the cybersecurity program can be developed ... The thought model encompasses the current computing disciplines identified by the ACM: computer science, computer engineering, information systems, information technology, and software engineering" (ibid.). Based on *Cybersecurity Curricula 2017* and on constituent needs, ABET has recently developed, published, and fielded cybersecurity program criteria (ABET 2020).

## Cyber in general education and electives

Few institutions require cyber security as part of their general education program. However, some do. Examples of such requirements include mandated general education courses at the United States Military Academy (Sobiesk et al. 2015) and the United States Naval Academy (Brown et al. 2012). Examples of cyber electives and cyber minors are found in (Sobiesk et al. 2015) and (Stockman et al. 2006).

## Extracurricular cyber opportunities

Outside the classroom, there are extracurricular competitive opportunities, training courses that often have associated certifications, and government frameworks. Three well-known educational extracurricular cyber security competitions are the college-level National Collegiate Cyber Defence Competition (2020) that includes roughly 200 institutions, CyberPatriot (2020) which involves 3000+ teams composed of high school and middle school students, and PicoCTF (2017) "a game designed to expose students to the science of computer security," which has over 17,000 middle and high school participants. Additionally, SANS CyberStart provides "a suite of challenges, tools and games designed to introduce young people to the field of cyber security" (SANS 2020). Hundreds of capture-the-flag competitions also take place every year in which competitors are faced with a plethora of real-world, concrete instances of computer security challenges (CTFtime 2020). Hundreds of cyber security conferences also take place every year, providing scholars and the private sector opportunities to share ideas, innovations, and research (Concise AC 2020). There are numerous training courses and certifications associated specifically with cyber security or that include significant security components. Some of the most prominent come from organisations such as SANS (2020), (ISC)$^2$ (2020), Cisco (2020), and ISACA (2020).

## Curricular elements of the holistic approach

The primary contribution of this chapter is a holistic, multi-level, multidisciplinary approach that provides all individuals a level of cyber education appropriate for their role in society. This model integrates and significantly builds on our previous work (Sobiesk et al. 2015; Hall and Sobiesk 2017; Blair et al. 2019). In the curricular elements of our approach, cyber education includes technical and non-technical content across the various levels, which includes:

- general education content: giving all students the basics of cyber
- disciplinary and interdisciplinary cyber electives, in areas like Political Science, Law, Cognitive Science, and Computing: providing opportunities to supplement one's education with cyber-related content
- elective or embedded-in-a-major cyber-focused threads, such as cyber security engineering or robotics: providing the opportunity to specialize in cyber at a level less than a minor but more than a single course
- cyber minors: including both technical and non-technical knowledge areas
- technical and non-technical cyber-related majors that prepare graduates to succeed in the Cyber Domain.

Figure 10.1, inspired by (Sobiesk et al. 2015), illustrates the various curricular levels of this approach. In the subsequent sections, we elaborate on each of the levels in detail as well as provide examples.

## Cyber in general education

We believe all educated individuals need at least a fundamental level of cyber education. To that end, we advocate integrating cyber into general education requirements. The key pedagogical technique is to consciously make cyber literacy and cyber security an institutional goal. With that, it becomes easier to purposely integrate cyber into as many places as possible in the general education curriculum and to ensure that every student's path includes sufficient coverage. This obviously includes computing and other Science, Technology, Engineering and Mathematics (STEM) disciplines, but cyber should also be addressed when covering most of the social sciences (such as political science, economics, international relations, and sociology) as well as in law, ethics, and social justice components, and in studies of human behavior.

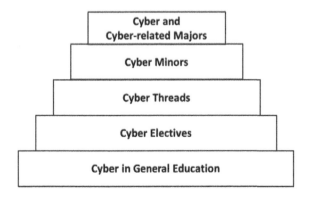

**Holistic Cyber Education: A Multi-Level, Multidiscipline Approach**

Cyber and Cyber-related Majors

Cyber Minors

Cyber Threads

Cyber Electives

Cyber in General Education

FIGURE 10.1 Curricular elements of the holistic cyber education approach

We realize that general education requirements will vary greatly by institution, with the USMA's being among the most stringent in the world. However, we believe that the concepts and vision illustrated through the following examples can provide inspiration and exemplars for almost any institution.

During their four academic years in attendance at the USMA, all cadets must complete a minimum of 40 academic courses, of which 27 are core general education courses spanning a variety of disciplines, including numerous courses in the humanities, social sciences, and STEM disciplines. Each cadet also chooses a major from across the same spectrum, but the core STEM requirements are so rigorous that all cadets, regardless of their chosen major, receive a Bachelor of Science degree.

There are two core general education courses assigned to specifically introduce cadets to computing and the Cyber Domain. The first course, CY105 Computing Fundamentals, introduces the principles and practices of computing along with foundational design and construction techniques for computer programming. The course also covers "legal, ethical, professional, and security issues and the challenges, opportunities, and attributes of the Cyber Domain" (United States Military Academy 2016). A second core course, CY305 Cyber Foundations, provides cadets

> [the] capacity and confidence to employ information technology – hardware, software, and networks – to empower people and organisations to acquire, manage, communicate and defend information, solve problems, and adapt to change. It provides a deeper understanding of sensor and communications technologies; computer processing, storage, and networks; cyberspace operations, planning and management; interaction of components in cyberspace; data-driven decision making; and the evolving legal and ethical framework surrounding use of IT and operating in the cyber domain. Cybersecurity issues are addressed throughout the course.
>
> *(ibid.)*

All cadets take the first course and get the content from the second course either by taking the course itself or by completing an engineering or computing major that provides equivalent content.

Several additional courses contribute to the integration of cyber across the USMA's general education curriculum. As examples, a required Probability and Statistics course exposes cadets to scripting, command line interface, and open source software as a part of coding in the R statistical language, and required courses in International Relations, Economics, Law, and even History and Philosophy, address the evolving aspects of those disciplines that are becoming interwoven with Cyber as a Domain. All this content is required as a part of the liberal education taken by all cadets and supports the Academy's goal that all graduates are able to "explain and apply Computing and Information Technology concepts and practices in the context of the Cyber Domain" (ibid.).

The USMA is continuing to evolve the integration of cyber across the required general education curriculum at West Point. Members of the USMA's faculty from many departments are working together to integrate content and concepts involving the Cyber Domain without adding additional required courses. We believe cooperation across disciplines is an essential element to holistically integrating cyber content into general education at any institution.

## Cyber electives in a variety of disciplines

Cyber electives increase accessibility to the subject, providing greater depth across a variety of disciplines. In our experience, this inspires a wider range of students to explore and learn about cyber from numerous valuable perspectives. It also naturally creates opportunities for students to develop multidisciplinary collaborative skills and mindsets.

The USMA offers many cyber electives as well as independent study opportunities. Cyber electives are offered in computing disciplines, interdisciplinary domains, and non-computing disciplines. Popular cyber electives include (ibid.):

- Computer Science course CS483 Digital Forensics
- Computer Science Special Topics course CS485 Ethical Hacking
- Cyber Engineering course CY450 Cyber Security Engineering
- Cyber Science course CY383 Secure Interface Design
- Cyber Science course CY460 Cyber Policy, Strategy & Operations
- Electrical Engineering Special Topics course EE485 Hardware Hacking
- Engineering Psychology course PL475 Human-computer Interaction
- History course XH341 Intelligence Cyber History
- Information Technology Special Topics Course IT485 Principles of Intelligence Analysis
- Law course LW462 Cyber Law
- Math course MA464 Applied Algebra with Cryptology
- Philosophy course PY326 Cyber Ethics

In addition to the cyber electives, cadets completing a cyber-related major can also choose a cyber topic for their senior capstone design experience. A recent example of a successful cyber-related capstone project was a cadet team that designed and built a "Vulnerable Web Server application … that packages instructional materials and pre-built virtual machines, created using Oracle VirtualBox, into interactive cybersecurity lessons" designed for non-computing high school and college students (Estes et al. 2016).

## Cyber threads

We define a thread to be a series of related courses that includes more than a single elective, but less than a minor. A thread provides opportunities for the students who do not have room in their schedule for a full minor but want greater study-in-depth in a discipline other than their chosen major.

The USMA curriculum offers each cadet the opportunity to experience an engineering thread as part of their education, ensuring exposure to the engineering thought and design process. For cadets in an engineering or computing major, this engineering sequence content is part of their major's required courses. The remainder of the cadets, however, are required to take a three-course thread in addition to their major. One of these three-course threads is Cyber Engineering. The Cyber Engineering Thread is as follows (United States Military Academy 2016):

- CY300 Programming Fundamentals covers "fundamental computing concepts that will allow them to design, build and test small to medium programs using a high-level programming language."
- CY350 Network Engineering and Management "addresses the analysis, design, building, and testing of modern computer networks."
- CY450 Cyber Security Engineering teaches cadets to "design, build and test secure networked computer systems" including a "hands-on experience with current network security tools and techniques" and a culminating exercise where cadets "design, build and test defensive measures to protect a production network from intrusions."

Essentially, the Cyber Engineering Thread can be viewed as (1) programming; (2) networking; and (3) securing.

## Cyber minors

A cyber minor is typically a set of related courses that together provide a depth of study that is not quite as extensive as a cyber major, but involves more courses, and is typically a more purposeful learning experience, than a thread. A cyber minor often may be used to complement an academic major or to enrich the interdisciplinary experience. Similar to electives, a cyber minor inspires a wide range of students with various backgrounds to study cyber from diverse academic perspectives. A cyber minor will, by its nature, encourage students to take courses across multiple disciplines and to develop multidisciplinary collaborative skills and mindsets.

At the USMA, a stated goal for the Cyber Security Minor is to achieve a "balance of both technical and non-technical knowledge and skills, as well as application" (ibid.). The minor builds on the Cyber Engineering Thread by requiring the two technical courses CY350 Network Engineering and Management and CY450 Cyber Security Engineering discussed above. Note that in preparation for these two courses, cadets must have taken the two cyber general education courses and CY300 Programming Fundamentals. In addition to the technical component of the Cyber Security Minor, a non-technical course must be chosen from the following three: CY460 Cyber Policy, Strategy & Operations, LW462 Cyber Law, or PY326 Cyber Ethics. Two additional elective courses are required from an extensive number of possibilities across a spectrum of disciplines.

## Cyber-related majors

Cyber-related majors fall into three general categories: (1) a stand-alone cyber major; (2) cyber-related technical majors; and (3) cyber-related non-technical majors. The technical and non-technical cyber-related majors are generally traditional majors that possess the potential to be cyber-related, depending on the focus of the curriculum or the student's curricular choices.

- *A stand-alone cyber major* is usually computing-based, having one of the computing disciplines as its foundation, and covers much of the multidisciplinary content described in CSEC2017, which we summarized in the Related Work section. Examples of stand-alone cyber majors include cyber security, cyber operations, computer security, information assurance, information security, and computer forensics.
- *A cyber-related technical major* is often computing-based, but also includes a significant variety of other STEM majors. Examples of cyber-related technical majors include: computer science, information technology, information systems, computer engineering, software engineering, electrical engineering, physics, mathematics, operations research, systems engineering, artificial intelligence, and data science.
- *A cyber-related non-technical major* encompasses a vast spectrum of other contributing disciplines. Examples of cyber-related non-technical majors include: political science, international relations, cognitive science, psychology, philosophy/ethics, law, and criminal justice.

At the USMA, we have all three categories of majors.

The USMA Cyber Science major is consistent with CSEC2017 and consists of the following five concentrations that share a ten-course common foundation (ibid.).

- The Cybersecurity concentration focuses on "the interdisciplinary study of people, processes, and technology to assure operations in the face of cyberspace risks."
- The Network Services concentration focuses on "building and securing the networks and services that are foundational to operating in Cyberspace."
- The Cyber Operations concentration focuses on "the low-level and technical skills that enable offensive and defensive cyberspace operations."
- The Cyber-Physical Systems concentration "provides a unique blend of depth in both hardware and software to exploit networked, physical systems that are controlled by algorithms."
- The Machine Learning concentration focuses on gaining insight using algorithmic tools that exploit large datasets and the Internet-of-Things.

The USMA's cyber-related technical majors include Computer Science, Electrical Engineering, Mathematical Sciences, Operations Research, Applied Statistics and Data Science, Physics, Systems Engineering, Engineering Management, and Systems and Decision Sciences. The USMA's cyber-related non-technical majors include Psychology, Engineering Psychology, Law and Legal Studies, Political Science, International Relations, Philosophy, and Defence and Strategic Studies. In addition, at the USMA, many cadets who take a traditional major supplement it with either our Cyber Engineering Thread or our Cyber Security Minor.

## Extracurricular elements of the holistic approach

Outside the classroom experiences are a critical component of a holistic cyber education approach. These activities provide experiential learning opportunities to apply concepts and skills from the classroom in a real-world environment. These experiences also offer the chance for developing communication, teamwork, and professional judgment skills as well as hands-on training experiences not always available in an educational environment. Outside the classroom cyber opportunities include internships, part-time jobs, research projects, student clubs, competitive events, conferences, training courses, and personal study.

At the USMA, cadets explore the Cyber Domain through participation in and attendance at cyber clubs, cyber-related conferences and training, summer internships across the U.S. Department of Defense and the U.S. private sector, through short temporary assignment to a U.S. Army cyber unit, and with assigned mentors. The following elaborate more of each of these USMA experiences.

The USMA has four cyber-related clubs:

- The Association for Computing Machinery Special Interest Group for Security, Audit and Control Club (SIGSAC) is open to all cadets with about 100+ participating. SIGSAC shares knowledge, cultivates technical skills, and develops leadership traits applicable to the Cyber Domain.
- The Cadet Competitive Cyber Team (C3T) consists of about 20 members selected through try-outs. They practice on an almost daily basis to prepare for, and compete in, numerous capture-the-flag competitions that improve their own computer and network security skills and serve as a form of outreach.
- The Cyber Policy Team is open to all cadets, with about 15 participating. This interdisciplinary club is dedicated to the study and application of cyber policy. The team competes at the regional, national, and international levels in various cyber policy competitions, including the annual Cyber 9/12 Student Challenge. The team's purpose is to encourage competition and a honing of cyber policy skill sets among the cadets.
- The Amateur Radio Club (HAMS) is open to all cadets, with about 50 participating. The aim of the club is to provide an educational environment which fosters enthusiasm for amateur radio and community service.

Several USMA cadets attend conferences such as ShmooCon, DEF CON - Black Hat, CyCon, and CyCon U.S. Attending these events allows cadets to encounter and interact with the larger cyber community of interest. In some cases, cadets even present results of their own research.

A few cadets participate in commercial cyber training with organisations such as described in the Related Work section. Other cadets experience cyber military training by either attending a military training course or by being assigned for a few weeks to a military cyber unit.

About 100 cadets participate each summer in cyber-related internships. All of these internships directly relate to the Cyber Domain, and many of them are associated with conflict in the Cyber Domain. As example, about 20 cadets conduct a summer internship with the NSA. Other cadet summer internships with a cyber focus include Facebook, USAA Cyber Operations Center, FBI, CERDEC, Lincoln Laboratories, and Amazon.

## A pervasive environment

One of the most critical aspects of a student's developmental experience is exposure to the culture, environment, and role models that facilitate their growth into professionals and leaders who possess the character and competence required to succeed in and adapt to the Cyber Domain. This includes interacting with members of the faculty and profession to receive mentorship, career guidance, and perhaps, most importantly, inspiration.

Based on the USMA's unique mission and goals, about 25 percent of the faculty are civilian with the remaining 75 percent consisting of some of the Army's very best officers, with advanced degrees, and who represent all branches of the Army. Across this diverse and enthusiastic organization, the Army also made the decision to place the 70-person Army Cyber Institute at the USMA, allowing for faculty with cyber expertise to be in at least nine different departments, and strongly contributing to the holistic, multidisciplinary cyber model adopted by the USMA.

## The U.S. Army Cadet Cyber Development Program

As a closing note, Army Reserve Officers Training Corps and USMA cadets have the unique opportunity to formally synchronize and track their cyber activities as part of the U.S. Army's Cyber Leader Development Program (CLDP), which includes a formal mentorship program. As described in (Army Cyber Institute 2020), CLDP identifies, develops, and tracks cyber leaders and is encouraged for cadets taking cyber-related majors or a cyber minor. Overall:

> CLDP provides a framework for cadets to pursue 800+ hours of impactful experiences outside the classroom through internships, conferences, clubs, and seminars. Cadets in CLDP pursue opportunities to attend advanced cyber training offered by SANS, Cisco, and other organisations ... Cadets in CLDP will also be favorably considered for the most challenging, technical Academic Individual Advanced Development opportunities at organisations

such as the NSA, U.S. Cyber Command, U.S. Army Cyber Command, and other institutions that have a cyber operations mission.

*(ibid.)*

Successful completion of the Cyber Leader Development Program results in the award of an Additional Skill Identifier on a cadet's permanent military record.

## Conclusion

This chapter addressed the moral imperative to integrate cyber into all levels of education—with the goal of providing all individuals a level of cyber education appropriate to their role in society. Toward this end, we described a holistic multi-level, multidisciplinary approach that incorporates the curricular and extracurricular elements of the student experience, complemented by a pervasive cyber-aware environment. While our approach and examples primarily focused on under-graduate education, we believe our principles and recommended practices easily extend to K-12 and graduate-level education.

## Disclaimer

The views expressed in this chapter are those of the authors and do not reflect the official policy or position of the U.S. Military Academy, the Department of the Army, the Department of Defense, or the U.S. Government.

## References

ABET. 2020. CAC General and Program Criteria. Baltimore, MD: ABET. Available at: www.abet.org.

ACM. 2013. Computer Science Curricula 2013. ACM/IEEE-CS Joint Task Force on Computing Curricula. Available at: www.acm.org/education/curricula-recommendations.

ACM. 2017. Cybersecurity Curricula 2017. Joint Task Force on Cybersecurity Education. Available at: www.acm.org/education/curricula-recommendations.

Army Cyber Institute. 2020. Cyber Leader Development Program (CLDP) Overview. Available at: https://cyber.army.mil.

Blair, J., A. Hall and E. Sobiesk. 2019. Educating Future Multidisciplinary Cybersecurity Teams. *Computer* 52(3).

Brown, C., F. Crabbe, R. Doerr, R. Greenlaw, C. Hoffmeister, et al. 2012. Anatomy, Dissection, and Mechanics of an Introductory Cyber-Security Course's Curriculum at the United States Naval Academy. In Proceedings of Conference Innovation and Technology in Computer Science Education. Haifa, Israel.

CISCO. 2020. CISCO Training and Certifications. Available at: www.cisco.com/c/en/us/training-events/training-certifications.html.

Concise AC. 2020. Cybersecurity Conferences 2020–2021. Available at: https://infosec-conferences.com.

CTFTime. 2020. Available at: https://ctftime.org.

CyberPatriot. 2020. Available at: www.uscyberpatriot.org.

Estes, T., J. Finocchiaro, J. Blair, J. Robison, J. Dalme, *et al.*2017. A Capstone Design Project for Teaching Cybersecurity to Nontechnical Users. In Proceedings of Conference. Information Technology Education. Boston, MA.

Hall, A. and E. Sobiesk. 2017. Integration of the Cyber Domain at the United States Military Academy. In Proceedings of International Workshops: Realigning Cybersecurity Education, Melbourne, Australia. doi:10.1145/3293881.3295778.

ISACA. 2020. Available at: www.isaca.org.

ISC$^2$. 2020. Available at: www.isc2.org.

Joint Task Force (JTF) on Cyber Security Education. 2017. Cyber Security Curricula 2017, Curriculum Guidelines for Post-Secondary Degree Programs in Cyber Security: A Report in The Computing Curricula Series. ACM/IEEE-CS/AIS SIGSEC/IFIP WG 11.8, Version 1.0, New York.

National Collegiate Cyber Defence Competition. 2020. Available at: www.nationalccdc.org.

NICE. (National Initiative for Cybersecurity Education). 2019. NICE Cybersecurity Workforce Framework. Available at: https://niccs.us-cert.gov/workforce-development/cyber-security-workforce-framework.

NSA. 2020. National Centers of Academic Excellence in Cyber Defence and in Cyber Operations. Available at: www.nsa.gov/resources/students-educators/centers-academic-excellence.

Parrish, A., J. Impagliazzo, R. K. Raj, H. Santos, M. T. Asghar, *et al.*2018. Global Perspectives on Cyber Security Education for 2030: A Case for a Meta-Discipline. In Proceedings of Conference on Innovation and Technology in Computer Science Education. Larnaca, Cyprus. doi:10.1145/3293881.3295778.

picoCTF. 2020. Available at: https://picoctf.com.

SANS. 2020. Available at: www.sans.org.

Sobiesk, E., J. Blair, G. Conti, M. Lanham, and H. Taylor. 2015. Cyber Education: A Multi-Level, Multi-Discipline Approach. In Proceedings of Conference Information Technology Education. Chicago.

Stockman, M., S. Leung, J. Nyland, and H. Said. 2006. The Information Technology Minor: Filling a Need in the Workforce of Today. In Proceedings of Conference Information Technology Education. Minneapolis, MN.

USMA. (United States Military Academy). 2016. Academic Program: Class of 2020 Curriculum and Course Descriptions (Red Book). Available at: www.westpoint.edu/academics/dean/strategic-documents.

# 11

# FIVE YEARS OF CYBER SECURITY EDUCATION REFORM IN CHINA

*Greg Austin and Wenze Lu*

In February 2014, President Xi Jinping declared that China wanted to become a cyber power. In 2015, the declaration led to a reset in national cyber security education policy to build the human capital assets needed. His maxim for guiding China in this sphere is "talent is the first resource; competition in cyberspace is ultimately talent competition" (Guangming Net 2018). Today, China continues its steady climb towards building its cyber security talent pool. Like many countries, China is a long way from achieving its goal. According to its own estimate for 2020 set out at least five years ago, it needs to overcome a deficit of 1.4 million people, even as the sector is expanding rapidly. Yet it produces no more than 20,000 graduates in the cyber security field annually. China's cyber defences are weak to very weak. It relies on foreign contractors for key elements of its cyber defence (Austin 2018: 54–5).

The main strategic tenets of China's cyber security education reform were set around 2015 and 2016. They have been summarised in the relevant chapter of *Cybersecurity in China* (ibid.), along with an overview of the severe institutional constrains on education in China. The first sections of this chapter revisit the main reforms by following up on the subsequent events and reporting on how particular initiatives have fared. The penultimate section addresses one of the main innovations in China's policy since the 2018 book was written: it showcases the explicit links between artificial intelligence (AI) and cyber security policies. The chapter concludes with an assessment of what China's experience in the past five years tells us about the dilemmas of national human capital formation in this field.

## The 2018 assessment

The 2018 analysis by Austin confirmed that "China faces many of the same dilemmas of cyber security education policy and delivery that other countries do" (ibid.: 37). These included pressures from rapidly changing technologies, dominance of the field of cyber security education by engineering, mathematics and computer science, inadequate consideration of social science dimensions, and poor technical infra-structure in tertiary institutions for "students to conduct even medium complexity simulations and experiments". The book also discusses substantial constraints of China's own making, such as a "rigid and authoritarian university system", "low levels of internationalisation" and the "intrusion of CCP supervision that affects student life and academic merit for teaching and research staff".

The country faced then, and now, a huge deficit in "cyber security talents" compared with demand (ibid.: 34). The deficit, in excess of one million, is condi-tioned by the "sheer size of the user population in China (individuals, business, and government agencies)". Another factor drawing talent away from commercial and user cyber security is the "government's insistence on a mass cyber surveillance system for internal security organised by the government": the largest such system in human history. The deficit was also conditioned by global competition for China's best talents, leading to a brain drain.

The main conclusion was that China was "not four decades behind" in cyber security education, but it had a monumental task ahead of it "to catch up to the education and research standards" of the United States.

Key initiatives reviewed in the 2018 assessment included:

- the move to nationwide mobilisation through a new policy
- elevation of cyber security to a level one discipline in the system of university administration (to stimulate transformation)
- creation of a new teaching and research base in the city of Wuhan
- ramping up of activities like cyber security week and student competitions.

The analysis was based on a wide range of sources from China, including the government, the education and business sectors. Similar sources have been used in the current chapter.

## Workforce and education

The workforce situation remains grim, according to several reports since 2018. The conclusions of a survey by the China Information Technology Security Evaluation Centre (CITSEC 2019a) are particularly telling. Excluding large information security firms/agencies or those involved in Internet services, the survey found that 50 per cent of the information security teams in government agencies and enter-prises have a staff of less than 20. According to the report, most respondents believe that their organisation's information security teams do not have enough people working and therefore do not function well. It also found that nearly 60 per cent of information security practitioners need to perform tasks unrelated to information security. For 34 per cent of this cohort (those who need to undertake unrelated work), it accounted for more than half of their daily time commitments. One of the most telling results was that government agencies and institutions accounted for the largest share of the "multiple roles" phenomenon, even though that sector accounted for only 17 per cent of all respondents. There is a shortage of various types of talents, especially for security construction and planning, and other organisational management roles. Consequently, the survey reported, respondents identified the lack of numbers of appropriately trained personnel resources as one of the most important reasons for information security incidents. Others included inadequate management, lack of security training and lack of funding.

The survey found that information security professionalisation is still in its infancy: no uniform professional standard for practitioners; a gap between job requirements and the qualifications and experience of practitioners; lack of employers' awareness of the importance of information security work and the need to develop such talents. More than half of the practitioners surveyed believe that senior management's lack of attention to information security is one of the main reasons for security incidents.

One of the other major complaints from practitioners was that their demand to improve their capabilities was generally not being met. One-third of practitioners surveyed say that their companies do not provide any funding for their training. The survey also found that only 18.5 per cent of employers can afford even half of the practitioners' training costs. The survey also identified deficiencies in several basic human resource management processes (such as the lack of incentives and poor promotion prospects).

Based on the survey results, the agency concluded that there were shortfalls between President Xi's cyber power ambition and China's workforce realities. It offered several recommendations. The first called for a systematic information security talent development plan. This would involve constructing a national system for cyber security education (including basic education, higher education, vocational training, and continuing education) that relied on a tripartite concept of professionals, reserve personnel and the general public. Second, the report recommended the coordinated execution of various talent development initiatives, including comprehensive planning of training, management and use of professionals, and reforming the performance evaluation and reward system. Third, the report proposed a multi-agent cooperation structure to build a cyber security talent ecosystem through closer collaboration between the relevant leadership departments, industry, academia and research institutes.

In one respect, the 2019 survey was itself a landmark compared with earlier ones. It was the first time any government agency had undertaken a systematic survey of the profession, which involved categorisation of work roles (six major categories and 14 sub-categories) (see Table 11.1). Of the six categories, operations occupying 62 per cent and security system construction occupying 32 per cent were the main two. The survey found that 46 per cent worked in private enterprises, 19 per cent in state-owned enterprises and 17 per cent in government agencies.

The percentage share indicated for content security almost certainly does not relate to government agencies, for which that is the primary mission. It is also likely that survey respondents who did not indicate this as a role may have been reluctant to do so.

**TABLE 11.1** Comparison of data on PhD completions

| Type of work performed | Tasks and responsibilities | (%) |
| --- | --- | --- |
| Regulatory governance | Strategy and regulation | 5 |
| | Information security law enforcement, supervision | 12 |
| Planning management | Strategic planning | 6 |
| | Organisation management | 21 |
| Security construction | Analysis and design | 15 |
| | Development and integration | 18 |
| Security operations | Security operations and maintenance | 22 |
| | Data disposition | 9 |
| | emergency response | 19 |
| | audit and evaluation | 18 |
| | security situation analysis | 4 |
| Content security | Content security | 8 |
| Scientific research education | Security research | 6 |
| | Training and teaching | 12 |

On gender balance, CITSEC (2019a) found that women account for around 23 per cent,[1] noting that was a significant increase of 14 per cent compared with the previous survey. Women were more often found in management positions than technical positions.

Reasons given for the persistence of the workforce problems included:

- the cyber security function does not create immediate economic benefits
- performance evaluation of cyber security professionals is underdeveloped and inconsistent
- absence of industry professional titles for expert talent.

The report identified limitations in the education system. It can only produce around 15,000 graduates each year, a rate that cannot support short-term needs. It said that the cycle of on-the-job training is too short and that many employers are "unwilling to invest sufficient resources for internal training or professional training": "only a small number of units provide adequate professional training to network security staff".

Of note, in what may be a reference to government agencies, the report noted that a "large number of key information infrastructure operating units are becoming less attractive to cyber security talent" and are subject to a severe brain drain. The main reason was that the "security function does not directly create economic benefits".

The report placed some hope in the China Information Security Evaluation Centre, where part of its mission relates to the setting of standards for professional qualifications and development, and the provision of professional education. The centre was, however, set up more than 20 years ago (1998), and has yet to achieve significant results. The report gave examples from the United States (the National Initiative for Cyber Security Education) and the United Kingdom for guidance on how China might strengthen its strategic planning and delivery of education services. In its conclusion, the short report cited the weak state of development of China's information security market as one major reason for the talent shortages. While this claim is well established, the figures cited are slightly puzzling: "the current domestic network security market is only three to four billion yuan, but the black and gray industry has reached 100 billion yuan". If the statistics are correct, they would represent a serious distortion of the market which would undermine attempts at professionalisation.

The CITSEC 2019 survey provided the foundation for a White Paper (CITSEC 2019b). The latter suggested some prospective growth in the number of cyber security professionals, based on its findings that the proportion of under-25s was 19 per cent of the total in the 2019 survey, which is 10 per cent higher than in 2018 (ibid.). But demand had also surged. A separate private sector study reported that the demand for cyber security talents has surged dramatically in the past year, as agencies and firms outside of the five main cyber cities (Beijing, Shenzhen, Shanghai, Chengdu and Guangzhou) increased (Zhaopin 2019).

The demographics of the country's cyber security workforce show severe distortions. According to the 2018 White Paper (CITSEC 2018), cybersecurity practitioners are comparatively young. The proportion of practitioners under the age of 40 is as high as 95 per cent.

Beijing, Guangdong and Shanghai are the three places with the highest demand for cyber security talents, accounting for just over 60 per cent of the total national demand in 2018 and 2019 (CITSEC 2018; 2019a) even though these areas represent a little over 10 per cent of the population. There is also a mismatch between the level of demand and the location of workforce supply. Beijing, Shenzhen, Shanghai, Xi'an and Chengdu are the cities where cyber security talents are mostly concentrated: approximately 79 per cent of the country's total in 2018.

A 2018 assessment published only a short time before a high-level work meeting chaired by Xi on cyber security and informatisation assessed that there are "still significant shortcomings in the current network security talent team [in the millions], which is far from meeting the needs of the rapid development of information technology" (Guangming Net 2018). It also reported an imbalance within the cyber security talent pool "between those specialised in technical support, management, risk assessment and testing" and those "adept in strategic planning, system design and understand both technical and business matters", describing the latter group as small in number. The author described the imbalance in other terms as well, noting that "relatively few are engaged in strategic planning and architecture design" and there is a "lack of high-end personnel who understand both business and technology". The talent pool, the report said, is "too large at the bottom and too small at the top".

The CITSEC White Paper (2019b: 59–60) made recommendations to the government to do a lot more:

- build a cyber security personnel training system
- increase investment in cyberspace security personnel training platforms
- expand the cyber security industry in local technology industries.

More specifically, the report suggested increasing investment in universal cyber security education, organising popular education and the advocacy of cyber security for young people and stimulating young people's interest in cyber security. It called for more reliance on special subsidies and talent recognition standards and implementation of a registration system for cyberspace security talents to facilitate management and human resource deployment. Overall, higher standards were needed all round.

Its recommendations for enterprises and government agencies included giving more emphasis to their network security personnel, giving full play to their professional capabilities, and paying attention to the promotion and implementation of corporate network security concepts and culture. To practitioners, the White Paper called for more attention to industry trends and to continuing education. It encouraged students to "intensify their studies, actively study relevant national strategies and laws and regulations, establish a correct outlook on security, development, and career, fully understand the interdisciplinary attributes of network security". For colleges, the recommendations called for closer adherence to professional characteristics, stronger collaboration with industry, and to meet a larger variety of needs for cyber security talent.

## Key policy milestones and reference points

Unlike many governments that prefer on-the-job skills development for cyber security over tertiary training and education, China places priority on tertiary education as the primary foundation of all workforce development in the field.

The 2016 National Cyber Security Strategy, China's first, highlighted education as one of nine strategic priorities while linking it very closely to development of the industry (CAC 2016). The most important education policy related to that position was in fact made in 2015 when the Ministry of Education (MoE) and the State Council Academic Degrees Committee agreed to elevate the discipline of cyber security to what the system calls a "first level discipline" (Hui and Tan 2016: 13). For undergraduates, this move meant that their degrees would be an "engineering degree". The agencies also formally declared the designation of first level discipline for doctoral studies in cyber security. When the decision was announced at the start of 2016, the government simultaneously disclosed that it had authorised 27 universities to implement both steps (MoE 2016; Austin 2018: 29). The main effect of designation as a first level discipline is that the MoE runs a teaching guidance committee for the development of the specialisation by the central government.

Not surprisingly, given that such policies need several years to take effect, the designation of "first level discipline" had little visible impact on domestic education delivery and outcomes by the end of 2019. As one measure of possible improvements, we can look at the number of PhD graduates in the field, as indicated in Figure 11.1. While the lack of visible impact in three years (2016–18) is not surprising, given the length of doctoral programmes, it reminds us that the impact of such policy measures will only be felt after considerable time (if at all).

It is worth noting that the CNKI database produced slightly different results in two samplings taken two years apart, one for the period to 2016 and the second for the period to 2019. The most likely explanation is that CNKI has modified the database or someone has added or deleted dissertations from the database.

In 2018, at a National Cyber Security and Informatisation Working Conference in Beijing on 20–21 April, President Xi Jinping offered an invocation to the country to do more, but there seems to have been few policy innovations, and a lack of recognition that the strategy was deficient. Speaking generally of all talents in the informatisation sector, he stated that China should formulate a comprehensive strategy that guides the development of talent. He called for the restructuring of systems and policies for talent development in order to nurture creativity and ingenuity in the workforce (Xinhua 2018a). Of note, he placed ideological considerations as the leading element of four principles to be observed.

In March 2019, the General Office of the Ministry of Education issued the most recent policy guidance, under the rubric of "Key points of work about education informatisation and cybersecurity in 2019" (MOE 2019a). Its main instructions on improving the "support capacity of cybersecurity talents" are listed in Table 11.2. The Ministry was asking for continued efforts in many specific initiatives.

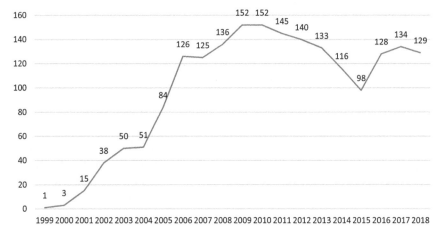

**FIGURE 11.1** China's PhD completions in cyber security, 1999–2018

**TABLE 11.2** 2019 policy guidance for China

Improve the capacity to cultivate talents and enhance their quality

Compile the Guide to Core Courses for postgraduate students

Enhance the guidance as to "double first-class" universities

Strengthen the construction of disciplines related to cyberspace security and artificial intelligence

Explore new ideas, systems, and mechanisms for training cyber security talents to build world-class cyber security colleges

Implement the "Excellent Engineer" Training Plan 2.0

Accelerate the construction of new engineering disciplines in the field of cyber security

Promote the collaboration between universities and the industry to cultivate cyber security talents

Encourage qualified vocational schools to set up cybers security-related majors

Expand the scale of training for cybers security talents

Continue to improve the national teaching standard system for vocational education

Carry out the second batch of work to revise teaching standards in high vocational schools

It included typical CCP mobilisation invocations, such as to further promote the implementation of the Opinions on Strengthening the Construction of Cyber Security Disciplines and the Training of Talents and Measures for Demonstration Projects of the Construction of First-class Cyber Security Institute (CAC and MoE 2017).

In September 2019, in a consultation paper promoting the development of the cyber security industry, the Ministry of Industry and Information Technology (MIIT) offered its insights into the education policy measures needed (MIIT 2019: 7). In a section on improving the talent training system, it called for the following proposals:

- more universities to establish cyber security colleges or cyber security-related majors
- to intensify the establishment of first-class cyber security colleges and development of teaching and research staff
- to strengthen vocational education to produce more graduates
- to promote the collaboration between universities and the industry by setting up joint laboratories for cyber security
- to support high-level cyber security contests
- to improve the talent discovery and selection mechanism.

Unusually, the MIIT paper called for more internationalisation of cyber security technologies and business, including measures for the most "powerful" companies to set up overseas R&D centres and joint laboratories, and to introduce high-end overseas talents and advanced technologies. The paper also pressed cyber security companies to participate in and organise influential international forums and exhibitions on cyber security and encouraged them to participate in the formulation of international cyber security standards.

In 2019, the government brought into effect a new regulation on information security standards that is likely to have a positive effect on enhancing business commitment to improving the workforce, thus potentially driving up education standards for cyber security. The regulation, dubbed MPLS 2.0, is a strengthened version of a system introduced in 2008 called the multi-level protection scheme (MLPS). It sets very broad definitions of the need for different levels of security for different types of information, largely with reference to national security and economic interests. The changes implemented through MPLS 2.0 extend and strengthen supervision and compliance processes (KPMG 2019).

## Universities approved for cyber security-related majors

By the end of 2018, "244 network security-related majors had been set up in 241 colleges and universities in China", according to a Chinese news report, citing Feng Huamin, Secretary General of the Cyberspace Security Teaching Steering Committee of the Ministry of Education (Xinhua 2019a).

On 25 March 2019, the MoE published the results of the filing and approval of new undergraduate majors in regular institutions of higher education in 2018 (MoE 2019b). The Ministry of Education approved 25 universities to set up cyberspace security majors and ten universities to set up information security majors. The difference between the two majors is not substantial. Table 11.3 shows a list of the institutions with new majors approved.

## Assessing quality

In November 2019, the Chinese Universities Alumni Association (CUAA) published a new ranking of the best Chinese universities for information security on a nine-point scale. Table 11.4 shows the rankings for the top ten universities (CUAA 2019). Two universities achieved equal top positions of 7-star rating, five attained 6-star rating, while another 16 were awarded a 5-star rating (ibid.). In 2017, the CUAA ranking awarded the top four universities a 6-star rating, and another 14 received a 5-star rating (CUAA 2017). Such ranking does not reveal anything about the top achievers, but it provides some indication of the likely numbers of high-end talents. Although no Chinese university was ranked at the two highest levels of excellence (8-star and 9-star), there seems to be an improvement in the quality of information security education since 2017, in the case of PLA University of Science and Technology and the National University of Defense Technology.

As observed by Austin (2018), it is surprising that Tsinghua and Beijing University, the country's two premier education and research universities, did not appear in the rankings. This reflects the enduring reality that "the centre of gravity in Chinese studies of information security broadly defined is not in Beijing, and nor is it in Shanghai, though these cities are prominent". The two cities figured more prominently in the results of the 2019 CITSEC White Paper, which reported that professional preference ranking the top five universities with cyber security majors are Beijing University of

**TABLE 11.3** Institutions with new majors approved in 2018

| Cyberspace security | Cyberspace security | Information security |
| --- | --- | --- |
| Tianjin University | Jinan University | Central Institute for Correctional Police |
| Jilin University | Shandong Normal University | Hebei GEO University |
| Shandong University | Hubei Institute of Technology | Changchun University of Technology |
| Huazhong University of Science and Technology | South China Normal University | Qingdao Institute of Technology |
| Beijing University of Electronic Science and Technology | Guangzhou University | Xuchang University |
| Harbin Institute of Technology | Chengdu Neusoft University | Yulin Normal University |
| Nanjing University of Science and Technology | Guizhou University of Science and Technology | Chongqing Institute of Engineering |
| Inner Mongolia University of Science and Technology | Yunnan University | Qinghai University for Nationalities |
| Shanghai University | Tibet University for Nationalities | Xinhua College of Ningxia University |
| Hangzhou University of Electronic Science | Gansu College of Political Science and Law | Guangxi University for Nationalities |
| Anhui University | Xinjiang University | |
| Anhui Normal University | Xinjiang University of Finance and Economics | |
| Fujian Normal University | | |

Posts and Telecommunications, Xi'an University of Electronic Technology, University of Electronic Science and Technology in Chengdu, Beijing University of Aeronautics and Astronautics, and Shanghai Jiaotong University (CITSEC 2019b). An interesting point is that the top 16 universities for cyber security education only account for 18 per cent of the practitioners. One explanation may be that most practitioners do not have degrees in cyber security.

Data from 2019 shows the following educational qualifications in Tables 11.5 and 11.6 from cyber security practitioners in a survey with a sample size of 4,344 (CITSEC 2019a: 79).

The lead official for cyber security education in China, Feng Huamin, offered a very bleak assessment in 2019 (Xinhua 2019a):

- the cyberspace security specialty and information security specialty are ambiguous in content and lack homogeneity within the specialties

TABLE 11.4 CUAA university rankings for the cyber security discipline, 2017 and 2019

| Tier 2019 | Tier 2017 | Name of institution | Star rating 2019 | Star rating 2017 |
|---|---|---|---|---|
| 1 | 1 | University of Science and Technology of China | 7 | 6 |
| 1 | n/a | National University of Defense Technology | 7 | n/a |
| 2 | 1 | Shanghai Jiaotong University | 6 | 6 |
| 3 | 1 | Wuhan University | 6 | 6 |
| 3 | 1 | Shandong University | 6 | 6 |
| 3 | 2 | Huazhong University of Science and Technology | 6 | 4 |
| 4 | 3 | University of Electronic Science and Technology | 6 | 4 |
| 5 | 2 | China Criminal Police College | 5 | 5 |
| 5 | 2 | Nanjing University of Posts and Telecommunications | 5 | 5 |
| 5 | | Beijing University of Posts and Telecommunications | 5 | 5 |

TABLE 11.5 Undergraduate majors of survey respondents

| Degree | (%) |
|---|---|
| Non-computer-related arts major | 13 |
| Non-computer science major | 11 |
| Computer-related major | 55 |
| Information and network security-related majors | 22 |

TABLE 11.6 Education level of survey respondents

| Education level | (%) |
|---|---|
| High school and below | 3 |
| College (including higher vocational) | 16 |
| Undergraduate | 65 |
| Master's degree | 14 |
| PhD | 2 |

- there is a lack of high-level professional teachers who have in-depth engagement with cyber security research
- the quality of teaching materials is uneven
- there is a lack of a good offensive and defensive training platforms, experimental opportunities, and exposure of students to actual network security problems.

In September 2019, Liu Changya, Director of the Development Planning Department of the Ministry of Education, offered another assessment of the state of cyber security education during the national Cyber Security Week in Tianjin (People's Daily TV 2019). To overcome the challenges of workforce development, he urged the country to establish new concepts, standards, models, methods, and technologies for network security and informatisation training. He introduced the five types of cyber security majors that constitute the total of 233 approved majors in Chinese universities as of that date: cyberspace security, information security, information and countermeasure technology, confidentiality technology, cyber security and law enforcement. He stated that seven universities had been selected to urgently deliver special training programmes for high-level talents. He referenced the impact of the National Standard for the Teaching Quality of Undergraduate Majors in General Colleges and Universities, released in 2018, in clarifying the discipline basis and personnel development intent of information security majors.

He offered useful data that shows impressive gains. In 2018, the five undergraduate majors in cyber security had 9,231 students enrolled, an increase from the previous year of 16 per cent (The Paper 2019). The number of new Master's students was 30,208 students, an increase from the previous year of 44 per cent. The number of new PhD students was 4,851, an increase of 18 per cent over the previous year. As at May 2019, he reported that 42 universities had set up academic departments specialising in cyber security.

At the same time, his speech also referred to problems previously acknowledged in earlier critiques over several years (Austin 2018), such as the decoupling of theory and practice, the lack of cooperation between business and educational institutions, and the lack of investment (even by cyber security companies) in skills development of the workforce (People's Daily TV 2019).

Liu offered three recommendations. First, the country should deepen the integration of business and education, especially through the establishment of a national security-integrated innovation platform for network security based on talent training and technological innovation. Second, there was a need to build a task-driven composite talent training model that would rely on disciplinary crossovers (integration of education in energy, security, transportation, sociology, and law) and other innovations such as a dual mentoring system. Third, he urged the strengthening of military-civilian integration and the integration of cyber security into the national security system.

## Demonstration projects for first-class cyber security institutes

In September 2017, the Office of the Central Cyberspace Affairs Commission and the Ministry of Education jointly published "Measures for Demonstration Projects of the Construction of First-class Cyber Security Institutes", setting an overall training regime and specific objectives for the cultivation of cyber security talents. In the 2017 China Cyber Security Week, which was held in Shanghai on 16 September 2017, seven universities were first selected for the demonstration projects. They were Xidian University, Southeast University, Wuhan University, Beihang University, Sichuan University, University of Science and Technology of China and the Information Engineering University.

The 2018 China Cyber Security Week, with the theme "cyber security for the people and cyber security through the people", opened in Chengdu, the capital of Sichuan Province, from 17 to 23 September 2018. The 2018 Cyber Security Week was co-organised by government authorities including the Cyberspace Administration of China, the Ministry of Public Security and the Ministry of Education. It was designed to promote Xi Jinping's grand vision of building cyber power, display important achievements in China's cyber security, and raise the public's cyber security awareness. A series of forums and an expo were included in the cyber security week. At the 2018 China Cyber Security Week's sub-forum on personnel training in relation to cyber security, experts from the universities that were selected as Demonstration Projects of the Construction of First-class Cyber Security Institutes introduced their education and training of cyber security talents. See Box 11.1 for examples.

---

## BOX 11.1 EXAMPLES OF INNOVATIONS IN TERTIARY STUDIES

- *Sichuan University*: The College of Cyber Security at Sichuan University is a national cyber security talent base. It proposed the "Cyber Security Outstanding Talent Plan" in 2017, which aimed at attracting potential cyber security talents who are in their second year of high school studies. The college can grant special admissions for these students. According to Xingshu Chen, Deputy Head of the College of Cyber Security at Sichuan University, the College recruited 13 students in 2018, and 12 of them were granted admissions by reducing the *Gaokao* entry requirements for them. The College built an experimental class for students recruited by the "Cyber Security Outstanding Talent Plan" to give them individualised training. To carry out multidisciplinary training, the College designated two supervisors with different specialist subjects for each student.

- *Beihang University*: Liu Jianwei, the Head of the School of Cyber Science and Technology at Beihang University, stated that their school had signed strategic cooperation agreements with 12 cyber security companies, such as DBAPPSecurity (安恒信息), Tencent (腾讯), Eversec (恒安嘉新), and Bangcle (梆梆安全). The school had established six research laboratories, including the cryptography and application laboratory, the system security laboratory, the network security laboratory, the content security laboratory, the application security laboratory, and the cyberspace security governance laboratory. Moreover, in terms of international partnership, Beihang University had signed cooperation agreements with the International Civil Aviation Organization (ICAO), Russia's Information Technologies, Mechanics and Optics (ITMO) University, and the National University of Sciences and Technology (NUST) of Pakistan to jointly train graduate students in the field of cyberspace security.

- *Xidian University*: The School of Cyber Engineering at Xidian University attempts to run talent contests to promote cyber security education. According to Li Hui (李晖), the Head of the School of Cyber Engineering at Xidian University, the School holds a contest to choose 40 special talents for cyberspace security from the whole university every year.
- *Southeast University*: On 15 March 2018, the Ministry of Education approved the undergraduate major "Cyberspace security" of Southeast University. It means Southeast University became the first university in Jiangsu Province to offer the undergraduate major of "cyberspace security". This is another landmark after the university was established as one of the seven universities of "Demonstration Project in the Construction of First-class Cyber Security Institute" by the Office of the Central Cyberspace Affairs Commission and the Ministry of Education in September 2017. In terms of talent development, the School of Cyber Science and Engineering at Southeast University added the major of cyber security to its independent enrolment since 2018. The school attempted to make full use of independent enrolment to pick young students with potential in cyber security. On the other hand, the university paid great attention to the joint degree education of the Bachelor's degree, Master's degree, and the PhD, and established the special talent training system with Southeast University characteristics and in line with the international standards.
- *University of Science and Technology of China*: In June 2018, the School of Cyberspace Security at the University of Science and Technology of China set up the "Wang Xiaomo Cyberspace Technology Talents Class" (王小谟网络空间科技英才班) to select students with potential in cyber security. There are currently two types of students enrolled in the class. The first is students who are much younger compared to the usual college students, with the entrance age younger than 15. The second is excellent college freshmen.

In March 2019, one China's leading cyber security companies, Qihoo 360,[2] announced its own initiative to set up a training base in Beijing in partnership with Shandong Zhongqi Chuangyou Technology.[3] The base will use the 360 standard curriculum system and framework for collaboration between business and education providers. The Qihoo training base will build on previously developed and wide-ranging training and education activities. These activities already have existing partnerships with leading universities, such as Peking University, Tsinghua University and Wuhan University. The instructors are mostly front-line cyber security experts, professors and lecturers working in 360.

In July 2019, 360 announced the official rebranding of its "Cyber Security College" (set up in 2017) as a university to help better prepare the country for the era of information warfare (360 Security 2019a). It would build an advanced system for the training of cyber security talents across industry, and provide professional skills improvement for key positions in the Internet, medical, transportation, education, finance, power, water conservancy and other industries, as well as key positions in state agencies, public security systems, and the armed forces.

Qihoo has also established a certification system which it saw as filling the national need (360 Security 2019b).

During the 2019 China Cyber Security Week, which kicked off in Tianjin on 16 September 2019, China's top cyber security and education authorities added another four universities to the list of the Demonstration Projects of the Construction of First-class Cyber Security Institutes (Pengpai xinwen 2019). They are Huazhong University of Science and Technology, Beijing University of Posts and Telecommunications, Shanghai Jiao Tong University and Shandong University. Therefore, as of now, 11 universities have been selected as Demonstration Projects of the Construction of First-class Cyber Security Institutes.

## The national research bases of international cyberspace governance

On 5 July 2018, the State Internet Information Office and the Ministry of Education decided to set up the National Research Bases of International Cyberspace Governance. They aimed to give China's universities the full scope to take advantage of their teaching and research resources in the field of the Internet and encourage Chinese universities to further strengthen related theoretical research, discipline construction as well as talent cultivation. Ten universities were selected as the first batch of the National Research Bases of International Cyberspace Governance: Tsinghua University, Beijing University of Posts and Telecommunications, Wuhan University, Fudan University, Harbin Institute of Technology, Beihang University, Zhejiang University, People's Public Security University of China, Southeast University and Tongji University.

### The Wuhan base

One of the most radical institutional responses to the education deficit for cyber security is the plan to establish a new vocational college for non-degree studies in Wuhan. Wuhan may well be the leading city in China for academic research and teaching in the field. The college had an initial target of 10,000 students over an undefined period, but presumably in one year. It was announced in August 2017 with a projected cost of US$751 million (Xinhua 2017). It was part of a larger plan approved one year earlier by the Cyberspace Administration of China (CAC) for the establishment of a National Cyber Security Talent and Innovation Base (NCTIB) in the city on a site of 60 hectares (China Net Com 2019). Alongside the new college, the first phase of construction beginning in 2017 included an exhibition centre, an international talent community, infrastructure of the NCTIB, a supercomputer centre by Centrin Data Systems and a cybersecurity technology incubator set up by TusStar (China Youth Network 2017).

The process of identifying recruits proceeded quite well, but it appears that few, if any, have set foot in the new Academy. According to one report, as of July 2019, 38 classes comprising 1,500 students from the two universities were scheduled to move into the Academy, while the Cyber Security Training Centre has already recruited 20,000 registered students both online and offline (Huang et al. 2019).

Wuhan University and Huazhong University of Science and Technology have nearly 50 professors and instructors teaching in the National Cybersecurity Academy, and the number is estimated to double to 100 (Hubei Daily 2019).

In 2018, the Base began construction of a Joint Research Institute of Cyber Security, in which six companies have jointly invested (Hengan Jiaxin, Zhongke Shuguang, Digital Certification, Technological Technology, Tianrongxin and Open Source Network Security) (China Net Com 2019).

The first public use of the Base on the 20 July 2019 was an "introduction" of its offerings. More than 500 industry heavyweights and student representatives from home and abroad attended the opening event. The opening event also included a cyber security talent training forum to promote various talents and attract high-quality projects to the site. (Huang et al. 2019). The exhibition centre opened on 20 July 2019, serving as a platform for conference services, the reception and the showcase of exhibitions (Xinhua 2019b).

The construction of TusStar's cybersecurity technology incubator is expected to be completed in 2020. Centrin Data System's Wuhan supercomputing centre was to be fully completed by the end of 2019 (Hubei Daily 2018). As of March 2019, 91 companies (domestic and foreign) had registered to be part of the Base, with 43 contracted projects and a total investment of 327.2 billion yuan (China Net Com 2019). These included China Information Technology, France Source News, Aerospace Information, NSFOCUS, Evertrust Sincere, Daystar, Anheng Information, Blue Shield and Ansai Technology.

It was only in April 2019 that a Steering Committee for the Base was established in Wuhan, and the first working meeting was held. The committee includes well-known experts from education, science and technology and industry (Huang et al. 2019).[4]

In early 2020, a high-level Party group was convened at the provincial level to provide better strategic direction and ensure that the Academy would meet its target of teaching students in 2020 (Xie 2020). The group, led by Ma Guoqiang, Deputy Secretary of the Hubei Provincial Party Committee and Secretary of the Wuhan Municipal Party Committee, was named the Leading Group for the Construction of the Provincial National Cyber Security Base. The meeting called for a strengthening of the connection with the central state ministries and commissions, and the establishment of more projects. The intent should be, the group affirmed, to set a world standard in cyber security training. The meeting also called on Wuhan University and Huazhong University of Science and Technology to strengthen communications and share resources.

## AI and cyber security

While the view that AI will become increasingly valuable in cyber security defences is already current outside China (CAICT 2018; 2019), few countries have given AI much attention in their main public documents framing their cyber security education policy. For example, President Trump's Executive Order on America's Cybersecurity Workforce (White House 2019) does not mention AI. The US National Cyber Strategy (White House 2018) only mentions AI technology as something that needs to be defended, not as an integral component of its cyber defences or its cyber security education policy. That said, cyber defence is an important part of international AI research, including by the US government. For China, the efficiencies offered by AI applications to cyber security offer the only possible pathway to overcoming its severe human capital deficit in this sector, estimated to be in excess of one million posts.

A White Paper (CAICT 2018) on AI security has two short sections relevant to education: "Situation of the Construction of Artificial Intelligence Talents at Home and Abroad" and a section on "Improving Talent Training and Improve Employment Skills". The paper observed that despite China's achievements in education for artificial intelligence in recent years, there is still a "large gap compared with developed countries, notably the United States and Britain" (ibid.: 35). These education systems have significant advantages, especially in long-established artificial intelligence-related majors and research directions in their well-known universities. Citing data from the Tencent Research Institute, "2017 Global Artificial Intelligence Talent White Paper", the CAICT report observed that of the top 20 research universities in the world for AI, the United States occupies 14, and sits in the first eight places. In terms of industrial talent, as of 2017, the total number of qualified professionals in the United States was "about twice that of China": "approximately 78,000 employees in 1,078 artificial intelligence companies compared with approximately 39,000 employees in 592 Chinese companies".

The CAICT paper made three recommendations to improve AI security education, with the goal of strengthening the construction of artificial intelligence technology and industrial talents to reduce the risk of hindering the development of the industry caused by talent shortage (ibid.: 41). First, it called for the robust implementation of existing AI education policy measures proposed by the Ministry of Education. The measures included establishing artificial intelligence-related majors in qualified universities, expanding enrolment quotas, strengthening professional education and vocational education, providing access to artificial intelligence professionals, granting financial support for key universities to build research and innovation centres and, finally, focusing on the nurturing of research talent. Second, the paper proposed AI companies to establish training institutions or jointly build laboratories with universities, carry out technology and applied research, and cultivate available talents through practical training. Third, and perhaps a little controversially, the paper recommended a heavier reliance on foreign AI talents through intensifying recruitment to China, setting up research and development centres abroad, and attaining core technologies through foreign investment and acquisitions.

## Conclusion

In the five years since Xi's declaration of China's cyber power ambition, China has made technocratic adjustments to its education policy for cyberspace security. It has not moved decisively towards the multidisciplinary approaches that were advocated elsewhere in this book. It has not been able to achieve radical breakthroughs in the quality and volume of education outcomes that it so desperately needs. China is not alone in this respect, yet there appears to be a number of constraints arising from its unique social and political order that will frustrate its efforts to adjust to the wide range of requirements outlined elsewhere in this volume, compared with other countries.

The Chinese domestic assessments of the state of play of their education policy presented in this chapter show little prospects for a quick turn-around from the prevailing skills deficit. The impulse of China to internationalise its cyber security education may be its best hope. This is not a widely supported goal nor a deeply developed impulse in the country. In fact, there are strong anti-globalising (supposedly patriotic) influences that run counter to the internationalising impulse. At the same time, there is a huge information deficit both for Chinese officials and analysts about the degree of dependence on non-Chinese actors in the delivery of cyber security in the country. There is no ready acceptance of the view that there can be no cyber security in China without radical internationalisation of the sector, especially in education policy.

## Notes

1  Percentages cited from all reports cited in this chapter are rounded to the nearest whole numbers.
2  360 describes itself as "China's largest and world's leading cybersecurity company, committed to providing world-leading products, services and solutions for personal security, social security, national defense security and national security".
3  The company describes itself as a "wholly-owned listed company under CIC Great Wall, with a deep knowledge of China's education sector, with vocational education as its starting point and focus on government, individuals and businesses provide one-stop education solutions". CIC is a wealth management fund.
4  Academicians of the Chinese Academy of Engineering, Shen Changxiang, Chairman of 360 Group Zhou Hongkun, Director of the Information Engineering Institute of the Chinese Academy of Sciences, Meng Dan, and other professionals have provided suggestions on the training of network security personnel and the construction of the base. Professor Jin Hai of Huazhong University of Science and Technology serves as the dean and the honorary dean is Professor Su Jinshu of the National University of Defense Technology.

## Acknowledgements

The authors would like to acknowledge research assistance provided by Kai Lin Tay in the final stage of completing this chapter.

# References

360 Security. 2019a. 360 Beijing Cyber Security Talent Base Officially Launched. 360 website. 14 March. In Chinese. Available at: https://university.360.cn/c/wz/t/wzxq/a rticle/360bjwlaqrcjdzsqd.html.

360 Security. 2019b. Create Authoritative Security Talent Certification: 360 Cyber Security Occupation Certification Registration Formally Launched. 11 September. In Chinese. Available at: www.freebuf.com/company-information/214092.html.

Austin, G. 2018. *Cybersecurity in China: The Next Wave*. New York: Springer.

CAC. 2016. *National Cyber Security Strategy*. Beijing: Cyberspace Administration of China.

CAC and MoE. 2017. Measures for Demonstration Projects of the Construction of First-class Cyber Security Institutes. The Office of the Central Cyberspace Affairs Commission and the Ministry of Education. In Chinese. Available at: www.moe.gov.cn/srcsite/A16/s3342/201708/t20170815_311176.html.

CAICT. (China Academy for Information and Communications Technology). 2018. Artificial Intelligence White Paper. In Chinese. Available at: www.caict.ac.cn/kxyj/qwfb/bp s/201809/t20180918_185339.html.

CAICT. (China Academy for Information and Communications Technology). 2019. China's Cyber Security Industry White Paper. In Chinese. Available at: http://m.caict.ac. cn/yjcg/201909/t20190918_211485.html.

China Net Com. 2019. Hubei: Double High Focus on Training of Cyber Security Talents and Industrial Development. 27 March. In Chinese. Available at: www.cac.gov.cn/2019-03/27/c_1124246685.htm (accessed 4 February 2020).

China Youth Network. 2017. Construction of Cyber Security Base Entered a Substantive Stage. 23 August. In Chinese. Available at: http://news.youth.cn/jsxw/201708/t20170823_10572006.htm (accessed 4 February 2020).

CITSEC. (China Information Technology Security Evaluation Center). 2018. 2018 Cyber Security Talent Development White Paper. Hangzhou Anheng Information Technology Co., Ltd. and Hunting.com. In Chinese. Available at: www.cac.gov.cn/2018-12/28/c_1123919726.html.

CITSEC. (China Information Technology Security Evaluation Center). 2019a. Survey Report on the Status of China's Information Security Practitioners 2018–2019. 6 September 2019. Available at: www.itsec.gov.cn/zxxw/201909/t20190906_36022.html.

CITSEC. (China Information Technology Security Evaluation Center). 2019b. 2019 Cyber Security Talent Development White Paper. China Information Technology Security Evaluation Center, Hangzhou Anheng Information Technology Co., Ltd. and Hunting. com. Available at: www.itsec.gov.cn/zxxw/201909/t20190906_36022.html.

CUAA. (Chinese University Alumni Association). 2017. Alumni Association 2017 China University New Discipline Rankings. 18 August 2017. Available at: www.cuaa.net/paiha ng/news/news.jsp?information_id=133226.

CUAA. (Chinese University Alumni Association). 2019. Alumni Association 2019 China Computer Related Majors Ranking. In Chinese.. Available at: www.cuaa.net/paihang/news/news.jsp?information_id=135786 (accessed 4 February 2020).

Guangming Net. 2018. Ensuring the Security of National Cyberspace. Available at: www.ca c.gov.cn/2018-04/14/c_1122679939.html.

Hu, J. 2019. Sub-forum of 'Cultivation and Discipline Construction of Cyberspace Security Talents' Held in Tianjin. *Legal Daily*. 19 September. In Chinese. Available at: www.itsec. gov.cn/zxxw/201909/t20190906_36022.html.

Huang, J., S. B. Guo and X. X. Cai. 2019. Transformation of the National Cyber Security Innovation and Talent Base Three-Year Blueprint. In Chinese. Available at: www.dong xihu.gov.cn/html/xwzx/lkgyw/2019/0719/114650.shtml (accessed 4 February 2020).

*Hubei Daily*. 2018. Centrin Data Centre Becomes Wuhan City's "Super Brain" . 12 March. In Chinese. Weibo. Available at: www.weibo.com/ttarticle/p/show?id= 2309404216784671643161 (accessed 4 February 2020).

*Hubei Daily*. 2019. Hubei Province's Cyber and Information Security Work Has Entered the Stage of Combat Phase. 20 September. In Chinese. Xinhuanet. Available at: www.hb. xinhuanet.com/2019-09/20/c_1125017605.htm. (accessed 4 February 2020).

Hui, Z. and Q. Tan. 2016. Cyberspace Security in the Era of Data Economy: Global and Chinese Contexts. In Z. Hui and Q. Tan (eds). *Annual Report on Development of Cyberspace Security in China*. In Chinese. Beijing: Social Sciences Academy Press.

KPMG. 2019. MLPS 2.0 Insights and Strategies. Available at: https://home.kpmg/cn/en/ home/insights/2019/05/mlps-insights-strategies.html.

MIIT. (Ministry of Industry and Information Technology) . 2019. Guidance on Promoting the Development of the Cyber Security Industry. In Chinese. Available at: www.cac.gov. cn/2019-09/27/c_1571114011459248.html.

MoE. (Ministry of Education). 2016. The Academic Degrees Committee of the State Council Agrees to Add Cyberspace Security. Notice of Doctoral Degree Authorization at Level 1. Decree [2016] No. 1. In Chinese. 28 January 2016. Available at: www.moe.gov. cn/s78/A22/A22_gggs/A22_sjhj/201603/t20160304_231944.html.

MoE. (Ministry of Education). 2019a. Key Points of Work About Education Informatisation and Cybersecurity in 2019. In Chinese. Available at: www.moe.gov.cn/srcsite/A16/ s3342/201903/t20190312_373147.html.

MoE. (Ministry of Education). 2019b. Results of the Filing and Approval of New Under-graduate Majors n Regular Institutions of Higher Education in 2018. In Chinese. Available at: www.moe.gov.cn/srcsite/A08/moe_1034/s4930/201903/t20190329_376012.html.

Pengpai xinwen. 2019. The Number of First-Class Cyber Security College Construction Demonstration Projects Increased to 11 Universities. 9 September. In Chinese. Available at: https://baijiahao.baidu.com/s?id=1644897288385187746&wfr=spider&for=pc.

*People's Daily TV.*. 2019. Exploring the Talent Training Model of "Network Security + X". People's Daily Online-IT Channel. 17 September. In Chinese. Available at: http://it. people.com.cn/n1/2019/0917/c1009-31357753.html.

The Paper. 2019. Director of the Development Planning Department of the Ministry of Education: Exploring the Dual-Tutor System for Training Cyber Security *Talents*. 17 September. In Chinese. Available at: www.sohu.com/a/341380535_260616.

White House. 2018. National Cyber Strategy of the United States of America. September. Available at: www.whitehouse.gov/wp-content/uploads/2018/09/National-Cyber-Strategy.pdf.

White House. 2019. Executive Order on America's Cybersecurity Workforce. 2 May 2019. Available at: www.whitehouse.gov/presidential-actions/executive-order-americas-cyberse curity-workforce/.

Xie, H. 2020. Hubei Province Held Provincial National Cyber Security Base Construction Leading Group Meeting. *Hubei Daily*. 13 January. In Chinese. Available at: www.cac.gov. cn/2020-01/13/c_1580458156252104.htm.

Xinhua. 2017. China Starts Building Internet Security Institute. 23 August. Available at: news.xinhuanet.com/english/2017-08/23/c_136549729.htm.

Xinhua. 2018a. Xi Jinping Attends National Network Security and Information Work Conference and Delivers Important Speech. 21 April. In Chinese. Available at: www.gov. cn/xinwen/2018-04/21/content_5284783.htm.

Xinhua. 2019a. There Is a Large Gap of Cyber Space Security Talents in China. China News Portal. 18 September. Available at: www.chinanewsportal.com/news/2019/0918/1739/5d820bda8a9caa1d2fbedecd.

Xinhua. 2019b. National Cyber Security Talent and Innovation Base Exhibition Centre Has Been Put into Use. 20 July. In Chinese.. Available at: www.xinhuanet.com/politics/2019-07/20/c_1210205370.htm (accessed 4 February 2020).

Zhaopin. 2019. 2019 Cyber Security Talent Market Research Report. Zhaopin and Qi'anxin Industry Security Research Center. In Chinese. Available at: http://js.ifeng.com/a/20190807/7603981_0.shtml.

# 12

# FUTURE RESEARCH ON THE CYBER SECURITY SKILLS SHORTAGE

*Tommaso De Zan*

When I was preparing my PhD research proposal in the fall of 2016, studies on the cyber security skills shortage (CSSS) were scant. The shortage was starting to emerge in the policy discourse, but the lack of scientific investigation on the matter made the writing of my literature review a particularly daunting task. Four years later, the situation has greatly improved and today both policy and research have begun to deal with the CSSS more consistently. We certainly know more about the CSSS than four years ago, but we still have a long way to go to produce solid research and policy outputs.

This chapter reflects upon future directions that research on the cyber security skills shortage might take and argues that it should primarily concentrate on two aspects: (1) the incidence of the shortage; and (2) the effectiveness of policy interventions, which are the topics of the two first sections of this chapter. The third and final section discusses the need to anchor analysis on the cyber security skills shortage in more established research traditions in the social sciences, such as labour economics, skills policy and impact evaluation. The chapter updates and revisits a discussion on issues and reflections first examined in the report "Mind the Gap: The Cyber Security Skills Shortage and Public Policy Interventions" (De Zan 2019).

## Getting to know the shortage: incidence, contours and causes

Research on the CSSS needs to redouble its efforts to analyse the incidence, characteristics and causes of the shortage. Doing this would benefit both knowledge development and policy-making. It would benefit knowledge development because, among all skills issues, skills shortages have received the least attention by researchers – only 12 papers on this topic were written between 1994 and 2017 – and have the least developed evidence base (McGuinnes, Pouliakas and Redmond 2018). In addition, it would enormously help policy-making, as having a clearer idea about this sector shortage is the necessary first step before launching policy interventions aimed at solving this problem.

The CSSS is now fully acknowledged by governments and often discussed in mainstream media outlets (De Zan 2019; Nachreiner 2019). At almost every conference frequent references to the shortfall of cyber security professionals are made. Yet, we still know very little about it. The main issue is that we probably do not even realise how scarce our knowledge of the shortage is.

Most of the public debate on the CSSS has been driven by private sector reports, which are often cited by media or by governments in justification of their policies. Table 12.1 gives an example of one commonly cited set of estimates from the International Information System Security Certification Consortium (ISC)[2]. However, these reports have used methodologies which make their results scientifically unsound. There have been various issues with these reports, for example, there have been various quantifications of the shortage at the international level, but most of the time it has been unclear how these figures have been computed. The fact that predictions of the shortage have been constantly, and *unpredictably*, on the rise is a warning sign that should make us reflect on how these calculations were done in the first place. Above all, it should make us reflect on whether it is safe to rely on these estimates as the foundation of our research papers and national policies.

Moreover, CSSS research has relied heavily on survey methodologies, but often the questionnaires have been so vague and poorly formulated that we should be careful if we assertively claim that, given these results, there is absolutely no doubt that a shortage in cyber security is underway. When most Chief Information Security Officers (CISOs) answer positively questions, such as "Do you think there is a lack of cyber security skills at your work?", this does not provide hard evidence of the presence of a shortage. The question, and its related answer, might be interpreted in different ways. If a CISO answers yes, she might mean that there is not enough IT security personnel in her team, but this might be due to several causes, for example, dysfunctional HR recruiting processes or the unavailability of further funds within the budget to invest in human capital rather than lack of available talent.

Criticising the results of some reports of shortage does not mean denying shortages do not exist. It would be irresponsible to posit that because research so far has not followed high scientific standards, we should roll out the presence of the CSSS. Indeed, if one looks beyond this industry reports, there is enough evidence confirming that the labour market is experiencing difficulties at the intersection

**TABLE 12.1** Shortage of workers according to (ISC)[2]

| 2015 | 2017 | 2018 | 2019 |
|------|------|------|------|
| 1.5 million (by 2020) | 1.8 million (by 2022) | 2.93 million (in 2018) | 4.07 million (in 2019) |

Sources: Frost and Sullivan 2017; (ISC)2 (2018; 2019).

between cyber security supply and demand. However, it seems obvious that so far, no measurement or description of the shortage has been able to effectively and comprehensively capture the presence, scale and nature of the problem. In the words of the US government, "While there is not an exact number to describe it, the shortage of cyber security professionals is happening and is clear" (The Secretary of Commerce and the Secretary of Homeland Security 2017).

Luckily, not everything that we know about the presence of the shortage has a weak foundation. Some governments have produced stronger evidence on it, and more should be done to build upon these methodologies and findings to achieve better conceptual clarity. The best example of CSSS analysis possibly comes from the Australian Sector Competitiveness Plan (AustCyber 2018). The Plan presents a battery of indicators that more strongly produce evidence ascertaining the shortage of cyber security professionals in the Australian labour market:

- Wage premium
- Recruitment failure rate
- Recruitment time
- Job market depth
- Size of the current workforce
- Composition of the workforce according to NICE's (National Initiative for Cybersecurity Education) categories
- Number of job vacancies and breakdown according to NICE's categories and by experience requested
- Forecast of the additional workforce the Australian economy could require in the medium-term
- Cyber workforce demand and supply.

This shortage analysis punches above its weight because it assesses the problem holistically and does not stop to analyse the issue only from a labour market perspective, but also includes how the education and training system is shaping the national supply of cyber security professionals. Relevant data includes the number of established cyber security degrees, student demand for cyber security courses, a comparison of salaries between the industry and the education system (to prove the point that education is facing tough competition from the private sector in attracting capable experts who can teach cyber security) and finally awareness of the cyber security sector and careers among Australian students. Furthermore, the Plan does not stop to attest the presence of the shortage but goes deeper into the analysis of its causes. As any serious analysis of the shortage should do, it outlines how the shortage is compounded by issues within the education system (students' demand, among others) and in the labour market as well (employers' high requirements, among others).

In sum, the Australian Sector Competitiveness Plan represents a step forward in the analysis of the CSSS. A possible suggestion would be to use the Plan as a reference to research other national shortages and then, depending on stakeholder's appetite for an even fuller understanding, integrate additional methodologies that could further enrich how this phenomenon unfolds. The Plan's analysis should be complemented with quantitative surveys and qualitative interviews to both employers and cyber security students to understand both what happens when students leave the education system and in the workplace.

As noted already, survey research has been used extensively, but with mixed results. This does not mean, however, that this type of methodology is not suitable to study the shortage. Rather, it should be used better. Indeed, when proper and unbiased questions are asked, surveys are a rich source of information and well equipped to give a more nuanced understanding of the reasons for the shortage rather than labour market indicators, which only attest to the presence of a shortage or not. Moreover, a lot could be gauged from the use of in-depth interviews with employers in different sectors and with different recruitment needs. Interviews would enable richer data to be collected on the mechanisms that are impeding a correct match between supply and demand. They would more precisely determine the extent to which the current situation is compounded by issues within the labour market or by problems related to the development of graduates in the education and training system. Most likely, they would find the shortage to be worsened by multiple factors.

The analysis of the shortage should not omit a much richer investigation of what happens when graduates leave the education and training system and attempt to enter the labour market. Much has been written on issues that are beleaguering cyber security education. Some of these issues include the need to better integrate cyber security in computer science degrees, the need to promote alignment between educational offers and labour market demands, to develop multi-disciplinary expertise and to encourage educators to promote a more hands-on education (Conklin, Cline and Roosa 2014; University of Phoenix, (ISC)[2] and (ISC)[2] Foundation 2014; Gagliardi et al. 2016; Catota, Morgan and Sicker 2019; Crumpler and Lewis 2019). Nonetheless, less is known about when cyber security students start to search for a job after they graduate. In the context of a shortage such as the one claimed in cyber security, one would expect cyber security graduates to be in high demand of being "poached" by employers on campus, even before entering the labour market. However, there is some evidence that this is not happening. In the UK, for example, at least one-third of cyber security graduates do not end up in cyber security, but transition to other sectors (Malan, Lale-Demoz and Rampton 2018). While this is not necessarily bad for the economy – cyber security graduates might have developed skills and knowledge that make them employable and valuable in different sectors – it is important to further investigate the causes and consequences of this "leakage". If a leakage is occurring and its scale is more consistent than we think, governments might even come up with more innovative solutions to increase student demand in cyber security, but these policies might be worthless if students do not enter the sector in the end.

In further studying the incidence of the shortage, there should be more clarity on the type of cyber security professionals the labour market that is missing and at what experience level. In countries such as Australia and the US, there is now evidence stemming from the analysis of online vacancies that most open positions are for those specialists with at least 3–5 years of professional experience. See Tables 12.2 and 12.3.

In my own research, I was often told that "the shortage is happening everywhere and at all levels", meaning it is occurring both horizontally, across various job roles and tasks, and vertically, at different experience levels. Some believe that the deficit is greatest and of most consequence at the "super expert" level (Libicki, Senty and Pollack 2014), among those specialists who have to deal with advanced persistent threats, multi-wave attacks in complex environments, or situations of comprehensive data destruction.

This should be investigated as a matter of priority. Whether the shortage is happening more at a mid to senior level rather than at the junior level is important to calibrate the right policy response. If the labour market is missing young professionals, it would be easier to locate the main thrust of the shortage problem within the education and training system. If employers do not find young graduates to enter the firm, it is probably the education and training system that is not attracting students to the field and not preparing them for a job in the sector. But when employers struggle to recruit mid or senior professionals with a mix of knowledge and expertise in multiple domains (e.g. in cyber security and finance or cyber security and insurance), they would be better off refraining from criticising

TABLE 12.2 Cyber security years of experience requirements in the Australian labour market (%)

| Mission | 0–2 years | 3–7 years | 8+ years |
| --- | --- | --- | --- |
| Securely provision | 13 | 56 | 31 |
| Operate & maintain | 16 | 59 | 25 |
| Oversee and govern | 9 | 51 | 40 |
| Protect and defend | 10 | 54 | 36 |
| Analyse | 16 | 52 | 32 |
| Collect & operate[1] | 15 | 37 | 49 |
| Investigate | 22 | 49 | 30 |

Source: AustCyber (2018).
Note:[1] The sum of the percentages in this row and the next is 101, due to rounding.

TABLE 12.3 Cyber security years of experience requirements in the US labour market (%)

| Years experience | 0–2 | 3–5 | 6–8 | 9+ |
| --- | --- | --- | --- | --- |
| % | 15 | 46 | 22 | 17 |

Source: Burningglass (2019).

the education and training system for not fulfilling its role. The education and training system is not suited to forming "super experts" as the structure of the schooling system, the limited amount of time and the overall purpose of education make it very difficult, if not impossible, to form such specialists then. Creating super experts entails a partnership between educators and employers and should be thought as a medium- to long-term objective. These professionals should be formed in multiple learning environments where the workplace and other professional training settings should be considered as conducive to honing specific cyber security knowledge and skills as the classroom.

Finally, there are various claims suggesting that the shortage is occurring worldwide. This is because there exists quantification of the worldwide shortage. However, these quantifications lead us to assume that a shortage exists everywhere and that the nature of the CSSS is identical in every single country. While it is possible that the shortage in a country is similar to a shortage elsewhere, uncritically assuming so is not helpful. Having a battery of common indicators that could help us identify the issue does not mean that the problem is due to the same causes. For example, two countries could have a limited supply of cyber security graduates coming out of the education system, but the reasons for the shortage can be different. One country could have a limited number of students entering cyber security higher education degrees, but another country might not have enough cyber security degrees to satisfy student demand. In this case, the problem is the same, but their basic reasons are different and so must be their policy remedies. It follows that every government must start from a careful definition and analysis of its *own* shortage problem if it wishes to seriously tackle it. Using an analysis of the UK or the Australian labour market as a basis to solve a national problem is unlikely to work. Despite this conviction that a shortage is happening worldwide, today one can claim there is enough evidence of the shortage in very few countries, including Australia, Italy, Japan, the UK (including Scotland) and the US. Whether and to what extent the CSSS is plaguing other countries worldwide is something that research and policy are necessary to find out.

## Policy effectiveness: conducting rigorous impact evaluations

Another key area of research is on the effectiveness of policies that are designed and implemented to reduce the CSSS. There is now ample recognition that governments can put forward any policy, but if they are unaware of their outcomes, it is as if these policies have never been implemented. It is important to run rigorous evaluations of cyber security workforce development policies as their effects might not be obvious. The example of cyber security competitions helps to elucidate why this is the case.

Among the plethora of policy interventions deployed to mitigate the shortage, national administrations have been particularly fond of cyber security competitions, which possibly are now more widespread than any other policy instrument. The Five Eyes countries and the European Union have heralded cyber security competitions as effective solutions to do the following: encourage young people to pursue a cyber security career, nurture students' interest, attract talented individuals to the field and, ultimately, meet demands for cyber security skills while generating a self-sustained cyber security workforce (see Table 12.4).

Notwithstanding the enthusiasm that surrounds them, however, if one takes a closer look at the mechanisms through which competitions supposedly "work", it is apparent that their effects might not be so obvious or at least have not been thoroughly investigated. This is evident from a quick review of the scientific literature.

On one side, there are researchers who found a positive relationship between attending competitions and career interest. Dabney et al. (2012) found that those participating in Open Start-up (OST) clubs/competitions and reading/watching science content at least a few times a year are more likely to be interested in a STEM discipline at university. Similarly, Melchior et al. (2018) found that the participants of the First Inspiration and Recognition of Science and Technology programme in the US continue to report greater average gains on STEM-related attitudes and interests as they are 3.0 times more likely to show gains on interest in STEM careers. Finally, Dunn and Merkle (2018) analysed the survey data from the CyberPatriot contests and found that interest in cyber security as an academic or employment career grew meaningfully across multiple dimensions, such as perception of career tasks, interest and awareness, and view of self.

TABLE 12.4 Cyber security key goals in Five Eyes countries and the EU

| Country | Comment |
| --- | --- |
| Australia | "Expanding the national annual Cyber Security Challenge Australia … will also help generate a sustained national pipeline of cyber security professionals" (Australian Government 2016). |
| Canada | "Youth are a vital talent pool to meet cyber security skill demands" and "This collaboration of National Youth Cyber Education Programs seeks to promote education and awareness in technology education and foster excellence in students pursuing careers in cyber security or other science, technology, engineering, and mathematics (STEM) areas" (CyberTitan 2019). |
| European Union | "Many countries launched national cyber security competitions targeting towards students, university graduates or even non-ICT professionals with a clear aim to find new and young cyber talents and encourage young people to pursue a career in cyber security" and "to help mitigate this shortage of skills" (ENISA 2019). |
| United Kingdom | The Initial Strategy cites Cyber Discovery as a programme aimed at supporting skills capability "by identifying and engaging young people and nurturing their interest in cyber security as a future career path" (HM Government 2018). |
| United States | "Cybersecurity competitions have been increasingly popular tools for attracting talented individuals and federal agencies should make greater use of them, including for professional development" (The Secretary of Commerce and the Secretary of Homeland Security 2017). |

Nonetheless, other studies found this correlation not to be so strong or even inverse. Welch and Huffman's (2011) statistical analysis detected no difference between a group of participants attending a competition and a control group of non-participants in relation to their aspirations for a science career. Tobey et al. (2014) find that competitions might be constraining the number of entrants in the field and discouraging the involvement of those with no prior experience. Hence, competitions might be better at further engaging those already committed to cyber security rather than those who are exploring it as a career possibility. Miller et al. (2018) discover that, if a student attends any STEM competition, there is a 5 per cent greater likelihood she/he will be interested in a STEM career at the end of high school. However, further analysis showed that STEM competitions seem to retain already interested students rather than bringing on board new ones.

To sum up, one can conclude that evidence on the ability of competitions to nurture cyber security career interest is at best mixed. This does not mean that cyber security competitions are not useful instruments to relieve the shortage, but that claims of policy effectiveness must be substantiated with solid evidence and policy outcomes must not be assumed. If policy outcomes are not evaluated, the obvious risk is that policies could have negative effects which had not been foreseen or could not be as efficient as originally envisaged.

Luckily, awareness is emerging among stakeholders that evaluations are key to mitigating the CSSS. For instance, the UK government's Initial Cyber Security Skills Strategy devotes an entire chapter to the importance of implementation and measurement of cyber security education interventions (HM Government 2018: Chapter 9). Of the US government's imperatives, there is now the need to establish metrics to measure the effectiveness and impact of cyber security workforce investments (The Secretary of Commerce and the Secretary of Homeland Security 2017). De Zan points out that solid and systematic evaluations would establish evidence-based frameworks to guide the formulation of cyber security skills shortage strategies, a sentiment which is similarly expressed in the White Paper of the Task Force on Cybersecurity Professional Training and Development of the Global Forum on Cyber Expertise (De Zan 2019; Garcia-van Hoogstraten and Bate 2019).

If awareness is followed by concrete willingness to establish evaluations mechanisms, luckily interested stakeholders have ample references and support to make these evaluations right. Policy evaluation is now recognised both as an academic discipline and as a field of practice. There are numerous textbooks providing the theoretical foundation of the field, including, for example, *The SAGE Handbook of Evaluation* (Shaw, Greene and Mark, 2006) as well as academic degrees, such as, for example, the Master's Degree in Evidence Based Intervention and Policy Evaluation at the University of Oxford, among others (Department of Social Policy and Intervention 2020). In the policy world, some international organisations conduct evaluations as one of their core tasks. It is not by chance that organisations such as the World Bank or the Asian Development Bank have recently published informative practical guides on how to do impact assessments (Gertler et al. 2016; White and Raitzer 2017). Impact evaluation has also attracted the attention of the non-for-profit sector with organisations such as Better Evaluation (Better Evaluation 2020); finally, the private sector has also the expertise and is very involved in doing various types of evaluations for the public sector (Ipsos MORI 2020; Kantar Public 2020). In sum, if administrations are keen to know if what they do actually works, there is certainly an abundance of knowledge and expertise to do so.

However, as implementing policies without measuring their effects is clueless, doing poor evaluations would also be of very little utility. This is because only when done properly are impact evaluations good instruments to find out the efficacy of a policy. Fully-fledged evaluations can correctly estimate whether a policy has produced the intended effects only through a mix of qualitative and quantitative methods of data collection and analysis, especially in the context of randomised control trial (RTC) designs (Trochim 2006; Owen et al. 2011; Gertler et al. 2016; White and Raitzer 2017). RTCs are the "gold standard" for evaluating policies, although other quasi or natural experiments designs can also provide enough evidence on policy outcomes. Doing RTCs and other types of experimental designs requires proven expertise, money and planning. Planning is particularly important as the most solid evaluations require measurements before a policy is implemented, and not only after completion. In sum, when deciding on doing evaluations, administrations and/or researchers should be aware of what they are undertaking. These are tools that could greatly improve the way cyber security policy-making is done, but if not conducted properly, they are unlikely to do much to enhance our understanding on how to reduce the shortage.

## Disciplinary home for the cyber security skills shortage: a "dream team of experts"

Future research on the CSSS would benefit from being solidly anchored in more established research traditions in the social sciences. Previous research in other fields can help direct research efforts and avoid starting from scratch the investigation of issues that have been already studied in other sectors and fields.

For example, the first section has already talked about the importance of determining the scale and nature of the shortage, however, this is nothing new in skills mismatch research. Today, private sector research is driving the public debate with most online media outlets citing the same industry reports over and over. I suspect that the debate would be different if interested stakeholders engaged more often with what has been previously written on issues in skills shortage measurement. Various authors have already underscored that it is difficult to distinguish between genuine and over-emphasised shortages (Cappelli 2015; McGuinness et al. 2018) and unfortunately measuring the CSSS has not been less complicated, as shown above. Reading the previous literature on skills mismatch measurement would have prompted interested individuals to assume a more critical outlook regarding the notion of the shortage and this could have initiated more serious investigations of the issue a while ago.

There is another example that helps to illustrate why getting closer to other research fields would be useful. The shortage seems to be compounded by issues occurring in the labour market and workplace, namely, when employers are reluctant to offer adequate training opportunities to their employees. In labour market economics, there is ample literature that has analysed what makes firms decide to train their employees or not and what incentives they need to do that (Acemoglu and Pischke 1999; 2001; Brunello and De Paola 2004; Keep 2006; Boeri and van Ours 2008). Although this literature might be at times overly theoretic and difficult to grasp, it is certainly better than starting from scratch and building from new what labour economists have been dealing with for many decades now.

The cyber security skills shortage is not an easy topic for researchers to deal with as it requires a unique blend of expertise. Labour economists and education specialists might not engage with cyber security as they perceive the topic to be too technical or they are simply not aware that cyber security supply and demand are not meeting at the moment. Cyber security experts are not generally concerned with education or labour market policies. Public policy specialists (especially from national security think tanks) have tried to fill the gaps, but they lack the theoretical depth of labour economists and educationalists, as well as the foundational and practical knowledge of cyber security experts. That we are failing to gather together people with complementary knowhow is evident on many occasions. For example, I have rarely (if ever) found myself at conferences or workshops where experts from different *relevant* disciplines – labour economics, education, public policy and cyber security specialists – were gathered together to discuss the shortage from their own unique view and perspective. Most of the time, one attends events where educationalists talk education or economists discuss economic issues and expertise is confined in silos. Engaging in and discussing what one knows are certainly responsible, but do not offer chances for knowledge development or policy problem-solving. The CSSS requires a "dream team" of experts that, combining their knowledge of the labour market, education and training systems, cyber security and public policy, would open the debate and base it on more solid theoretical and empirical background knowledge. If concrete willingness to solve the shortage emerges, it is paramount to create multidisciplinary groups of experts who can leverage their own unique disciplinary expertise and bring to the table the pieces of knowledge that are necessary to solve the CSSS puzzle.

## Conclusion

The cyber security skills shortage is a problem which has now been extensively debated and is increasingly recognised by governments worldwide. The relevance of the shortage in this sector makes it an important opportunity to further analyse a type of skills issue which has been under-researched in the scientific literature. Studying the shortage in cyber security can be useful to expand our knowledge of how to cope with problems that are likely to be recurring in the era of pervasive digitisation, automation and artificial intelligence, which are likely to irreversibly change the labour market and the education system. This chapter has argued that two lines of research can be particularly useful to improve the knowledge base of the CSSS: the incidence of the shortage and the effectiveness of policies designed to curb it.

First, more efforts should be devoted to study the incidence of the shortage. Our current knowledge base is flawed because shortage claims derive from reports that are scientifically weak. Thankfully, however, there have been more solid examples of CSSS research, such as the Australian Competitiveness Plan, and more should be done to build on its foundation to achieve a more complete understanding of this policy issue. In addition to online vacancy analysis, using quantitative surveys and qualitative interviews would be useful to give us a more nuanced understanding of the shortage. In this line of inquiry, it is important to rapidly find out what the labour market most badly needs. If it is true that what it is lacking are "super experts", then strategies to cope with the shortage require an unprecedented level of coordination and collaboration among academia, industry and governments. Finally, research energies should be directed to know whether and how the shortage is happening in countries that are not usually the subject of this sort of research.

Second, research should be conducted on the effectiveness of the cyber security skills shortage policies. It should not be assumed that what governments (or experts) think work, necessarily does. The example of cyber security competitions was given to prove this point. Cyber security competitions are now widely used and backed up by government as part of their cyber security workforce strategies. They are tasked primarily to increase students' interest in a cyber security career and potentially supply the pipeline of professionals. Nonetheless, evidence from a review of the literature is mixed. This does not mean that cyber security competitions are not useful in mitigating the shortage, but also it does not mean that they certainly are. Uncertainty regarding their outcomes means that their effects should not be assumed and should be rigorously evaluated so their structure or implementation are altered if ineffective, or are scaled up, if instead they indeed reach their objectives. Therefore, there is the need to create a solid evaluation culture and perform evaluations with those designs – before and after experiments, quasi or natural experiments – that are most useful in finding out whether a policy works or not.

Finally, the chapter argued that the cyber security skills shortage should not be seen in isolation from the rest of skills issues and should be anchored to establish social science disciplines, such as labour market economics, skills policy and impact evaluation. Some of what is happening in the cyber security sector has occurred, or at least has been discussed, in other fields, so there is no need to reinvent the wheel when insights from other disciplines and sectors are available. In this regard, a "dream teams of experts" composed of labour economics, education, cyber security and public policy specialists should be gathered so to combine their expertise in an attempt to have a common and solid conceptualisation of the CSSS.

# References

Acemoglu, D. and J. S. Pischke. 1999. The Structure of Wages and Investment in General Training, *Journal of Political Economy*. doi:10.1086/250071.

Acemoglu, D. and J. S. Pischke. 2001. Minimum Wages and On-the-Job Training. IZA. Available at: http://ftp.iza.org/dp384.pdf.

AustCyber. 2018. Australia's Cyber Security Sector Competitiveness Plan – 2018 Update – Driving Growth in Australia's Cyber Security Sector. Available at: www.austcyber.com/file-download/download/public/415.

Australian Government. 2016. Australia's Cyber Security Strategy: Enabling Innovation, Growth & Prosperity. Available at: https://cybersecuritystrategy.homeaffairs.gov.au/AssetLibrary/dist/assets/images/PMC-Cyber-Strategy.pdf.

Better Evaluation. 2020. About Us. Available at: www.betterevaluation.org/en/about.

Boeri, T. and J. van Ours. 2008. Education and Training. In *The Economics of Imperfect Labor Markets*. 1st edn. Princeton, NJ: Princeton University Press.

Brunello, G. and M. De Paola. 2004. Market Failures and the Under-Provision of Training. Available at: www.oecd.org/els/emp/34932691.pdf.

Burningglass. 2019. Recruiting Watchers for the Virtual Walls: The State of Cybersecurity Hiring. Available at: www.burning-glass.com/wp-content/uploads/recruiting_watchers_cybersecurity_hiring.pdf.

Cappelli, P. H. 2015. Skill Gaps, Skill Shortages, and Skill Mismatches: Evidence and Arguments for the United States. *ILR Review* 68(2): 251–290. doi:10.1177/0019793914564961.

Catota, F. E., M. G. Morgan and D. C. Sicker. 2019. Cybersecurity Education in a Developing Nation: The Ecuadorian Environment. *Journal of Cybersecurity*, 5(1). doi:10.1093/Cybsec/Tyz001.

Conklin, W. A., R. E. Cline and T. Roosa. 2014. Re-engineering Cybersecurity Education in the US: An Analysis of the Critical Factors. In *Proceedings of 2014 47th Hawaii International Conference on System Sciences*. IEEE, pp. 2006–2014. doi:10.1109/HICSS.2014.254.

Crumpler, W. and J. A. Lewis. 2019. The Cybersecurity Workforce Gap. Available at: https://csis-prod.s3.amazonaws.com/s3fs-public/publication/190129_Crumpler_Cybersecurity_FINAL.pdf.

CyberTitan. 2019. What is CyberTitan – CyberTitan – ICTC Canadian Youth Cyber Education Initiative. Available at: www.cybertitan.ca/index.php/about/what-is-cybertitan/.

Dabney, K. P., R. H. Tai, J. T. Almarode, J. L. Miller-Friedmann, G. Sonnert, *et al.*2012Out-of-School Time Science Activities and Their Association with Career Interest in STEM, *International Journal of Science Education, Part B*. 2(1): 63–79. doi:10.1080/21548455.2011.629455.

Department of Social Policy and Intervention. (2020) Evidence Based Intervention and Policy Evaluation Master's Programmes. Available at: www.spi.ox.ac.uk/evidence-based-intervention-policy-evaluation-masters-programmes (accessed 4 January 2020).

De Zan, T. 2019. Mind the Gap: The Cyber Security Skills Shortage and Public Policy Interventions. Available at: https://gcsec.org/wp-content/uploads/2019/02/cyber-ebook-definitivo.pdf.

Dunn, M. H. and L. D. Merkle. 2018. Assessing the Impact of a National Cybersecurity Competition on Students'Career Interests. In *Proceedings of the 49th ACM Technical Symposium on Computer Science Education - SIGCSE '18*, pp. 62–67. doi:10.1145/3159450.3159462.

ENISA. 2019. Supporting IT Professionals — ECSC. Available at: https://europeancybersecuritychallenge.eu/about.

Frost & Sullivan. , 2017. 2017 Global Information Security Workforce Study - Bench-marking Workforce Capacity and Response to Cyber Risk. Available at: www.isc2.org/-/media/B7E003F79E1D4043A0E74A57D5B6F33E.ashx.

Gagliardi, F., C. Hankin, J. Gal-Ezer, A. McGettrick and M. Meitern. 2016. Advancing Cybersecurity Research and Education in Europe: Major Drivers of Growth in the Digital Landscape. Europe Policy Committee Association for Computing Machinery. Available at : www.acm.org/binaries/content/assets/public-policy/2016_euacm_cyberse curity_white_paper.pdf.

Garcia-van Hoogstraten, C. and L. Bate. 2019. White Paper: Task Force on Cybersecurity Professional Training and Development. Available at: https://cybilportal.org/publica tions/white-paper-task-force-on-cybersecurity-professional-training-and-development/.

Gertler, P. J., S. Martinez, P. Premand, L. B. Rawlings and C. M. Vermeersch. 2016. *Impact Evaluation in Practice*. 2nd edn. Washington, DC: World Bank.

HM Government. 2018. Initial National Cyber Security Skills Strategy: Increasing the UK's Cyber Security Capability. Available at: https://assets.publishing.service.gov.uk/governm ent/uploads/system/uploads/attachment_data/file/767515/Cyber_security_skills_stra tegy_211218.pdf.

Ipsos MORI. 2020. Policy and Evaluation. Available at: www.ipsos.com/ipsos-mori/en-uk/policy-and-evaluation.

(ISC)$^2$. 2018. Cybersecurity Professionals Focus on Developing New Skills as Workforce Gap Widens: (ISC)2 Cybersecurity Workforce Study 2018. Available at: www.isc2.org/-/media/ISC2/Research/2018-ISC2-Cybersecurity-Workforce-Study.ashx?la=en&hash= 4E09681D0FB51698D9BA6BF13EEABFA48BD17DB0.

(ISC)$^2$. 2019. Strategies for Building and Growing Strong Cybersecurity Teams: (ISC)2 Cybersecurity Workforce Study 2019. Available at: www.isc2.org/-/media/ISC2/Resea rch/2019-Cybersecurity-Workforce-Study/ISC2-Cybersecurity-Workforce-Study-2019. ashx?la=en&hash=D087F6468B4991E0BEFFC017BC1ADF59CD5A2EF7.

Kantar Public. 2020. Evaluation. www.kantar.com/public/uk/about/practice-area/evaluation.

Keep, E. 2006. Market Failure in Skills. *SSDA Catalyst*, 1. Available at; www.researchonline. org.uk/sds/search/download.do;jsessionid=5A30E0612A636657FF1C84177B85B5ED? ref=B62.

Libicki, M. C., D. Senty and J. Pollak. 2014. H4CKER5 WANTED: An Examination of the Cybersecurity Labor Market. Rand Corporation. Available at: www.rand.org/con tent/dam/rand/pubs/research_reports/RR400/RR430/RAND_RR430.pdf.

Malan, J., E. Lale-Demoz and J. Rampton. 2018. Identifying the Role of Further and Higher Education in Cyber Security Skills Development. Available at: https://assets.pub lishing.service.gov.uk/government/uploads/system/uploads/attachment_data/file/ 767425/The_role_of_FE_and_HE_in_cyber_security_skills_development.pdf.

McGuinness, S., K. Pouliakas and P. Redmond. 2018. Skills Mismatch: Concepts, Mea-surement and Policy Approaches, *Journal of Economic Surveys* 32(4): 985–1015. doi:10.1111/joes.12254.

Melchior, A., C. Burack, M. Hoover and Z. Haque. 2018. FIRST Longitudinal Study: Findings at 48 Month Follow-Up (Year 5 Report). Waltham, MA. Available at: https:// www.firstinspires.org/sites/default/files/uploads/resource_library/impact/first-longitudina l-study-summary-year-5.pdf.

Miller, K., G. Sonnert and P. Sadler. 2018. The Influence of Students' Participation in STEM Competitions on Their Interest in STEM Careers, *International Journal of Science Education, Part B* 8(2): 95–114. doi:10.1080/21548455.2017.1397298.

Nachreiner, C. 2019. Can CTFs Help Close the Cybersecurity Skills Gap?, Council Post. Available at: www.forbes.com/sites/forbestechcouncil/2019/11/22/can-ctfs-help-clo se-the-cybersecurity-skills-gap/#15607ed512b0 (accessed 5 December 2019).

Owen, K.*et al.* (2011) *The Magenta Book: Guidance for Evaluation.* London: HMSO. Available at: https://assets.publishing.service.gov.uk/government/uploads/system/uploads/attachm ent_data/file/220542/magenta_book_combined.pdf.

Shaw, I., J. Greene and M. Mark. 2006. *The SAGE Handbook of Evaluation.* London: SAGE Publications Ltd.

The Secretary of Commerce and the Secretary of Homeland Security. 2017. Supporting the Growth and Sustainment of the Nation's Cybersecurity Workforce: Building the Foundation for a More Secure American Future. Available at: www.nist.gov/sites/default/ files/documents/2018/07/24/eo_wf_report_to_potus.pdf.

Tobey, D. H., P. Pusey and D. L. Burley. 2014. Engaging Learners in Cybersecurity Careers: Lessons from the Launch of the National Cyber League. *ACM Inroads.* doi:10.1145/2568195.2568213.

Trochim, W. M. 2006. Introduction to Evaluation: The Research Methods Knowledge Base. Available at: https://socialresearchmethods.net/kb/intreval.php (accessed 24 September 2019).

University of Phoenix, (ISC)$^2$ and (ISC)$^2$ Foundation. 2014 Cybersecurity Workforce Competencies: Preparing Tomorrow's Risk-Ready Professionals. Available at: www.na tionalcyberwatch.org/ncw-content/uploads/2016/03/cybersecurity-report-1-1.pdf.

Welch, A. and D. Huffman. 2011. The Effect of Robotics Competitions on High School Students' Attitudes Toward Science. *School Science and Mathematics* 111(8): 416–424. doi:10.1111/j.1949-8594.2011.00107.x.

White, H. and D. A. Raitzer. 2017. *Impact Evaluation of Development Interventions: A Practical Guide.* Manila, the Philippines: Asian Development Bank.

# 13

# TWELVE DILEMMAS OF REFORM IN CYBER SECURITY EDUCATION

*Greg Austin*

In 2011, several researchers in the field of cyber security education captured the dilemma facing governments and other stakeholders around the world in the title of their article: "The Ephemeral Legion: Producing an Expert Cyber Security Work Force from Thin Air" (Locasto et al. 2011). They highlighted the constraints associated with various programmes in the United States, such as an Academic Centres of Excellence network. The authors made a series of complementary recommendations to try to promote the more rapid development of education in the field. One of their recommendations concerned the need to massively expand investment in related educational technologies and research into those educational technologies. And this was in the leading cyber power and the wealthiest country in the world. It raises the question for all other countries of their readiness to expand investment in technologies relevant to cyber security education and research into the educational uses of such technology.

Yet other researchers have noted fundamental weaknesses even in the very conceptualisation of cyber security education. Schneider (2013) suggested that change is needed on all fronts in how universities develop curricula in this field and deliver them. Conklin et al. (2014) have warned against any vision of cyber security education that is monochromatic: "The development of a single foundational curriculum that can meet all major requirements is not a possibility for a field as diverse as information security. Information security is a field that has both breadth and complexity."

These considerations in respect of tertiary level programmes sit alongside a myriad of other fundamental curriculum-type issues that any country faces in reorienting its educational and vocational training system to adjust to the threats of the cyber age. Some of these are spelled out in Chapter 2 in this book by Adam Henry on a future cybersecurity education framework that distinguishes between mission sets, level or expertise, and work roles in a fine-grained way that most existing national frameworks do not. But other chapters in the book add equally important overlays to that framework.

A brief list of these many requirements suggested by the contributing authors might include:

- a social and philosophical vision (what sort of cyberspace do we want?)
- multidisciplinarity (e.g. law, psychology, economics, management of cyber security)
- comprehensive scope (seating the cyber security in broader local, national and international environments)
- holistic approach (everything has a cyber reality and everyone studies cyber)
- personal attribute development related to novel cyberspace realities
- heavy involvement of practitioners
- leadership and oversight by professional associations
- reconciling sovereign security issues with the educational environment (open curricula and enrolment)
- above all, teaching must be research-based and seated in a university-like setting to deliver the precision and discipline needed to protect national and personal security and prosperity.

Critics might say that such a set of requirements sounds like a utopia of cyber security education. Or they might suggest that the various combinations of need laid out in this book cannot be imagined or found in a single locus of formal education; and that we have to rely on imperfect *laissez-faire* outcomes and labour market forces. Just as democracy is often described as a bad political system but the best available choice, so too we have become accustomed to the view that universities are inefficient at satisfying both market needs and broader social needs (especially around privacy protection) on the scale needed, but we want to keep a university system as the best available choice. We convince ourselves that we can achieve our aims by preserving the system without changing the paradigm. We resort to "branding solutions", such as "centres of excellence", that reinforce pre-existing university patterns of the technological dominance of the cyber security field. If the government and its intelligence agencies say a cyber security education programme is good, then surely little else is needed (irony intended). Moreover, critics might say that the large number of post-tertiary, non-university accreditation and certification options for information security have filled many of the gaps that formal education has left and we don't need too many more. They can also point to the proposition that advanced information science has penetrated most academic disciplines in traditional universities, and this includes considerations of information security. In short, how do stakeholders identify viable aiming points on the spectrum of reform and transformation for cyber security education?

It would be great if the challenges of cyber security education, digital literacy promotion and workforce development could be easily bounded and managed by a single government agency, by a peak professional body in the sector, or by a national education standards committee. One example of such a bounded problem managed by a single agency was the US ambition to land a man on the moon under the largely exclusively management of NASA. The challenges of security in cyberspace cannot be so bounded. Security in the information age and the teaching of it appear as unbounded a set problems, and as multi-dimensional, as we can find elsewhere in social policy, short of problems like ending poverty. While we can credit intelligence agencies and governments as the sources of one set of truths about security in cyberspace, we also need to recognise people like Edward Snowden and Mark Zuckerberg as pointing to a very different set of truths about security. The convergence between authoritarianism, war-fighting and emerging cyber security technologies further extends the suite of subjects that are worthy of considerable attention in education strategies at all levels.

The global political and social environment for policy reform in education for cyber security is more complex than for the subject of climate change. The latter as a subject for educators is relatively easy at almost every level of analysis compared with the challenges of security for cyberspace. The biggest difference is the pace of technological change and the economic disruption: change is much faster for the cyber emergency than for the climate emergency. Other differences include the day-to-day geopolitical confrontation in cyberspace, the daily economic losses, the direct negative impact of today's cyber activities on people's most intimate lives or their very physical survival – today or next week, not 2030 or 2050. Universities around the world and the civil society underpinnings of university education have not kept up with the comprehensive study of and education for social and moral life in the information revolution (and even less so than for the climate emergency). If we are talking dates and priorities, 1984 has already been and gone, and the futuristic prognostications of the book by that name, first published in 1949, now seem all too commonplace.

There at least 12 national level choice points (dilemmas) that are shaping the direction and trends in cyber security education that may help us analyse the challenges of reform. These dilemmas play out differently in each country and each community. Some figure explicitly in education strategies and some do not. They are all shaping outcomes in education policy, but for the most part their influence is playing out invisibly.

## Dilemma 1 What sort of information society do we want?

The question has been addressed at length by governments, philosophers, educators, practitioners and civil society. There is a set of answers to match every conceivable political philosophy. For the purposes of this analysis, the question is best answered in the negative. What don't we want? The discussion here is not meant to proffer a choice, but rather to expose subtle (or not so subtle) influences. Do we want to avoid an information society shaped largely by intelligence agencies? Are we content with an information society driven by technological serendipity and base consumer choices? The world loves Facebook but is it good for the world?

The choice we make on such questions will have to be a composite mish-mash of political and social compromise worthy of a liberal pluralist society. The point to note here in respect of the constraint on education policy is that in many countries, their governments, educators, legislators and civil society are involved in a pro-tracted abdication of judgement on what they don't want to see in their informa-tion society. There is either a lack of moral and political urgency about the importance of this subject; or a default setting favouring corporate interests and the technology innovators over the citizen or community. In this regard, the contrast between the European Union's deliberation of the General Data Protection Reg-ulation (GDPR) or on the regulation of Facebook stands in strong contrast to the attitude of many non-European countries, and even of many EU members states that favour an economic growth and pro-business policy agenda. In any country, the scale of social and political demand for educators to engage deeply with these issues, along with interest from students and journalists, will be a primary driver of education outcomes on security aspects of the information society. We can go so far as to say that the quality of university education in any country on these issues can stand as a fairly reliable measure of the social and political demand in a country for well-articulated and hotly debated approaches of the information society.

## Dilemma 2 What sort of security do we want in cyberspace?

The same sort of arguments can be made about the type of security we want in cyberspace. To what extent does the quality and character of debate on that issue invisibly shape education and workforce outcomes? Is there a default setting that favours intelligence and police agencies over other conceptions of citizen security? Do we tend to privilege the state's need to conceal information over the public right to know? Do we want technical security only (no viruses, please) or should we aspire to very high standards of privacy in handling of big data? As with the previous discussion, the sense of public policy urgency around these issues will determine the demand for education and its character. In this regard, the available pool of educators in cyberspace security in each country is also shaped by the quality and performance levels of intelligence and police agencies, as well as their social standing. It seems to be the case in the Five Eyes countries and Israel, that the high political standing accorded their cyber agencies has had a marked impact on the education demand and curriculum outcomes in those countries. Former personnel from these agencies seem to hold commanding positions in the infor-mation policy ecosystem, including for education, in these six countries. In coun-tries where the intelligence agencies are held in different regard, as in Germany and Japan, the influence of the intelligence and police imperatives on policy, including for cyber security education, is arguably less prominent.

## Dilemma 3 Evidence-base for national and sub-national policy

It is ironic that the knowledge society and its economy are protected by policies of governmental and corporate leaders that are underpinned by a very weakly devel-oped evidence base on most aspects of human capital development for cyber security. In spite of Herculean efforts by a small handful of researchers in the field of cyber security education and workforce development, we can safely say that there is little to no sustained, longitudinal or comprehensive research in almost all countries on the state of their cyber security education, development of professional skills, or workforce development. There may be a handful of exceptions.

For the past 12 years, committed researchers in this field have participated in the annual World Conference on Information Security Education (WISE). As entirely appropriate to such a conference, the topics researched were almost always about the common technical or management problem sets. The papers rarely analysed the unique national conditions or even shared international social circumstances that defined the problem set of human capital accumulation, either at the enterprise level of beyond it, at a regional or national level.

For example, Bishop et al. (2017), in the Proceedings of the tenth WISE, provide useful insights from researchers and practitioners on important issues of information security education; teaching information security; information security awareness and culture; and training information security professionals. They do not touch national policy or corporate planning for human capital in any significant way. Their work has a classic focus on cyber security awareness, an important but low-level (community-oriented) issue. In the 2018 Proceedings from the eleventh annual conference, there are the beginnings of a national level orientation. Furnell et al. (2018) provide a useful account of the United Kingdom's development of a national certification process for university education based on a body of knowledge and skill set considerations. In the same volume, von Solms and Futcher (2018) reveal that in the case of South Africa, engineering schools do not "traditionally cater for cybersecurity training in undergraduate or post-graduate studies" and they offer proposals for a "process followed to determine the body of knowledge" which the country might adopt for new courses.

Consolidated academic work beyond the fragmented and episodic coverage in journals has concentrated largely on professional practices of the technical providers rather than practices of human capital formation. For example, LeClair (2013) brings together 12 experts from across the cyber security spectrum and "shines a spotlight on operational challenges and needs across the workforce: in military, health care, international relations, telecommunications, finance, education, utilities, government, small businesses, and nonprofits". The focus of attention in each chapter is on the specific sub-sectors. While the book notes the "scarcity of information about the need to build a cyber workforce", it offers little by way of corrective. The book is focused almost exclusively on the United States, the world's only cyber superpower, and is therefore of less relevance to middle powers and small countries. A subsequent volume (LeClair 2015) again looks mainly at cyber security practices associated with protection of critical infrastructure in particular sectors, but it does have one chapter specifically addressing education and workforce development.

The best research on human capital formation for cyber security has been undertaken by government agencies (or for them) in the United States, primarily through a process of policy review. There is a mountain of examples. Going back many years, one could point to Evans and Reeder (2010). Yet in 2017, the Trump Administration declared a national emergency in cyberspace, identified the cyber workforce as a leading component of the new technological confrontation between the United States and China, and called for yet another report. The report and resulting policy changes included some radical provisions, especially in respect of training opportunities for government personnel, but there was not a lot of evidence of new research or breakthrough ideas capturing most of the issues canvassed in this book. The tone was well set in the 2019 Executive Order:

> America's cybersecurity workforce is a strategic asset that protects the American people, the homeland, and the American way of life. The National Cyber Strategy, the President's 2018 Management Agenda, and Executive Order 13800 of May 11, 2017 (Strengthening the Cybersecurity of Federal Networks and Critical Infrastructure), each emphasize that a superior cybersecurity workforce will promote American prosperity and preserve peace.
>
> *(White House 2019)*

There is a large amount of high quality research work on this subject available internationally that needs to be surfaced in public debates and policy formulation. Much of this has come from task forces in the United States, including through the National Initiative for Cybersecurity Education (NICE), but also in support of military personnel policies. Most countries must marvel at the reports of the Government Accountability Office picking apart the failure of Cyber Command to ensure that its personnel have reached the right level of accreditation for their designated roles (GAO 2019). However, the US case is like almost no other. And the labour market policy in all countries is determined largely by national and/or sub-national authorities according to the specific policy settings of the domestic economy. For this reason, studies of other countries' policies for reform of cyber security education can only provide broad pointers. They lack ready transferability.

The daunting dimensions of the research problem of workforce development were illustrated in a report by NICE on best practices in that area (NICE 2012). The report notes that there are three essential layers in studying the research foundations needed for workforce development: process, strategy and infrastructure. Within each of these three layers, there are identifiable best practices just for the research needed to underpin evidence-based policy. One important approach is to undertake risk assessments of each new education plan based on analysis of suddenly emerging gaps between new needs and existing supply. Another best practice is to use research to identify how "rapid fluctuation" in workforce supply of cyber security knowledge, skills and abilities (KSAs) affect downstream risks in infrastructure, financial stability and the physical environment. According to the NICE report, workforce planning needs to be supported by a Human Resources Information System on the cyber security work force. (Most countries do not have one.) Best practice would see this system being used for "easy drill-down into data to understand the impact of organizational changes on cybersecurity workload and better manage fluctuations in need". The approach would depend on "maintaining relevant [analytical] tools, which assist in the cybersecurity workforce planning effort". The report also identified that investing in enabling technology for cyber security work force analysis had proven to be a key differentiator in terms of available infrastructures.

In comparison with the ideal research environment for evidence-based policy on workforce development as advocated by the NICE report, the current status of the research environment at the national level in most countries would have to be assessed as highly underdeveloped. Their first priority in reorienting cyber security education policy would be to establish a Human Resources Information System on the cyber security workforce. If a country's stakeholders are serious about the challenges, another step might be to fund a sustained research stream in one or more research centres or policy institutions. But to be effective, that research funding support would not be a low-cost or low complexity exercise.

## Dilemma 4 Education policy choice points beyond the multiple curricula

Curriculum-related issues are only a small slice of the policy menu in cyber security formation faced by governments and industry stakeholders. Other very problematic choice points include how much money to invest in transformation of the education system or public information systems for cyber security. Or indeed, should these be transformed or simply incrementally altered? How many new students should be graduated through revamped programmes: double the current number of graduates or four times the current number? Should the spending and number ambitions be focused on vocational training, undergraduate education or graduate education? Which institutions are best able to deliver new educational outcomes at the pace and on the scale needed?

Are entirely new educational institutions, such as a National Cyber Security College, needed? An even thornier problem is that of drawing the line between government intervention and free market principles and free society principles, particularly in respect of university choices about curricula, degree structures and student places. And then, once all of the choices are made by universities and other delivery institutions, how can a single government escape its own cyber immaturity at the national level? If a country has immature cyber security cultures that permeate business and government, not to mention the wider community and even educational institutions, and if it has only a small cohort of educators in the discipline, it will inevitably stall in any effort to bring about a significant increase in indigenous cyber security workforce numbers who are better trained than the existing workforce.

## Dilemma 5 Measuring maturity in education systems for cyber security

Just as the concept of cyber security maturity is widely accepted internationally, we also need a concept of and models for maturity in cyber security education and training. There are two basic approaches that spring to mind. One is to create a baseline, matching existing knowledge sets to numbers enrolled and to see maturity in reaching new levels on these types of indicators. But this approach will come up against the very large number of sub-fields and specialisations, not to mention skill levels. Moreover, in most countries, such data is not readily available and most governments will never be able to ever afford to collect it.

The other immediately obvious approach is to compare existing and planned sets of skills and numbers relative to the types of threats a country faces. If we take the case of Australia, we know that the government, businesses and educational institutions see the current maturity level of cyber security education as inadequate relative to the types of threats. What we don't know is whether these actors view the maturity level as almost satisfactory or desperately weak. From the various surveys available in Australia and related research, one could make a case for an interpretation that the level of maturity in the country's cyber security education, especially in terms of throughput of potential workers, is – relative to the scale and scope of threats – weak to very weak.

This assessment in the case of Australia is quickly borne out by reference to a more detailed analysis of existing educational and training offerings relative to national needs. If we make the mistake of seeing these needs in aggregate terms (that is a "cyber security workforce"), then that argument might be challenged. On the other hand, if we take the essential step of breaking down the needs even into top tier sub-components, such as countering cyber crime, fighting cyber war, protecting critical infrastructure, providing online safety for children and the elderly, countering fake news, ensuring privacy, we can quickly see that there are no university degrees in the country and little training activity in professional settings that prepare students for these sub-disciplines with any depth (except perhaps for specialised training in the country's leading security intelligence agencies). Even within each of these sub-fields, there are unique problem sets of cyber security which need specialised education and training.

Everything mentioned above is true of technical aspects of cyber security education and training that relates to technical aspects, such as software, hardware, wireless, mobile, payload or network considerations. When we include issues of human-computer interaction, personnel security, systems management, enterprise compliance, identity and privileges management, legislation, or the many additional policy elements of a country's information security ecosystem, the level of maturity of the education and training in cyber security is even lower than for the technical aspects.

## Dilemma 6 Resilience and dependency: the missing link in education and training

There is yet another level of complexity. As Henry points out in Chapter 7, there are few universities that prepare graduates for the problem-solving associated with complex questions of system resilience at the national level in cyberspace, even though resilience is the main practical goal of all cyber security practice. Since 2009, the U.S. Department of Homeland Security (DHS) has identified the assurance of resilience as an integral component of cyber security practice (NIAC 2009). By way of example, one of the ten principles of cyber security and resilience advocated by DHS is the management of external cyber dependencies. There is almost zero specialisation on this topic (cyber resilience and dependency) in educational institutions, in most countries, and it is only weakly visible in the case of the United States. The main focal points for research work on this subject, at least in the English-speaking world, are the Idaho National Laboratory (INL) and the Argonne Laboratory (Thakur 2016; Austin 2017). These are not front-line teaching institutions.

## Dilemma 7 Immigration and off-shore workforces

All governments face a choice about the balance to be struck between producing a workforce through provision of education and training to home-grown students versus sponsored immigration of foreign nationals already having the knowledge and skills. How does a country develop an immigration programme to match the skills gaps in cyber security? This can be illustrated with reference to the case of Australia which started slowly but which by 2019 seemed to have struck a suitable formula. The question remains of what impact such programmes will have on the workforce deficit, including the available pool of educators.

Until quite recently, Australia had a general provision identifying workers with skills in information and communications technology as a category for special treatment in visa applications, and one such category (not further defined), was "information security specialist". (The Australian Computer Society has long held the role of verifying relevant certifications of intending ICT immigrants.) This single classification did not really reflect the demands for occupational diversity and security specialisation outlined in this book.

In a 2014 submission, the Australian Information Industry Association (AIIA 2014) reported "the absence of specific data to demonstrate non-compliance by the ICT industry" of the various tests imposed by the skilled worker visa process. The lack of data has persisted. There has been no public domain analysis done by anyone of the information security workforce brought to Australia under the programme, much less a study of how the structure of that workforce relates to the evolution of Australia's capabilities and throughput (graduation rates) for cyber security education and training. There has been no study available in the public domain of comparative salary levels for peer appointments of Australians (citizens or permanent residents) and immigrants in the sector. It is of some note that the AIIA submission suggests that Australian workers can be more expensive than non-Australians in peer posts, presumably with per qualifications.

According to 2019 data from the immigration authorities (Home Affairs 2019) and the Cyber Security Growth Centre (AustCyber 2019), there has been something of a disconnect in policy between the immigration programmes and the cyber defence needs of the country. The 2019 AustCyber Sector Competitiveness

Plan reported an escalating skills shortage, especially outside the two biggest states. The immigration data revealed no special attention to cyber security specialists among the 4,000 ICT professionals granted skilled worker visas in 2018–19, most of whom went to just three states, and an unusually high visibility of chefs and cooks (3,440 in the same year) compared with ICT professionals.

Table 13.1 shows a comparison and numbers for the top six nominated occupations for primary visa holders (temporary skilled residents) in Australia as at 30 June 2019 by nominated position location. The balance between the hospitality sector and the tech sector looks somewhat out of line with the cyber defence needs.

In mid-2019, a leading policy advocacy body noted that "ICT Security Specialist roles are still relegated to the short-term skilled occupation list (STSOL) rather than the medium and long term strategic skills list (MLTSSL) that allows TSS holders to stay in Australia for four years instead of two" (Braue 2019). The government has repaired that shortcoming and, by early 2020, the role was on the medium-term lists and available to more than ten different categories of possible visa entry.

It was only in November 2019 that the Australian government launched a new programme for independent immigrants targeted specifically at cyber security. The 'Global Talent Independent Program' (GTIP), announced one year earlier, would target seven "future-focused fields", including cyber security, fintech and quantum computing, in a programme scheduled to recruit 5,000 immigrants in its first year of operation. It followed the successful launch over one year earlier of the Global Talent Employer Sponsored (GTES) which focused on finding talents for "highly-skilled niche positions" that could not be filled by Australians or through other visa programmes, such as the short-term or medium-term skilled temporary resident. This programme could over 20 years or so make a solid contribution to reducing the country's estimated workforce deficit of "almost 17,000 additional cyber security workers by 2026" (as long as that estimate from AustCyber holds firm).

**TABLE 13.1** Top six nominated occupations for Temporary Worker Visas, Australia, 2019

| Nominated occupation | ACT | NSW | NT | QLD | SA | TAS | VIC | WA | Total |
|---|---|---|---|---|---|---|---|---|---|
| Cook | 90 | 1,550 | 60 | 600 | 90 | 40 | 1,130 | 520 | 4,080 |
| Chef | 50 | 1,530 | 40 | 480 | 50 | 30 | 960 | 350 | 3,490 |
| Developer Programmer | 10 | 1,950 | 0 | 140 | 20 | <5 | 870 | 100 | 3,090 |
| Café or Restaurant Manager | 40 | 1,230 | 40 | 550 | 50 | 20 | 550 | 250 | 2,710 |
| ICT Business Analyst | 10 | 1,370 | <5 | 130 | 20 | 0 | 930 | 110 | 2,570 |
| Software Engineer | 20 | 1,570 | <5 | 130 | 30 | 5 | 700 | 100 | 2,560 |

## Dilemma 8 Cost transfer of training from the private sector to the public sector

It is not unreasonable to ask questions about the private sector's long-term plan for developing public goods in structured development programmes to promote cyber security education and training. It is a common practice in the private sector in many fields to complain of government inactivity or non-performance when there is a shortage of skills in a workforce rather than take on what may well be the private sector's responsibility. In the case of Australia, for example, there is no national consensus in Australia on where the division of responsibility lies, except in those professions traditionally regulated by peak bodies, such as medicine, law, accountancy and engineering. In the cyber security sector, we need to be alert to the proposition that private businesses are shifting the blame for their own lack of investment in and engagement with universities and other education providers on to an overly sympathetic and overly interventionist government.

## Dilemma 9 Online education and training: international and domestic

There are almost no education and training needs for any country's cyber security sector that cannot currently be met, provided the price is right, by non-national providers, from countries as diverse as the United States, the United Kingdom, France, Israel, India, Russia and China. Much of that can be provided online. A mature cyber security formation policy in a given country would set priorities for where it needs to develop its own sovereign education and training capabilities. This could and should include: defence, foreign affairs, security agencies and the police. The highest priority mission sets for the highest level of sovereign capability for education and training include: cyber warfare, cyber espionage, cyber crime and critical infrastructure protection. This is where most governments must continue to spend the bulk of their money and planning effort in cyber security education reform. Yet most countries have only partial baselines for understanding the impact of government spending on education and training for these sensitive national sectors.

## Dilemma 10 Disruptive technologies

There is a marked difference between developing long-term education strategies for core skills in content-stable subjects (relatively speaking) like languages, physics, chemistry and mathematics compared with understanding education needs in content-dynamic subjects like contemporary politics, Islamic State terrorism, estimating global warming impacts of current $CO_2$ emissions, or cyber security. Opinions will differ about just how dynamic the content of cyber security education will be. It could be noted, however, that the Idaho National Laboratory sets a two-year time horizon on the likely beneficial outcomes of its research on resilience-critical national infrastructure in cyber space. This points us to policy settings that favour practical or on-the-job education strategies rather than those seated in slow-moving institutional frameworks. The primary locus of the best long-term cyber security education that takes account of the content-dynamic character of cyber security education needs may well be a new form of "cyber defence workshop" or what some in the United States are developing in the form of continuous cyber labs, where students have 24/7 access to live simulations and actual cyber events.

## Dilemma 11 Formal knowledge and education versus self-taught informal knowledge

There may be few fields of modern education where the knowledge, skills and abilities (KSA) of practitioners and theorists can be acquired as much by self-taught processes as in cyber security. We would probably all trust many committed hackers without formal education to know what he/she is doing in defence of an IT system more than we would trust a "doctor" lacking formal training to advise on medical interventions in a human being. The emergence of cyber space has been accompanied by a surge in the ability of people to become self-taught. This clearly has dangers as well as benefits. In practical terms, this risk is not handled well by most institutions since few have the ability to certify how much the KSA of individual cyber security operators is derived from formal education (and is therefore testable and hopefully reliable) and how much is derived from self-taught (often "seat of the pants") sources. A national education system for cyber security must provide a mechanism which understands both the strengths and weakness of the self-taught pathways and how these can be understood and managed.

## Dilemma 12 Critical thinking and personal resilience as the core abilities

Knowledge and skills for cyber security are tough enough challenges for formal cyber security education. What are the unique challenges of formal education for developing graduate attributes for the "A" in KSA: the "abilities"? This concept refers to a student's demonstrated capacity to achieve certain practical outcomes in a measurable or observable way when challenged with a concrete problem or challenge. In cyber security, there are two key aptitudes (not abilities) which need to be developed through formal education. These are critical thinking and personal resilience. Education for cyber security is more akin to education for other high pressure operational environments, such as surgery or for counter-terrorism operations, than it is akin to education for mathematics or science, which are more passive undertakings and which involve the student mainly as observer or analyst and not as an actor. Assuming that tertiary-level studies in cyber security should be expected to meet the "A" requirement in this spirit, modes of "study" do need to be adjusted to include mandatory learning and testing in cyber security operations akin to one-year practicums for architecture or medicine degrees.

# References

AIIA. (Australian Information Industry Association). 2014. Integrity in the Subclass 457 Programme: AIIA Response. Available at: www.aiia.com.au/documents/policy-subm issions/policies-and-submissions/2014/independent_review_of_integrity_in_subclass457_ 06_05_2014.pdf (accessed 26 February 2020).

AustCyber. 2019. Australia's Cyber Security Sector Competitiveness Plan 2019. Available at: www.austcyber.com/resource/australias-cyber-security-sector-competitiveness-plan-2019.

Austin, G. 2017. Are Australia's Responses to Cyber Security Adequate? Australia's Place in the World 2017, *CEDA*, pp. 50–61. Available at: www.ceda.com.au/Research-and-p olicy/All-CEDA-research/Research-catalogue/Australia-s-place-in-the-world    (accessed 26 February 2020).

Bishop, M., , L., Futcher, N. Miloslavskaya and M. Theocharidou (eds). 2017. Information Security Education for a Global Digital Society: In *Proceedings of the 10th IFIP WG 11.8 World Conference WISE 10, Rome, Italy, May 29–31, 2017*. Vol. 503.

Braue, D. 2019. As Skills Gaps Persist, CEDA Finds Temporary Migration Is "a Net Positive" for Australia. CSO Online. 17 July. Available at: www.csoonline.com/article/3504357/a s-skills-gaps-persist-ceda-finds-temporary-migration-is-a-net-positive-for-australia.html.

Conklin. W. A., R. E. Cline, and T. Roosa. 2014. Re-Engineering Cybersecurity Educa-tion In The US: An Analysis of the Critical Factors. In *Proceedings of the 2014 47th Hawaii International Conference on System Sciences*, pp. 2006–2014. IEEE.

Evans, K. and F. Reeder. 2010. *A Human Capital Crisis in Cybersecurity: Technical Proficiency Matters*. Washington, DC: CSIS.

Furnell, S., F. Piper, C. Ensor, *et al.*2018. A National Certification Programme for Academic Degrees in Cyber Security. In L. Drevin and M. Theocharidou (eds), *Information Security Edu-cation – Towards a Cybersecure Society. Proceedings of WISE 11, Held at the 24th IFIP World Com-puter Congress, WCC 2018, Poznan, Poland, 18–20 September*. Berlin: Springer, pp. 133–145. Available at: https://link.springer.com/chapter/10.1007/978-3-319-99734-6_11 (accessed 26 February 2020).

GAO. (Government Accountability Office). 2019. DOD TRAINING: U.S. Cyber Com-mand and Services Should Take Actions to Maintain a Trained Cyber Mission Force. Report no. GAO-19–362. Available at: www.gao.gov/assets/700/697268.pdf. LeClair, J. (ed.). 2013. *Protecting Our Future: Educating a Cybersecurity Workforce*. New York: Hudson Whitman/Excelsior College Press.

LeClair, J. (ed.). 2015. *Protecting Our Future, Educating a Cybersecurity Workforce* (Vol. 3). New York: Hudson Whitman/Excelsior College Press.

Locasto, M. E., A. K. Ghosh, S. Jajodia and A. Stavrou. 2011. The Ephemeral Legion: Producing an Expert Cyber-Security Work Force from Thin Air. *Communications of the ACM*, 54(1), pp. 129–131.

NIAC. (National Infrastructure Advisory Council). 2009.. Critical Infrastructure Resilience Final Report and Recommendations.Department of Homeland Security, September 8.

NICE. (National Initiative for Cybersecurity Education). 2012. Best Practices for Planning a Cybersecurity Workforce, White Paper Version 2.0. Department of Homeland Security, Cybersecurity Education Office.

Schneider, F. B. 2013. Cybersecurity Education in Universities. *IEEE Security & Privacy*, 11 (4), pp.3–4.

Thakur. 2016. Literature Review – Cyber Dependency at a Domestic and International Levels. Cyber Discussion Paper, No. 2, University of New South Wales. Canberra.

von Solms, S. and L. Futcher. 2018. Identifying the Cybersecurity Body of Knowledge for a Postgraduate Module in Systems Engineering. In L. Drevin and M. Theocharidou (eds)

*Information Security Education – Towards a Cybersecure Society. Proceedings of WISE 11, Held at the 24th IFIP World Computer Congress, WCC 2018, Poznan, Poland, 18–20 September.* Berlin: Springer, pp. 133–145. Available at: https://link.springer.com/chapter/10.1007/ 978-3-319-99734-6_11 (accessed 26 February 2020).

White House. 2019. Executive Order on America's Cybersecurity Workforce. May 2. Available at: www.whitehouse.gov/presidential-actions/executive-order-americas-cyberse curity-workforce/ (accessed 26 February 2020).

# INDEX

For Product Safety Concerns and Information please contact our
EU representative GPSR@taylorandfrancis.com Taylor & Francis
Verlag GmbH, Kaufingerstraße 24, 80331 München, Germany